MAKE MONEY

with

CONDOMINIUMS
AND
TOWNHOUSES

MAKE MONEY

with

CONDOMINIUMS

AND

TOWNHOUSES

GARY W. ELDRED, Ph.D.

WILEY

John Wiley & Sons

Copyright © 2003 by Gary W. Eldred, Ph.D. All rights reserved.

Published by John Wiley & Sons, Inc., Hoboken, New Jersey.
Published simultaneously in Canada.

For general information on our other products and services, or technical support, please contact our Customer Care Department within the United States at 800-762-2974, outside the United States at 317-572-3993 or fax 317-572-4002.

Wiley also publishes its books in a variety of electronic formats. Some content that appears in print may not be available in electronic books. For more information about Wiley products, visit our web site at www.wiley.com.

Library of Congress Cataloging-in-Publication Data:

Eldred, Gary W.
   Make money with condominiums and townhouses / Gary W. Eldred
     p. cm. — (Make money in real estate ; 1734)
   Includes bibliographical references and index.
   ISBN 0-471-43344-6 (pbk.)
   1. Real estate investment—United States. 2. Condominiums—United States. 3. Row houses—United States. I. Title. II. Series.

HD259.E43 2003
332.63'243—dc21   2003050160

Printed in the United States of America.

10 9 8 7 6 5 4 3 2 1

CONTENTS

MAKE MONEY

with

CONDOMINIUMS AND TOWNHOUSES

CHAPTER 1

The Lazy Investor's Way to Wealth

If you're like most people these days, you would like to find a safe investment that yields high returns. You probably know that you could profit big in real estate, but you hesitate to take on the part-time job of landlording. What to do? Invest in condominiums.

In the beginning you will need to put forth some effort to learn the market. Once you're past that step, though, the condos will operate on automatic pilot most of the time. Most condo investors I know put in less than 10 to 20 hours per year for each unit they own.

How can condo owners earn high real estate returns with minimum hassle? It's easy: Because the condominium association takes care of all exterior (and maybe some of the interior) maintenance for the units.

> **Condominiums and townhouses offer high returns, low risk, and minimal landlording.**

Condominiums Attract Better Tenants

You will gain a partner to help manage your tenants. The homeowners' association (HOA), as well as the individual homeowners who live in the other units, will keep an eye on the behav-

HOA communities attract good tenants.

ior of your tenants. Even better, as it turns out, well-run condo and townhouse developments actually attract a better class of tenants than comparably priced single-family houses and apartment buildings.

Why Condos Attract Better Tenants

Condos and townhouses tend to attract *low-maintenance* tenants because these residents actually prefer to live under the strict rules and more pleasant environment of a home-owning community. Think about it. If you were the type of person who likes to hang out at the swimming pool on Sunday afternoons and get rowdy, would you choose to live in a home-owning community or an apartment complex? If you plan to ask six of your closest friends to move in with you to help pay the rent, do you choose to rent in a townhouse community of homeowners, or would you try to rent a single-family house?

Experience shows that trouble-making tenants avoid *well-run* condo and townhouse developments because they know that they will not be able to get away with their antics.

Well-run HOAs   Take note that I emphasize well-run associations. To gain the "association effect," you must carefully select the projects and buildings in which to buy your units (a topic that will be covered in later chapters).

Good tenants prefer strict rules of conduct. Bad tenants avoid them.

Early on, I learned this lesson when I invested in a cheap condo unit in a building that had slid downhill. Apathy and lack of care prevailed. Rules went unenforced. Owners moved out. More unruly tenants moved in. Property values stagnated. Vacancies and turnover increased.

Happy Ending Fortunately, my mistake turned a remarkable profit. Eventually, the investors and homeowners elected a new board of directors for the HOA. We hired a new management company. We developed new rules with teeth in them (daily accelerating fines for repeated offenses). Within three years of our project turnaround, our units had appreciated by 40 percent. In fact, for investors who are willing to accept a little more risk and put in a little more effort, the turnaround play can yield big profits within a period of a few years.

> **Turnaround projects can yield thousands in quick profits.**

The One Easy Test: Who's Moving In, Who's Moving Out

How can you tell whether a project offers a promising future? How can you tell before you buy whether the HOA will prove to be an asset that helps you attract and retain good tenants? Again, I will go into this topic in more detail later. But one helpful way is to learn who's moving in, who's moving out, who's selling, and who's buying. In other words, before you commit to a building or development, review the demographics (age, occupation, incomes, and household composition) of the owners and the residents. From these data you can figure out whether the project is moving upscale, holding its own, or sliding down.

> **You will learn how to own rental properties without becoming a landlord.**

Your Procedures Count, Too!

Of course, even with a watchful and well-run HOA, you can't just rent to the first person who's willing to write you a check. Later I'll tell you exactly what you need to do to enjoy carefree rent collections from the perfect tenant.

Can Investors (Lazy or Not) Really Build Wealth with Condos and Townhouses?

William Nickerson wrote the all-time classic get-rich-in-real-estate book (*How I Turned $1,000 into a Million in My Spare Time*) more than 45 years ago. Since then, hundreds of similar books have promised to show readers how to build wealth in real estate. These authors have urged their readers to buy fixer-uppers, foreclosures, apartment buildings, and single-family houses.

> **Condos and townhouses represent an overlooked opportunity.**

Yet not one such book tells readers how to build wealth with condos and townhouses. Indeed, I plead guilty to this neglect. My own best-selling book, *Investing in Real Estate, Fourth Edition* (Wiley, 2003) focuses exclusively on single-family houses and small apartment buildings.

Why Such Neglect?

Why have real estate authors shied away from recommending condos and townhouses as investments? Presumably condos usually do not appreciate as fast as houses. "When condos become in short supply in an area and prices start to appreciate, more complexes are built and the oversupply cycle begins again. Houses, however, can't be built quickly (if at all) in most areas because very little land remains."[1]

> **Authors and experts fail to tell the whole story.**

Although this quotation was written by other authors, it's similar to the explanation I have given over the years when my readers and seminar attendees ask about condos and townhouses. "Condos don't appreciate as fast as

---

1. Ralph Warner and Ira Serkes, *How to Buy a House in California* (Berkeley: Nolo Press, 1990), 3/24.

houses. Condo prices can suffer when a glut of new apartments floods the market." Okay, that's the bad news.

Experience Trumps Cliché   Now here's the good news. When I reviewed the actual experience of investors (including myself), I found that total returns have often exceeded the returns from owning single-family houses. Why? How? Here are the reasons.

◆ Because of periodic oversupply, it's easier to buy condos at a steeply discounted bargain price.
◆ In nearly all markets, condos yield more cash flow than houses for each dollar invested.
◆ Condos typically yield more tax shelter for each dollar invested.
◆ Condos present less risk of cash flow shock (i.e., new roof, exterior paint job, major electrical upgrade, etc.).
◆ Condos/townhouses often prove easier to rent and consequently suffer lower vacancies.
◆ Condos require much less managerial time and effort.

When you compare investment choices, you must compare the *total* returns, not just the so-called average rate of appreciation. You must also compare the time, trouble, and energy that you will put forth to oversee and look after the investment. When you look at this total picture, you will find (as I have) that condos and townhouses can help you achieve very strong returns, an inflation-protected stream of income, and a multimillion-dollar net worth.

> You can sometimes earn higher profits with condos than you can with single-family houses.

It's Your Choice!   By pointing out the fact that you can make money with condos and townhouses, I am not urging you to forgo single-family houses or apartment buildings. I am not arguing that you will necessarily earn more with condos than you could with other types of real estate. No one can say for sure how *you* will do with any type of investment—real estate or anything else.

However, I am urging you to weigh the merits of condo investing against your financial goals and personal resources. Too many investors pass up real estate because they don't want the supposed hassle of landlording. Other investors who choose real estate pass up condos and townhouses because they erroneously believe that a low appreciation will make condos an inferior investment. Do you hold either of these beliefs?

If so, you're in for a pleasant surprise. In the following pages, you will gain a newfound appreciation (no pun intended) for condos and townhouses. In the end, you may choose not to follow through. But if you do pass up this opportunity, you will not be able to justify your decision with the usual reasons. There's simply no question that over the next 5 to 15 years, well-selected condos and townhouses will reward investors with very handsome returns for relatively little effort.

> **Condos and townhouses often yield higher *total* returns.**

How You Will Profit with Condos

In the remainder of this chapter, I detail more closely the how and why of the rewards of investing in condos. Essentially, you can profit in six ways.

1. Appreciation
2. Mortgage paydown
3. Cash flow
4. Tax shelter
5. Value creation
6. Diversification

Now we look at each of these sources of profit with more precision.

Appreciation

The evidence clearly shows that over the long term, condos do appreciate. Those who argue in favor of houses over condos only allege that houses appreciate at a faster pace. No one claims that condos won't appreciate at all.

The Historical Record

I traced some condo and townhouse prices back to the 1970s and then compared the same units to the prices at which they're selling today.

As you can see from Figure 1.1, the least appreciating complex tripled in value, whereas several others have multiplied in value four to eight times over. In fact, although I researched records from all over the country, I could not find any units that had not at least doubled in value since 1980. In other words, the absolute worst record equaled an average rate of appreciation of about 3 percent a year.

But before you shout, "Three percent? That's lousy!" you need to consider that the rewards of 3 percent appreciation are really quite generous. That's because nearly all investors leverage their returns.

	Sales Prices ($)	
Condominium Development	1970s	2000s
Sabal Point (Miami, FL)	50,000	375,000
Forest Edge (Reston, VA)	25,000	180,000
Faulkner Station (Columbia, MD)	22,500	140,000
Mount La Jolla (San Diego, CA)	60,000	425,000
University Park (Irvine, CA)	25,000	200,000
Sudley Station (Manassas, VA)	26,500	180,000
Louis Park (Stockton, CA)	14,900	140,000
Treasure Isle (Foster City, CA)	29,000	245,000

Figure 1.1 A Sampling of Condo Price Appreciation.

> **Condos and townhouses give investors strong gains through appreciation.**

To buy a $100,000 condo, an investor might invest only $20,000 of his or her own money (often less). When that $100,000 unit moves up to $103,000, the investor has actually experienced a 15 percent return on invested cash—and that's just from first-year appreciation:

$$15\% = \frac{\$3,000}{\$20,000}$$

After five years, still assuming 3 percent a year, the property is then worth $115,900. Therefore, year six appreciation equals

$$0.03 \times \$115,900 = \$3,477$$

And the rate of return on original cash invested increases to

$$17.38\% = \frac{\$3,477}{\$20,000}$$

> **"Low" rates of appreciation yield high rates of return.**

When I read in the financial press that by registering a *total* return of 10 to 12 percent a year, "stocks outperform all other types of investments," I don't know whether to laugh or cry. As you can see, the weakest performing condo record in the country has out-earned stocks by a wide margin—*just from appreciation!*

What Does the Future Hold?

"Okay, Eldred," you might say, "you're talking history. I want to know what's going to happen in the future. Don't you understand that we're in a real estate bubble? All of the financial press is talking about it."

I realize the financial journalists are trying to compare real estate prices to the inflated high-tech stock prices of early 2000. In

> **The bubble theory of real estate prices is full of hot air.**

fact, I am interviewed by such journalists almost weekly. I will tell you from firsthand knowledge that the great majority of these journalists couldn't value a property or calculate an investment return if their lives depended on it.

I have attempted many times to explain that the values of rental real estate are supported by a real and provable stream of income, whereas many of the high-flying tech stocks never earned a nickel of profits. Even solid companies like Microsoft, Intel, and Cisco Systems were valued at absurd multiples of 60, 80, or 100 times actual earnings. The term *bubble* means no underlying fundamentals to support the price of the investment—as in the Florida land boom of the 1920s that the Marx Brothers spoofed in their movie *Coconuts*.

Will today's housing prices stall (or even drop some) within the next year or two? Possibly. Will condo and house prices crash, as did the NASDAQ and S&P 500? Absolutely not. Will condo and home prices continue to set record high prices 5, 10, and 20 years from now? Barring economic or national collapse of the United States, positively, yes.

More Historical Perspective   With talk about a housing bubble, or as the *Wall Street Journal* recently wrote, "Homes no longer are the place to put your money," you need to gain more historical perspective on the decade-by-decade performance of home prices since the end of World War II.

Among all of the lessons history teaches, none is more certain than the fact that home prices will go up. Regardless of how high you think prices are today, they will be higher 10 years from now and much higher 20 or 30 years into the future. Don't make the mistake of believing that home prices have reached their peak. Before you put faith in the naysaying of so-called economic experts, take a quick trip through some of their faulty predictions from years past:

> **The bubble theory for real estate first appeared in the *1940s*!**

◆ "The prices of houses seem to have reached a plateau, and there is reasonable expectancy that prices will decline" (*Time,* December 1, 1947).

◆ "Houses cost too much for the mass market. Today's average price is around $8,000—out of reach for two-thirds of all buyers" (*Science Digest,* April 1948).

◆ "If you have bought your house since the War . . . you have made your deal at the top of the market. . . .The days when you couldn't lose on a house purchase are no longer with us" (*House Beautiful,* November 1958).

◆ "The goal of owning a home seems to be getting beyond the reach of more and more Americans. The typical new house today costs about $28,000" (*Business Week,* September 4, 1969).

◆ "Be suspicious of the 'common wisdom' that tells you to 'Buy now . . . because continuing inflation will force home prices and rents higher and higher' " (*NEA Journal,* December 1970).

◆ "The median price of a home today is approaching $50,000. . . . Housing experts predict that in the future price rises won't be that great" (*Nations Business,* June 1977).

◆ "The era of easy profits in real estate may be drawing to a close" (*Money,* January 1981).

◆ "In California . . . for example, it is not unusual to find families of average means buying $100,000 houses. . . . I'm confident prices have passed their peak" (John Wesley English and Gray Emerson Cardiff, *The Coming Real Estate Crash,* 1980).

◆ "The golden-age of risk-free run-ups in home prices is gone" (*Money,* March 1985).

◆ "If you're looking to buy, be careful. Rising home values are not a sure thing anymore" (*Miami Herald,* October 25, 1985).

◆ "Most economists agree . . . [a home] will become little more than a roof and a tax deduction, certainly not the lucrative investment it was through much of the 1980s" (*Money,* April 1986).

◆ "We're starting to go back to the time when you bought a home not for its potential money-making abilities, but rather as a nesting spot" (*Los Angeles Times,* January 31, 1993).

◆ "Financial planners agree that houses will continue to be a poor investment" (*Kiplinger's Personal Financial Magazine,* November 1993).

◆ "A home is where the bad investment is" (*San Francisco Examiner,* November 17, 1996).

◆ "Your house is a roof over your head. It is not an investment" (*Everything You Know about Money Is Wrong,* 2000).

◆ "Homes no longer are the place to put your money. With the recent run-up in prices, don't expect much more appreciation" (*Wall Street Journal,* January 20, 2003).

> **The federal government is creating home-buying programs to bring another 10 million individuals and families into the ranks of homeowners.**

As you can see from these quotations, the financial press has warned against investing in real estate for more than 50 years. Fortunately, most Americans have ignored these naysayers. The rates of homeownership continue to set new records.

More important, the president of the United States and the secretary of the U.S. Department of Housing and Urban Development (HUD) are working to develop even more outreach programs that will push demand for homes (condos and houses) even higher. With respect to condos and townhouses specifically, the future looks especially attractive for these three reasons:

1. Favorable demographics
2. Higher affordability
3. Inflation-protected income

Favorable Demographics   The overwhelming demographic fact of the United States remains population growth. Over the next 20 years, the number of people living in the United States will increase by 35 to 50 million (depending on birth rates, mortality, and immigration). But within that overall larger population, the age groups and household sizes that tend to prefer condos and townhouses will grow much faster.

> **Emerging population demographics favor condos and townhouses.**

The demographics of condo buyers are heavily weighted among persons under age 35, persons over age 55, singles of all ages, and DINKs (double income, no kids) of all ages. Although some overlap does exist among these demographic categories, here's how each group's numbers are expected to increase by 2013.

- *Echo boomers.* Beginning in 2003, the "echo boomers" begin turning 25 at the rate of 4 million persons a year. The echo boomers follow the baby bust era of 1965 to 1977, when births averaged only 3.4 million persons a year.
- *Baby boomers.* Whereas the echo boomers exceed the baby busters by about 15 percent, the baby boomers outnumber the 1930 to 1946 generation by 100 percent. During the next decade, around 40 million boomers will turn 55—up from around 22 million during the 1990s.
- *Single persons.* More Americans are choosing to live alone. By 2013, their numbers will jump by 7.5 million to 10.0 million persons.
- *DINKs.* Americans continue to live in smaller families. Many married women of childbearing age are either deferring or declining to give birth. For these DINKs, who prefer urban action over crabgrass and suburbia, central city condos rank high among their housing choices.

When compared to the 1990s, the era that we're entering now will almost double the number of people who fit a condo buyer's demographic profile. Younger adults, older adults, and

> **Echo boomers, retiring baby boomers, and no-children households will explode demand for condos and townhouses.**

adults without children (married or unmarried) will boost their total numbers by perhaps 40 million people. In addition, more Americans want secure, low-maintenance living. The "lock and leave without worry" attitude will draw more buyers to condos.

Overall, during the coming decade, demand for condos and townhouses by homebuyers (and second-home buyers) will break all previous records.

Higher Affordability   Have you looked at the prices of single-family houses lately? Over the past five years, house prices in most cities have jumped by 50 percent or more. In the higher-cost big cities, entry-level prices for modest two- or three-bedroom houses can easily top $300,000. The entry-level price for a house sits at about twice the entry level price of a condo.

Consider the West Point Grey–Kitsalano neighborhoods of Vancouver, British Columbia. In 1980, one could buy a decent (but far from extravagant) single-family home in these areas for around $100,000. Today, that same house carries a price tag of $500,000 (Canadian dollars). On the other hand, a comparably sized condo that sold for $100,000 in 1980 would sell today at around $300,000. A bare-minimum house (essentially site value) would cost $400,000, whereas one can buy an entry-level condo for $100,000 to $125,000.

These figures illustrate two points that apply in many (if not most) cities throughout the United States and Canada.

♦ Unless they buy a condominium, a large percentage of potential homebuyers are priced out of homeownership in the more desirable neighborhoods.
♦ In most of the more desirable neighborhoods, house prices have outpaced condo prices—but this trend won't likely continue.

> **Millions of hopeful homebuyers cannot afford to buy a decent single-family house in a desirable location.**

The first point is rather obvious. The rapid run-up in house prices has blocked many hopeful homebuyers from what were once considered middle-class neighborhoods. Even low mortgage interest rates won't make $300,000 to $500,000 houses affordable to average to above-average earners. Although house prices in your area may sit far lower than in Vancouver, San Francisco, Chicago, or Washington, D.C., I'm sure that you will find that the basic relationship holds. In the more desirable areas of town, condos and townhouses provide lower entry-level prices. In a word, condos rank higher in affordability.

The second point deserves more explanation. Suppose that you accept the premise that houses will continue to appreciate at a higher rate than condos. You estimate 6 percent for houses, 3 percent for condos. Table 1.1 shows how the numbers would evolve over periods of 5, 10, 15, and 20 years.

Someone once quipped that a trend that can't continue, won't continue. What you see here is a trend that can't continue. At different rates of appreciation, a house more than triples in value over 20 years, but the condo doesn't quite double. The house price increases by $693,000; the condo price increases by $82,075.

Even if we assume that people much prefer houses to condos, at some point condo prices become so *relatively* cheap that peo-

Purchase Price	5 Years	10 Years	15 Years	20 Years
$300,000 (6% appreciation for houses)	$404,400	$545,700	$736,200	$993,000
$100,000 (3% appreciation for condos)	$116,100	$134,935	$156,743	$182,075

Table 1.1   Why Housing Appreciation Cannot Continue to Outpace Condo Prices

> **Condo prices will play catch-up to home prices during the next decade.**

ple would say, "Sure, we would like to own a house, but we can't afford it. And even if we could afford it, we don't think we would be willing to pay such a steep price premium."

You can play with the numbers any way you want. But the essential principle remains. Over long periods of time, houses (on average) cannot and will not always appreciate faster than condos. In fact, given the changing demographics of the population (younger, older, fewer households with kids), you might even see some real price softening in those large, 3,000-square-feet to 10,000-square-feet McMansions that became so popular during the 1990s and remain so today.

During the late 1960s through the early 1980s, condo prices actually appreciated faster than houses in many cities. Subsequently, though, overbuilding and excessive numbers of apartment conversions flooded the market. Condo prices stagnated or fell. In Boston and Houston, some owners could not sell their units for 50 cents on the dollar. Nevertheless, long-term condo investors who bought at the peak of those earlier boom-and-bust times have still seen their unit prices double or triple in value.

After this brief digression, let me return to my basic point. Whether we are talking houses or condos of an earlier boom era, never simply extrapolate the past into the future. On average, neither type of dwelling can outperform the other decade after decade without end. As to the decade that lies before us, the fundamental facts support good appreciation for well-selected condos and townhouses.

> **Never project the past into the future without first studying market fundamentals.**

Strongly Competitive Yield: Investor Demand Up to now, you've seen that the homebuyer demographics and affordability will accelerate the demand for condos. But I also forecast a ballooning demand for condos by investors (which is why I wrote this book).

What do retirees need most during retirement? A safe, inflation-protected stream of income. In today's investment climate, where can retiree-investors obtain this needed income stream? Nowhere but rental properties—not stocks, not bonds, not annuities, not certificates of deposit. And for the great majority, not an employer pension.

◆ *Not stocks*. The current dividend yield on the S&P 500 sits at less than 2 percent. Put $100,000 into a diversified portfolio of stocks and you collect $2,000 a year.

◆ *Not bonds*. On relatively low-risk, long-term bonds that are suitable for retirees, the investor could earn 4 to 7 percent—for an income of $4,000 to $7,000 a year. That's not bad in today's market, but it is still woefully inadequate because bond interest does not protect against inflation. At an inflation rate of just 2.5 percent a year, after 10 years, the real value of that $5,000 in interest income has been sliced to $3,895; after 20 years, it offers only $3,030 in yearly spending power. Even worse, if interest rates fall, the corporation can probably call (redeem) the bond.

> **The retired investors may be forced to replace their bonds with ones that carry a lower interest rate.**

◆ *Not annuities*. Currently, many retirees are rushing to annuities because for $100,000 they can buy an income for life of $500 to $600 a month. But annuities offer a double bad deal: (1) The income stream will not grow with inflation, and (2) if the retiree drops dead tomorrow, the entire $100,000 vanishes into the insurance company's vault. The heirs of the retiree receive nothing.

Okay, back to rental properties. If a retiree paid cash for a $100,000 condo, he would probably net after expenses $500 to $600 a month for the first year—about the same as an annuity. But that's where the similarity ends. For as long as that retiree lives, his net rental income will increase by around 4 percent a year (more in some years, less in others). Here's how the numbers look:

Net Income from Rental Condo (4 percent Rent Increases)

	Year 1	Year 5	Year 10	Year 15	Year 20	Year 25
Amount	$500	$610	$745	$910	$1,110	$1,357

Income from Annuity

	Year 1	Year 5	Year 10	Year 15	Year 20	Year 25
Amount	$500	$500	$500	$500	$500	$500

> **Annuities guarantee *lower* real incomes as you get older.**

Now why would anyone choose an annuity that virtually guarantees that you will become poorer as you get older? It could get much worse for annuity holders relative to condo investors. The 4 percent rent increase above assumes that the Consumer Price Index (CPI) advances about 2.5 percent a year. Rents typically increase about 1.5 percent above the CPI to account for both inflation and wage increases due to gains in productivity.

Recently, inflation has settled down. But what if we returned to the 5 to 12 percent a year inflation we experienced throughout most of the 1970s and 1980s? At, say, an 8 percent increase in rents (6.5 percent gain in CPI), here's how our two retirees fare:

Net Income from Rental Condo (8 percent increases)

	Year 1	Year 5	Year 10	Year 15	Year 20	Year 25
Amount	$500	$745	$1,109	$1,651	$2,458	$3,660

Income from Annuity

	Year 1	Year 5	Year 10	Year 15	Year 20	Year 25
Amount	$500	$500	$500	$500	$500	$500

Although 6.5 percent inflation seems rather far-fetched right now, that's also how such figures would have seemed in the 1950s and early 1960s. Yet forecasting inflation is not the point. Rather, the retired investor needs to *prepare for an inflation-protected* income.

> **Retirees must prepare for the possibility of inflation.**

> **Annuity buyers liquidate their wealth. Condo investors continue to build their wealth— even while drawing a larger monthly income.**

That retiree never needs to worry about the cost of living outpacing the ability to pay.

If you believe the inflation issue to be of idle concern, revisit the experiences of those "safety-conscious" retirees of the 1970s and early 1980s who held most of their savings in 4 percent and 5 percent U.S. government bonds. Inflation devastated their wealth and standard of living.

Before leaving the topic of annuities versus investment condos, let's return to capital preservation. As noted, with a life annuity you give up your capital for a fixed monthly payment for life. How foolish is that? With a condo, you not only achieve a lifetime of inflation-protected income but your initial capital grows in value as the condo appreciates. Here's how the two retirees fare in terms of capital preservation and growth.

Capital Preservation and Growth

Year	Condo Investor (3% Appreciation)	Annuity Investor
1	$100,000	$0
5	116,161	0
10	134,935	0
15	156,743	0
20	182,000	0
25	211,501	0
30	245,684	0

Now you know what's even better. The appreciated condo passes to the retiree's children (or other heirs) completely free of capital gains taxes. Talk about a win-win situation!

Summing Up

During the next 10 to 20 years, the twin issues of demographics and affordability clearly indicate that homebuyers will boost demand for condos. In addition, retirees who want to earn an inflation-protected income and grow their capital for their heirs will also enter the investor condo market in record numbers. Together, these growing sources of buying power (homebuyers and investors) will undoubtedly continue to push up condo prices to successive new highs.

Moreover, as we move forward in the next chapter to calculating cash flows, equity build-up, and total returns, you will see even more clearly why condos really do provide the lazy way to wealth for those investors who want little or nothing to do with either property management or property maintenance.

CHAPTER 2

Bulls, Bears, and Cash Cows

You know that during the next 10 to 20 years, increasing numbers of buyers will keep condominium prices moving upward. In and of itself, condo/townhouse appreciation will give you a nice return on your cash investment (down payment). Fortunately, though, appreciation tells only part of the profit story. As mentioned in Chapter 1, you will also make money with condos through the other key components of your total investment return:

- ◆ Mortgage paydown
- ◆ Cash flow
- ◆ Tax shelter
- ◆ Value creation
- ◆ Diversification

Let Wall Street obsess over bulls, bears, and the flip-flops of the Dow Jones Industrial Average. As a condo investor, you can sit back, relax, and enjoy your cash cow. As your rent collections flow in, your tenants will buy property for you.

The Mortgage Paydown

Assume for a moment that you do not want to invest in condos (or anything else) primarily for appreciation. Naturally, like all investors, you want your investments to increase in value. But *you* want to make money, even if the prices stagnate.

You undoubtedly remember the late mania on Wall Street where so-called investors threw money at any crazy idea that came along. Did the companies touting these hotshot ideas really follow a business plan that had been tested by reason or experience? "No matter," such investors replied. "I don't care whether the company ever makes any money. I just want to see the stock price quadruple over the next six months and sell out for a bundle."

No investment can appreciate indefinitely without an underlying cash flow to support it.

After seeing such craziness, you've probably learned the lesson that many investors forgot: Buy the investment because it represents good value today. Graciously accept the appreciation as icing on the cake. Now, with that constraint, ask yourself this question: How would a condo investment perform if its value held firm over a period of 15 to 30 years and you merely paid off the mortgage from the rents you collect?

Wealth without Appreciation

Before we begin, let me clarify a point. In my college town, entry-level condo prices begin at $40,000 for a one-bedroom unit in a decent building. In San Francisco or Manhattan, a similar-sized unit might sell for $300,000 (or more). Unfortunately, these huge price differences that exist throughout the United States and Canada make writing a book with actual examples more difficult. So, in my effort to make examples easy, I will generally assume that an investor buys a condo priced at the easy-to-work-with figure of $100,000.

Throughout the country, condo prices vary, but the principles of condo investing hold true.

Regardless of the price levels in your area, the principles illustrated still apply. All you need to do is adjust the figures in the examples up or down to better fit the properties and places that match your own investment plans.

Double your money in five years. Triple within 10 years. Quintuple in 15 years.

With that caveat in mind, let's look at how a property that fails to appreciate will still help you build wealth. Assume that you put $20,000 down on that $100,000 condo/townhouse unit. You finance $80,000 for 15 years at 6.0 percent interest. Your mortgage payment equals $675 per month. To see how your mortgage payoff would increase your equity position in this property, take a look at Figure 2.1. Even without appreciation, your original $20,000 investment doubles in 5 years, triples in 10 years, and increases fivefold by the end of year 15. Because 15-year mortgages build wealth so much quicker than do 30-year mortgages, I generally encourage investors to choose this alternative over a 30-year mortgage—if they can handle the higher payments of the 15-year loan.

Nevertheless, the 30-year mortgage will still multiply your wealth—it just takes longer. Your equity build-up accrues more slowly with a 30-year loan not only because you pay less per month but also because 30-year loans require a higher rate of interest. In this instance, I'm assuming a 30-year loan interest rate of 6.5 percent and a payment of $505.60 per month. As you can see from Figure 2.2, with the 30-year mortgage it takes a full 15 years to double your money. You don't triple your original $20,000 in-

Year	Property Value ($)	Mortgage Balance ($)	Equity ($)
1	100,000	80,000	20,000
5	100,000	60,802	39,198
10	100,000	34,914	65,086
15	100,000	0	100,000

Figure 2.1   Equity Build-up from Mortgage Paydown (15-Year).

Year	Property Value ($)	Mortgage Balance ($)	Equity ($)
1	100,000	80,000	20,000
5	100,000	74,834	25,166
10	100,000	67,814	32,186
15	100,000	58,040	41,959
20	100,000	44,527	55,473
30	100,000	0	100,000

Figure 2.2 Equity Build-up from Mortgage Paydown (30-Year).

vestment until around 22 years. Your fivefold increase comes at the end of year 30, when your outstanding mortgage balance drops to zero.

Add to Your Principal Payments

> **Thirty-year mortgages build wealth—but at a slower pace.**

Because mortgage paydown accrues so slowly with a 30-year amortization, many investors tack on an extra $100 or so to their mortgage payments each month after the first few years. In other words, rather than completely pocket rent increases, they send some (or all) of that money to the lender. If, say, you begin your mortgage prepay in year 5, by year 15, your equity (not counting appreciation) would jump up to $63,000. With this $100 per month prepay, your money would triple within 15 years.

> **Use rent increases to quickly pay down the mortgage and build wealth faster.**

Certainty over Uncertainty

We will look at more mortgage payback alternatives later. For now, these payback calculations show that you don't need appreciation to multiply your wealth when investing in income-producing real estate. The rents you collect and pay to the lender automatically build equity as the outstanding loan balance evaporates. As long as the condo doesn't decline in value, you're guaranteed a nice return by simply letting your tenants buy you a property.

In fact, when I offered my *Stop Renting Now* seminars, attendees would sometimes say to me, "We can't decide for sure whether we want to buy or continue renting."

I answered, "You're asking the wrong question. The real question is whether you will *rent* or *own*. Every time you write a rent check, you are buying—except that your landlord becomes the owner, not you. So, rather than buy a property for someone else, commit to buy *and own* a home for yourself." It's amazing to me how many would-be investors overlook this basic point. Your condo wealth will grow because your tenants essentially buy your properties for you.

> **Your renters will *buy* real estate, but you will *own* it.**

Plan Your Wealth Building: Stocks versus Condos

When the stock market was flying high, most investors thought that their stock investments would grow without end at the steady rate of 10 to 12 percent a year. Millions of people were punching wealth-building numbers into their calculators. "Great!" they thought. "By the time we reach age 55, my 401(k) will be worth more than $500,000."

> **No one can predict the amount of wealth that you *might* accumulate with stocks.**

No Certainty with Stocks My, how times have changed. Slowly, investors are realizing that the stock market doesn't guarantee its returns. After hitting a peak in 1929, 25 years passed before the Dow Jones Industrial Average crossed that threshold again. After hitting a new peak in 1964, 18 years passed before the Dow permanently moved above that previous high. In early 2000, the market peaked at a record high.

When will it surpass that achievement—2005, 2010, 2020? Of course, no one knows. So how can one *plan* to build savings in the market when one can't count on accumulating any specific amount of wealth within any stated time period, whether measured in years or decades? The answer is, you can't. No one can.

The Condo/Townhouse Advantage   Do you know of any well-managed condo unit or townhouse that would sell at a price today that's less than what it sold for 10, 20, or 30 years ago? True, the short run may offer some ups and downs. But with rare exception, any period of 5 or 10 years will show an upward drift in unit value.

> **Real estate offers nearly certain returns from mortgage paydown.**

Over a decade or longer, you can *conservatively* count on selling your condo for at least the amount you paid for it. Consequently, you can predict the minimum amount of condo wealth you will have accumulated at any distant point in the future. You can conservatively assume the unit value will equal the price you paid. You can calculate the mortgage balance as of any selected date. To calculate the nearly certain wealth, merely subtract the mortgage balance from the purchase price.

History does not permit anyone to say the same thing about stocks. Whether you invest in the stocks of individual companies or in an index fund, neither you (nor anyone else) can predict within any tolerable degree of certainty the amount your stock investment will be worth at any given point in the future. Anyone who believes that they can plan a systematic wealth-building program in stocks needs to get a reality check.

> **You can't *plan* to build wealth in stocks.**

Depending on the term of your mortgage and the payback schedule, a condo will guarantee a fivefold increase of your original investment within 15 to 30 years. No stockbroker in the country will make you that kind of promise.

Cash Flow

Most people who buy stocks do so because they believe that their stocks will increase in value. Most investors who buy condos believe that the units will increase in value, but they primarily buy them to secure rent collections and cash flow. That's why condos offer a far safer investment alternative than stocks.

At current valuations, stocks do not come close to providing enough income to investors to justify their price. The greater fool theory reigns supreme. What is the greater fool approach to investing? It's the belief that income (dividends) don't matter. Investors may think to themselves, "Why should I care about dividends? Why should I care about corporate earnings? I'm holding for appreciation. As to the price at which I'm buying, it doesn't matter. I know some fool will come along and pay me even more than I paid."

> **Fools believe that they can sell their stocks at higher prices to even greater fools than themselves.**

When you *invest* to make money, reject this greater fool theory. Pay close attention to income, because income supports the foundation on which the value of an investment is built.

> **Speculators need favorable price movements to make money.**

You can certainly speculate. Income doesn't matter to speculators because they merely bet on a movement in price. Even though a few speculators (like George Soros) hit it big, the majority go bust (as did Long Term Capital Management, Richard Neiderehoffer, and the millions of people who bought the dot-coms and high-tech stocks of yesteryear).

Condo Investors Earn More Cash Flow

In Chapter 1, you saw how a retiree could obtain more income from rents than from any alternative type of investment (stocks, bonds, annuities). At that point of the discussion, we assumed that this investor paid cash for the condo. However, you will probably finance your units. To illustrate how to calculate your before-tax cash flow (BTCF) on a property you finance, start with the following data:

1. You buy today at a purchase price of $100,000.
2. You place $20,000 down. (Later, you'll learn how to buy with 10 percent down or less.)
3. You finance your purchase with a 30-year, fixed-rate mortgage of $80,000 at 6.5 percent interest.
4. Your mortgage payment equals $505.60 per month.
5. Your monthly expenses total $2,500 a year (including HOA fees).
6. You collect $850 a month in rents.
7. Rents and expenses each increase by 3 percent a year.

Again, these precise figures may not correspond exactly to your area. But remember, they illustrate a principle and technique. You will simply need to work through similar calculations with whatever numbers seem reasonable for the properties you investigate. With that said, you can see the cash flows for this property in Table 2.1. In the first year, this property throws off $1,633 in cash

Year	Rents ($)	Expenses ($)	Mortgage Payment ($)	BTCF ($)
1	10,200	2,500	6,067	1,633
5	11,842	2,898	6,067	2,877
10	13,749	3,358	6,067	4,324
15	15,962	3,892	6,067	6,003
20	18,532	4,511	6,067	7,954
30	25,000	6,085	0	18,915

Original investment equals $20,000. Mortgage payments based on $80,000 loan at 6.5 percent for 30 years.

Table 2.1 Annual Condominium Cash Flows (3 Percent Increases)

against your original investment of $20,000. In real estate lingo, that's called a cash-on-cash return of 8.1 percent.

$$\text{Cash-on-cash return} = \frac{\$1,633}{20,000}$$
$$= 8.1\%$$

> **Pay off your mortgage and kick the condo cash flow into high gear.**

But that's nothing compared to the cash flows and cash returns that will result over the longer term—even at just a 3 percent rate of increase in rent collections and expenses. As Table 2.1 shows, after 5 years, cash-on-cash jumps to 14.4 percent; and after 10 years, to 21.62 percent. Of course, the real kicker in cash flow comes when you get your mortgage paid off.

In Table 2.2, you can see the same types of cash flow calculations shown in Table 2.1. In this case, the figures assume an increase in rents and expenses of 5 percent a year. Although today 5 percent increases may seem rather optimistic, who knows what the future will bring? During the 1970s and 1980s, the Federal Reserve was working furiously to bring rent increases (and other prices) *down* to 5 percent a year.

Year	Rents ($)	Expenses ($)	Mortgage Payment ($)	BTCF ($)
1	10,200	2,500	6,067	1,633
5	13,087	3,208	6,067	3,812
10	16,790	4,115	6,067	6,608
15	21,541	5,280	6,067	10,194
20	27,638	6,774	6,067	14,797
30	45,520	11,157	0	34,363

Original investment equals $20,000. Mortgage payments based on $80,000 loan at 6.5 percent for 30 years.

Table 2.2   Annual Condominium Cash Flows (5 Percent Increases)

> **Earn indecent cash flows in later years.**

In any event, most experts are now projecting that over the next two or three decades rent increases will average somewhere between 3 and 5 percent a year. For people who want to invest to earn decent cash flows now (and positively indecent cash flows later), no safe investment (other than real estate) will produce such juicy yields. Why worry about where the stock market will sit 10, 20, or 30 years from now? You can virtually guarantee a cash-rich future by investing in two or three condos today.

How to Jump the Hurdle of Negative Cash Flows

With rents softening and home prices climbing, I constantly hear complaints from potential investors about negative cash flows. In some high-priced areas of the country, a $200,000 condo unit might bring in rents of only $1,250 to $1,500 a month. With 20 percent down, the mortgage payments plus expenses might easily consume all of your rent collections.

> **Even with negative cash flows today, you are building a strong, positive cash flow future.**

But that will happen only during the first several years of ownership. After five years or so, your rent collections will surpass the expenses. Although it's less than an ideal situation, you're still building a cash flow future that will yield more income than any other safe investment you can imagine.

Buying Growth   Sixteen years ago, California investor Leigh Robinson, in his popular book, *Landlording,* wrote,

Because rents used to be tied fairly closely to property values, setting rents was simple. The rule of thumb for an unfurnished house or duplex was that the monthly rent should equal one percent of its fair market value. A

$25,000 house, for example, would rent for $250 a month, and the tenant would pay for all the utilities and tend to the minor repairs. For multiple-family dwellings larger than duplexes, the rule of thumb was that the monthly aggregate of rents would approximate 1.2% of the value of the property, a figure which is the reverse of the common yardstick that the value of multiple units should equal seven times their annual gross rents. Each apartment complex in a $40,000 fourplex, then, would normally have rented for $120 per month.

Those old rules of thumb, which took into account decent cash flow return on the investment, simply do not apply now as much as they once did, for property values have outstripped rents significantly in most areas. Today, an $80,000 house may rent for any sum of money, from $400 to $800, from one-half of one percent of the property value to a full one percent, and a multiple-family dwelling may rent for as little as one-half of one percent to as much as 1.4% of its value.[1]

Did you notice the figures that Robinson used in his examples? A $25,000 house, a $40,000 fourplex, an $80,000 house, and rents of $400 to $800 a month for a California house! Robinson intended to lament the fact that rental properties (in high-cost areas) don't yield the same level of cash flows in the early years of ownership that they used to. Looking backward, you can see why.

Growth in Housing Prices and Rent Levels   In California and other high-priced areas, my 3-percent-a-year assumption for growth looks pathetic. From the mid-1980s on, rents and home prices in the Golden State have pushed ahead (on average) by 6 to 12 percent a year—with home prices moving up faster than rents.

---

1. Leigh Robinson, *Landlording* (El Cerrito, CA: Express, 1987), 91.

What Does the Future Hold? Will California, the District of Columbia, and New York City investors still achieve those outsized returns from growth during the next 10 to 20 years? No one knows for sure. But in the race between rents and prices, rents will begin a round of catch-up sometime shortly.

> **Rents are set to play catch-up.**

Right now, in high-cost areas, low interest rates are pushing housing prices further out of reach for the middle class. Sooner, rather than later, the vice of unaffordability will begin to squeeze more younger households into condos and apartments (as I argued in Chapter 1). Condo prices and apartment rents are destined to climb to new highs. The facts clearly indicate that today's negative cash flows will morph into high positive cash flows within a few short years.

Change the Financing on Your Properties For ease of illustration, my cash flow examples assumed a 6.5 percent 30-year mortgage. But (at least presently), investors can pick up adjustable-rate mortgages (ARMs) at interest rates of 4.0 to 6.0 percent. To avoid negative cash flows, use an ARM. If that doesn't appeal to you, try to obtain some type of hybrid ARM that guarantees your interest rate for three to five years and then readjusts yearly.

> **Lower your interest, lower your monthly payments. Increase your cash flow.**

You might consider using a higher down payment. Any low- to moderate-priced condo—even in Los Angeles or Brooklyn—will yield a positive cash flow with 30 to 40 percent down. If you can't come up with that amount of cash, join with a money partner.

Switch Locations As pointed out earlier, you can invest in a condo across town or across the country. Because the HOA handles nearly all the tough maintenance and management tasks of the complex, you won't need to drive by your property once a month to make sure the tenants haven't wrecked the place.

Invest in areas
with lower
housing prices.

Although my experience with long-distance ownership of single-family houses and apartment buildings suggests that such fears are greatly exaggerated, you may feel differently. If so, owning a condo will ease your mind. If your tenants fail to walk the straight and narrow, you can rest assured that the HOA will let you know about their offenses.

In many cities throughout the country, you can still achieve positive cash flows with 20 percent down—or less. Seldom will such cities show the same historically high appreciation rates as California or New York, but they offer astute investors a very strong value play. Get on the Web. Check out property prices and rent levels in Orlando, Terre Haute, Tallahassee, Topeka, or Atlanta. All of these cities currently offer condos at prices low enough to yield positive cash flows.

Buy at a Bargain Price/Create Value   What if you could buy a $200,000 condo for $160,000? You could certainly generate a positive cash flow at that bargain price. What if you could buy an outdated or uncared-for condo at a price of $160,000, dress it for success, and then rent it out? Creating value through improvements will also contribute to cash flow. Are these possibilities realistic? Absolutely. You will learn how to achieve both of these cash flow boosters later on.

Buy a high-value
property at a
bargain price.

Condos versus Single-Family Houses
As noted earlier, my previous books on investing generally recommend investing in single-family houses and small apartment buildings. I stand by that advice if you've got the time and money and are willing to put in the extra effort that these types of income properties require. Nevertheless, in terms of cash flow, in most markets, condos significantly outperform single-family houses.

In Vancouver, for example, I recently looked at a $100,000 condo that was leased for $800 per month. The lowest-priced house in the area cost $400,000. Yet the house would rent—at the

> **Condos/town-houses typically yield more cash flow than houses per dollar of investment.**

outside—for no more than $2,250 a month. The house would cost far more in annual operating expenses, property insurance, and property taxes.

Go out and look in your market. You may not find differences quite so great as those found in Vancouver. But you will certainly find that condos and townhouses produce noticeably more cash flow—per dollar of investment—than single-family houses.

Shelter Your Cash from the IRS

All types of income-producing real estate offer investors three outstanding opportunities to shelter the cash they earn from their properties from the grabbing hand of the Internal Revenue Service (IRS).

- ◆ Depreciation
- ◆ Section 1031 Tax-Free Exchange
- ◆ Cash-out refinancing

In addition, homeowners (condo owners) may earn up to $500,000 of tax-free capital gains. No other investment yields these same strong wealth-building benefits.

Depreciation

When you invest in a rental condo, house, or apartment building, tax law permits you to deduct from your rent collections an expense called *depreciation*. This expense differs from other expenses, such as property insurance, maintenance, plumbing repairs, and yard care. To pay those expenses, you need to write a check. As a result, they draw down your positive cash flow.

> **Depreciation—the expense that puts money into your pocket.**

With depreciation, you never write a check because it's a *noncash* statutorily mandated deduction against your revenues.

How Depreciation Boosts After-Tax Cash Flow (ATCF)   Reconsider Table 2.1, in which the condo unit yielded a BTCF of $1,633. To move from BTCF to ATCF, we use the following technique:

BTCF	= $1,633
+ Principal	= + 867
− Depreciation	= −2,909
Taxable Income	= −2,143

We add mortgage principal back to BTCF because the IRS doesn't consider principal repayment a deductible expense. Principal simply pays back money you borrowed. As shown in the next section, tax law does permit you to deduct depreciation in the amount of $2,909—thus leaving you a tax loss on the property of $2,143.

Now here's how this depreciation tax loss helps boost your ATCF. Subject to certain exceptions for high wage earners, you can

> **Depreciation lowers your taxes.**

use your $2,143 "loss" from your condo to offset $2,143 of your otherwise taxable earnings from your job or other investments. If your top marginal tax bracket (state and federal combined) is 35 percent, this loss permits you to cut your income tax bill by $750.

$2,147	(deductible loss)
0.35	marginal tax bracket
$ 750	(tax savings)

Your total ATCF gains from this property during the first year of ownership equal $2,383.

$$
\begin{aligned}
\text{BTCF} &= \$1,633 \\
+ \text{Tax savings} &= \underline{750} \\
& \$2,383
\end{aligned}
$$

With this tax savings figured in, your cash-on-cash return increases to 11.9 percent.

$$
\begin{aligned}
\text{Cash return} &= \frac{\$2,383}{\$20,000} \\
&= 11.9\%
\end{aligned}
$$

Naturally, the exact numbers vary across deals. But in every case, depreciation will help you boost your after-tax cash returns.

How to Calculate Your Tax Deduction for Depreciation

To actually calculate the amount of depreciation for residential income properties, first split the purchase price between land and buildings. Say that $100,000 condo actually costs you $80,000 for the unit and $20,000 for your share of the land on which the units have been built as well as common areas, such as parking areas and green space. The law then assumes that your unit will completely wear out over a period of 27.5 years, leaving you with only an interest in the land. The values of the condo buildings—according to tax law—will then equal zero. So, even without spending one extra nickel (above your normal maintenance and capital improvements), Congress gives you a noncash tax deduction for this $80,000 unit (purchase price less land) of $2,909.

$$
\begin{aligned}
\text{Depreciation} &= \frac{\$80,000}{27.5 \text{ years}} \\
&= \$2,909
\end{aligned}
$$

Allocating land value. For purposes of tax law, you'll want to allocate as much value to the unit and as little value to the land as seems legally defensible. The higher the amount you can depre-

Split your purchase price between land and buildings.

ciate, the larger the amount of your tax deduction. Generally, the IRS will accept an 80/20 allocation without question. In some instances, you may even be able to justify a 90/10 split. The agent who sells you the condo and the appraiser who values the property for the mortgage lender will be able to assign reasonable values to the unit and the land. Typically, land value climbs as a percentage of the purchase price only if you buy a unit that's situated on a very expensive site—such as oceanfront.

Condos' advantage over houses. In high-cost cities, condos frequently give you a substantial income tax advantage over single-family houses. That's because the land on which the house sits can easily account for 50 to 80 percent of your purchase price—especially at the low to moderate end of the single-family price range. (This point excludes newer homes in suburban areas, where land values tend to be lower.)

For each dollar invested, condos provide larger deductions for depreciation.

For example, a $350,000 house in Berkeley, California (if you could find a house at that price), would probably give you *at best* a 20/80 house/land allocation. Of your $350,000 purchase price, $280,000 would represent the value of the site. Your tax deduction for depreciation would amount to only $2,545, even though you paid $350,000.

$$\text{Depreciaton} = \frac{\$70,000 \text{ (house value)}}{27.5 \text{ years}}$$
$$= \quad \$2,545$$

In a head-to-head comparison with single-family houses, condos will generally give more depreciation for each dollar invested.

Tax-Free Exchanges

When you own a corporate stock that has a big run-up in price, you may think that now is the time to sell before the market stalls or turns down. But selling creates a serious problem. Because of federal income tax law, you will lose a big part of your gain to the U.S. Treasury due to the capital gains tax. As a result, many stock market investors hold their stocks long after they should have sold them because they can't bear the thought of immediately throwing away part of their profits in taxes.

> **Tax-free exchanges help you pyramid real estate wealth without sharing profits with the IRS.**

In contrast, real estate investors need not face this dilemma. As will be explained later, for many investors an installment sale can help them defer and perhaps reduce the amount of their profits they lose to taxes. Just as important, but not nearly as well known, real estate investors can also eliminate or defer federal income tax liabilities by trading up. These two techniques—installment sales and exchanging—give owners of income properties a substantial tax advantage over investors who choose stocks, bonds, and most other types of real or financial assets.

Exchanges Don't Necessarily Involve Two-Way Trades Due to lack of knowledge, most real estate investors who do at least have some awareness of tax-free exchanges believe that to use this tax benefit, they must find a seller who will accept one or more of their currently owned properties in trade. Although this does represent one way to enter into a tax-free exchange, it is not necessarily the most commonly used exchange technique. Most exchanges, in fact, actually involve at least three investors.

The Three-Party Exchange Three-party exchanges outnumber two-party "trade-in" exchanges because it's usually difficult to find an owner of a property you want who will accept the

Exchanges don't necessarily involve trades.

property you plan to trade up. True, it's sometimes possible to negotiate a two-way trade by convincing an unwilling seller to accept your property in trade and then turn around and sell it. But doing so may cause you to spend too much negotiating capital that you could devote to other issues such as a lower price or owner-will-carry financing.

Instead, most serious real estate investors arrange a three-party exchange through the following steps: (1) locate a buyer for the property to trade; (2) locate a property you want to buy; and (3) set up an escrow whereby you deed your property to your buyer, the buyer pays cash to your seller, and your seller conveys his or her property to you. In effect, no property has really been exchanged for another property. Because of this anomaly, John Reed (a leading expert on real estate exchanges) suggests renaming this technique the "interdependent sale and reinvestment" strategy.

Exchanges Are Complex but Easy   As you might suspect, anything that involves federal tax laws will be entangled in a spider web of rules and regulations, and Section 1031 Exchanges (as

Use an exchange pro.

they are called in the Internal Revenue Code) are no exception. However, even though exchange rules are complex, exchange transactions are relatively easy to administer when you work with a professional who is experienced in successfully setting up and carrying out tax-free exchanges.

Reed says the total extra costs (including attorney fees and escrow charges) of conducting an exchange should run less than $2,000. Professional Publishing Company (now owned by Dearborn Financial in Chicago) even publishes standard forms that may be used to complete the required paperwork. Even if you rely on standard forms, use a tax or realty exchange pro. Be aware, too, that the great majority of certified public accountants and real estate attorneys know little about Section 1031 Exchanges. Unless

> **Contact your local investors' exchange club.**

your accountant or lawyer has definitely mastered this area of the law, ask to be led to someone who has this expertise. (If you live in at least a midsize city, there's probably an exchange club whose members include investors and commercial realty brokers who will be able to recommend competent and experienced professionals.)

Note: Some accountants and lawyers have frequently told me things like "Oh, you don't want to get involved in something like that" or "That's more trouble than it's worth" or "Sure, I can handle it, no problem." In my inexperienced days I simply accepted such comments without question. "Surely, I can count on the wisdom and good faith of my accountant or lawyer," I told myself. (Those of you who have worked with lawyers and accountants can now stop laughing. I have already confessed to my early naïveté.) The points here are twofold: (1) To hide their own ignorance, lawyers and accountants who do not understand an issue will often advise against "getting involved with that" whatever "that" may be, so as not to disclose that they really don't know what they are talking about; or (2) depending on how much they need the business (or perhaps they just don't want to lose you as a client), accountants and lawyers frequently claim competency in areas where they lack expertise.

> **Pepper your tax counsel with penetrating questions.**

Either or both of these tendencies can cost you. (Yes, you can sue for malpractice, and I have done so. But it's not a recommended course of action.) To reduce the chance of professional error, misinformation, or just simple bad advice, don't let your accountant or attorney bluff you. Ask them a lot with detailed and specific questions about the issue at hand and their actual experience in successfully dealing with these issues. Whatever you do, don't naively accept the counsel of any professional (lawyer, accountant, real estate agent, medical doctor, and so on). These are people with serious limitations; they are not demigods. Require them to *earn* your trust and respect through knowledge and performance, not expect it simply because they list a string of initials after their names.

Are Tax-Free Exchanges Really Tax-Free?   Some people quibble with the term *tax-free* exchange. They say that an exchange doesn't eliminate taxes but merely defers payment to a later date. This view is misinformed on four counts:

1. The exchange itself is tax-free if you follow the rules (see the following section).
2. Whether you must pay taxes later depends on how you divest yourself of the property. If you hold it until your death, the property passes into your estate free of any capital gains taxes.
3. As another alternative, you could arrange a sale in a later year in which you have tax losses that you can use to offset the amount of any capital gain.
4. If Americans are sensible enough to elect legislators who understand the importance of productive investment, we may eventually see the income tax, or at least the capital gains tax, abolished.

The most important point is that exchanges eliminate capital gains in the year you dispose of a property by trading up. Whether you pay in future years will depend on how savvy you are in developing tax-avoidance strategies and the tax law that exists in some future year. By exchanging, you eliminate a definite tax liability in the year of disposition and accept an uncertain and contingent future tax liability. That's a tax trade-off you should always be willing to make. (For specific Section 1031 Rules, see Box 2.1.)

Stated as simply and briefly as possible, Section 1031 tax-free exchanges must comply with five principal rules:

1. *Like-kind exchange.* Here's another source of confusion: The tax law states that only exchanges of "like-kind" properties qualify for the preferred tax treatment. However, "like-kind" doesn't mean fourplex to fourplex or even apartment building to apartment building, as some people believe. The concept is actually much broader and includes "all property [types] held for productive use in a trade or business or for investment." As a matter of law, one is permitted to exchange nearly any type of real estate for any other type of real estate and still arrange your transaction to fall within Section 1031 guidelines.

2. *45-day rule.* If all parties to an exchange are known and in agreement, you can close all properties simultaneously. Otherwise, you can use a delayed exchange procedure that specifies two separate deadlines. One of these is the 45-day rule, which says you must identify the property you want to acquire within 45 days after the date of closing with the buyer of your present property (i.e., before midnight of the forty-fourth day).

3. *180-day closing.* The second time requirement states that you must close on your acquisition property within 180 days of closing the disposition of the property you are trading up.

4. *Escrow restrictions.* Tax-free exchanges generally require exchange proceeds to be paid into and distributed out of an escrow arrangement. The escrow agent must be completely independent of you (e.g., not your attorney, real estate agent, bank officer, spouse, company's employees, or anyone else who is subject to your exclusive control or direction). Most important, you must not be able to withdraw any money from this escrow or otherwise pull out of the exchange agreement prior to the date the escrow agent has scheduled disbursements and property conveyances.

5. *Trading up.* To gain the benefit of a tax-free exchange, you must trade for a property of equal or greater market value. Trading down or accepting a cash "boot" exposes you to a liability for capital gains taxes. If because of this tax liability your seller doesn't want to trade down or accept a cash sale, then you (or your realty agent) can create a "daisy chain" of exchange participants until a property owner is found who wants to cash out or trade down real estate holdings and is willing to pay the capital gains tax. (A seller who has planned a total tax strategy may not have to pay any taxes despite realizing taxable income from a specific transaction. Also, because heirs receive properties on a stepped-up basis, they will incur little or no capital gains tax liability unless they sell the inherited property for substantially more than its estimated market value at the time it entered the deceased's estate.)

(continued)

Box 2.1　Section 1031 Exchange Rules.

To keep lawyers and accountants fully employed, the tax law embellishes the preceding rules with various details, definitions, regulations, and requirements. As noted earlier, the trick is not only to use an experienced exchange pro to guide you *before* you enter into any purchase or sale agreement but also to keep the exchange process in legal compliance throughout each step until all closings are completed.

Box 2.1 *(Continued)*

> **Tax-free exchanges do permit you to legally avoid capital gains taxes—maybe forever.**

Homeowners Receive Tax-Free Gains

Because government policy favors homeownership over renting, Congress has provided homeowners with a gigantic tax break. However, as the following discussion shows, real estate investors can also integrate this benefit into investing strategies.

Under current tax law, you can sell your principal residence and pocket up to $500,000 tax-free (if married filing jointly). If you're single, your maximum untaxed profit is capped at $250,000.

Although generally the law requires you to have lived in the home for two of the past five years, it does not limit the total number of times that you may use this exclusion. It merely limits you to one capital gains exclusion every two years. In other words, over the next 24 years, you could buy and sell a personal residence (condo or house) up to 12 times—and escape capital gains taxes every time (subject, of course, to the limits).

> **Weigh the tax advantages of living in your investment.**

Flipper's Paradise For investors who would like to buy properties, improve them, sell, and move up to bigger and better, this law offers a "flipper's paradise." Granted, most people do not want to change residences every few years. But for those willing to tolerate this inconvenience, even an 8- or 10-year plan could easily help you gain $500,000 to $1 million in tax-free profits.

This is exactly how Suzanne Brangham, author of *Housewise* (HarperCollins, 1987), earned a fortune. Starting with a $40,000 condominium, over a period of 16 years, she rehabbed herself up to a $1.8 million mansion. In contrast to Suzanne's day, the beauty of the law now is that when you sell that last flipper property, you can avoid paying taxes. (Under previous tax law, homeowner capital gains were primarily deferred, not excluded.)

Tax-Free Capital   In addition to flipping condos (or houses), you might benefit from this law in another way. Suppose you own a home with a substantial equity. The kids are gone and you want to downsize. You can now (without the previous once-in-a-lifetime, age 55 restriction) sell that large, expensive house and unlock your equity tax-free (up to $500,000). Then, you can split the cash proceeds into several piles. Use part of this money as a down payment on a lower-priced replacement home as well as several condo income properties. Finance all of the newly acquired condos with 15-year mortgages. With property appreciation and mortgage payoff quickly building your net worth, you'll be set for life within a relatively short time frame— and still avoid most of the hassles of landlording.

> **Use your home equity to acquire investment condos.**

A Great Way to Begin Your Investing   This law also gives first-time homebuyers a great advantage. Buy a condo (or house). Use the favorable low- or no-money down first-time buyer mortgage programs. Live in the property for two years.

Then buy another personal residence using a low down payment owner-occupied type of mortgage. Hold the original condo as a rental for three years. Then sell it and pocket the capital gains tax-free. Use this cash to reinvest in one or more other rental properties. Remember, to profit with a tax-free gain, you only need to

> **You can use the homeowner exemption for capital gains with rental properties.**

live in the property for two of the previous five years prior to the date of sale.

Gain Tax-Free Cash with a Cash-Out Refinance

The hypesters of Wall Street persistently advise investors to stay away from real estate because it supposedly lacks liquidity. Wall Street insiders (as so often is the case) do not know what they are talking about.

Not only can you quickly and easily pull cash out of your condo (or other property) investments, but you can also do so free of all income taxes. Simply arrange an equity line of credit or a cash-out refinance.

As noted previously, you can't deduct mortgage principal repayments as an expense against your rent collections. But you gain

> **Refinancing give you tax-free cash.**

far more from that rule than you lose. Because you aren't allowed to deduct principal as an expense, you need not count mortgage proceeds (or any other type of borrowing) as income. As your equity wealth accumulates, you can borrow and spend (or hopefully reinvest) it completely without paying taxes.

You cannot gain this benefit with any other type of investment.

Summing Up

The fortunes of the bulls and bears on Wall Street continuously swing with the movement of the Dow. Is the market going up? Is the market going down? These investors persistently worry whether the stock market will give them the appreciation they're hoping for—the appreciation needed to make their stocks pay off.

As a condo investor, you can pitch such worries into the dust bin of history. Apart from the fact that the condo almost certainly will go up in value lies this more important point: You don't need appreciation to make your condo investment pay off. You will reap more than satisfactory gains from mortgage paydown, cash flows, and tax-sheltered or tax-excluded cash withdrawals. (We haven't even talked about the benefits of lower risk and diversification.)

Alas, these superior returns won't just appear for the asking. You must choose your condo/townhouse projects and units wisely. I now turn to that topic.

CHAPTER 3

Get to Know the Development

Thirty million Americans now live in condos, co-ops, and town-houses. Twenty years ago, that figure was just 10 million. As evidenced by this exploding popularity of community living, a large majority of investors and homeowners who have bought into these developments do express overall satisfaction.

Condo Communities Appeal to Buyers of All Incomes

Surprisingly, in the early years of condos and townhouses, experts believed that this type of housing would primarily serve younger individuals, couples, and families who couldn't afford to buy a house. Of course, condos still serve this purpose, but they've also become widely accepted as a lifestyle choice for homebuyers in all price ranges. On Longboat Key, Florida, for example, you can buy an exquisite waterfront (canal, not Gulf of Mexico) single-family house for $750,000. Yet many homebuyers opt for a condo that sports a price tag upward of $2 million (with some condos going for as much as $6 to $8 million). Do not believe for a minute that condo living necessarily implies something inferior to a house. A large percentage of condo residents prefer this style of living.

> **Condos are a lifestyle choice for all price ranges.**

When you invest in a rental condo, you may find many tenants who could easily afford to lease (or buy) a house but choose the rental condo because of the advantages it offers—not because it's in some way cheaper. Case in point: A surgeon friend of mine who earns well into six figures has rented a townhouse for the past three years. She could easily afford to buy an upscale single-family house; but as a single woman, she wants nothing to do with repairs, maintenance, and yard work. In fact, she has tried to buy the townhouse that she's leasing. Alas, the investor-owner won't sell.

Key Sources of Satisfaction and Dissatisfaction

"We have moved 12 times in 15 years," says Major Art Shapiro of the U.S. Marines.

> We have lived in all types of houses. But we like this townhouse development best. We have great privacy, the neighbors always stop to say, "Hi, how are you doing?" and that sort of thing. As for security, we feel very safe, even with our six-year-old. The homeowners' association keeps everything in top condition, too. I've never even seen a McDonald's sack or cigarette package lying on the ground. We really don't have any complaints. We love it.

> **Most owners and residents of condos express high levels of satisfaction.**

Condo resident Sam Dolnick agrees. "I love taking walks around the complex and looking at the green space and realizing I don't have to mow all that grass. We've got swimming pools; an exercise gym; courts for tennis, badminton, and basketball; and 11 acres of landscaped

> **Some projects are losers. But not necessarily the ones you might think.**

grounds. It's a great way to live. The homeowners' association takes care of everything."

As you can imply from these quotations, most condo and townhouse residents favorably view their developments and their HOAs. Nevertheless, no one would argue that all buildings and communities satisfy equally. You must not buy randomly. Before you commit to a development, building, or specific unit, check it out thoroughly in terms of the complex itself and how the unit pricing ranks competitively. Your best investment relates to a unit's relative desirability when measured against its price.

Features and Price

One author of a popular book on buying condos (written primarily for first-time homebuyers) goes through a list of dos and don'ts. For example, this author tells readers:

- ◆ Buy a property in the best possible location.
- ◆ Always look for the lowest-density development.
- ◆ Buy a unit that's easy to resell.
- ◆ Don't buy into a complex (building) with high monthly fees.

If you've read any guidebooks on homebuying or investing, you've probably run across authors and experts who likewise give you a concrete list of do-and-don't advice. Unfortunately, this approach to advising errs egregiously. Why? Because it ignores *relative* pricing. When real people buy or rent, they make trade-offs and compromises. They shop and compare. Then they choose their best value based on their wants, needs, preferences, and budget.

> **Buyers (and renters) shop for their best value.**

What if you were reading a book that advises you how to buy a car? The author tells you:

- ◆ Buy a car that gives you the best gas mileage.
- ◆ Always make sure the trunk includes a large storage area for suitcases.
- ◆ Look for the longest warranty.
- ◆ Make sure the car shows good resale value.
- ◆ Buy a car that ranks highly in safety and crash protection.

Most people would find these features desirable. But sometimes features conflict with each other (large trunk, safety, good gas mileage). Some features may not actually fit your needs or preference (large trunk, long warranty). If you're like many of us, you can't afford every desirable feature you prefer—even if you could find them all available in the same vehicle.

Your Best Opportunity

Perhaps first-time homebuyers need some handholding. They may feel like they need someone with more experience to tell them exactly what features to look for and which locations are best. For investors, that approach clearly won't work. Markets change constantly. Neighborhoods change. Population demographics change. Condo prices and rent levels change. Your best buy yesterday may not prove to be your wisest buy tomorrow.

> **Good buys depend on relative prices.**

Resale Potential

Consider this advice: Buy for the best resale potential. It sounds reasonable until you realize that nearly every unit will show strong resale potential at the right price.

Imagine that you find a unit that looks out into the complex dumpster. Similar-sized units in the complex sell for $125,000. For the past six months, the owner of this unit with the impaired view has been asking $119,000 but has found no takers. Now facing financial distress, this owner has morphed into a highly motivated seller. You believe that you can easily find a tenant for the unit who will pay $875 a month. You offer the distressed seller $75,000. The seller counters at $100,000. You ease up to $82,500. The seller again counters at $95,000. Eventually you both agree to $90,000, providing you can close within 21 days.

Good Buy

Have you violated the "resale potential" rule? This unit was up for sale for six months. Clearly, it lacks resale potential. Right? Sorry, wrong. The unit lacks good resale potential at a price of $119,000. But I bet that it offers very great resale potential at a price of $100,000.

> **At the right price, nearly all units show good resale potential.**

You can't judge the resale potential of a unit by the quality of its features alone. Primarily, resale potential relates to the asking price for those features. Alternatively, perhaps you could figure out a way to remedy the features that give rise to market resistance (move the dumpsters, beautify the fencing and landscaping around them, maybe even move a window within the unit).

No Simple Rules

Savvy investors realize that no one can rightfully give them a list of simple rules to follow that spell out features to avoid and features to look for. Instead, to invest most profitably, learn to accurately compare complexes and units on a full range of features, prices, and relative values. Learning to detail the comparisons represents one of the core competencies that I want you to absorb from this book.

Why Stress This Point?

Each year I talk with hundreds of beginning real estate investors. Seldom does anyone ask me a question that can be answered from a technical or factual standpoint (e.g., tax rules for a section 1031 Exchange, the number of echo boomers pouring into the housing market). Rather, I most often receive such questions as:

◆ Which make the best investments, condos, townhomes, or single-family houses?
◆ Which is better, an adjustable-rate mortgage (ARM) or a fixed-rate mortgage?
◆ Do vacation homes make good investments?
◆ Should I rent my properties to college students?
◆ Should I rent my properties to HUD Section 8 tenants?
◆ What types of neighborhoods make the best investments?

I know many real estate authors and seminar leaders who love to play the role of enlightened guru. When faced with questions similar to those listed, they give a pat answer. The "student" walks away satisfied and the guru puffs his chest a bit more.

> **Beware of real estate gurus who try to wow you with pat answers to complex questions.**

In reality, no one (guru or otherwise) can answer any of those questions until they know the facts and figures of the actual choices available in the market at that time. The basic rule is not to avoid buying units that face a dumpster or garbage area. Rather, it's never buy units with undesirable features vis-à-vis other units—unless you can negotiate a price discount that's large enough to give you a good buy.

Admittedly, I sometimes let my biases, preferences, and experiences color my advice. But please never accept my concrete experiences (or anyone else's) as displaying the ultimate truth.

You will find your own best opportunities when you ferret out deals based on the specific properties and relative prices that are available when and where you decide to invest. As we move through this and later chapters, you will learn such points of comparison as:

- ◆ The character of HOAs
- ◆ HOA finances
- ◆ Unit features and design
- ◆ Parking and storage
- ◆ Project layout and design
- ◆ Recreation facilities
- ◆ Physical condition
- ◆ Declaration and bylaws
- ◆ Rules for everyday living

In each and every case, you must weigh these features against the price you can negotiate and the price at which you could buy a competing property.

The HOA

In the early 1970s, when the condominium movement in the United States and Canada first began to take off, many homebuyers had not prepared themselves for community living. Nor had they prepared themselves for managing the legal, financial, and personal issues that fall within the responsibilities of the HOA. As a result, HOAs frequently encountered all types of serious problems, such as:

◆ Homeowner discord
◆ Dictatorial association boards
◆ Lawsuits
◆ Inadequate budgeting
◆ Inadequate maintenance

> **Practical experience and improved condo law has greatly improved condo living.**

Fortunately, today, more than 30 years of experience have dramatically improved the operation, efficiency, and effectiveness of HOAs. In addition, most states are now enacting their umpteenth revised condo statute. These laws continually fine-tune the rules that guide the performance of HOAs. As long as you do some basic checking before you buy, you now run little risk of getting into an HOA that's rife with value-destroying problems.

The Organizational Structure

For a snapshot look at the way most HOAs are set up, refer to Figure 3.1. This organizational chart indicates that all unit owners vote to elect the board. The board then exercises wide discretion (subject only to state statute and the condo complex's legal charter, i.e., its declarations and bylaws over the individual members and the association itself).

As a *prospective* buyer, you enjoy no rights against any officer or committee member to extract information about the operations of the condo project. However, as a matter of practice, I have generally found that many of the officers, committee members, and management staff will informally share their thoughts about the HOA. In addition, the selling unit owner is obligated by law to deliver a "resale package" (more on that later) to serious buyers. These documents detail the most important legal and financial facts about the HOA.

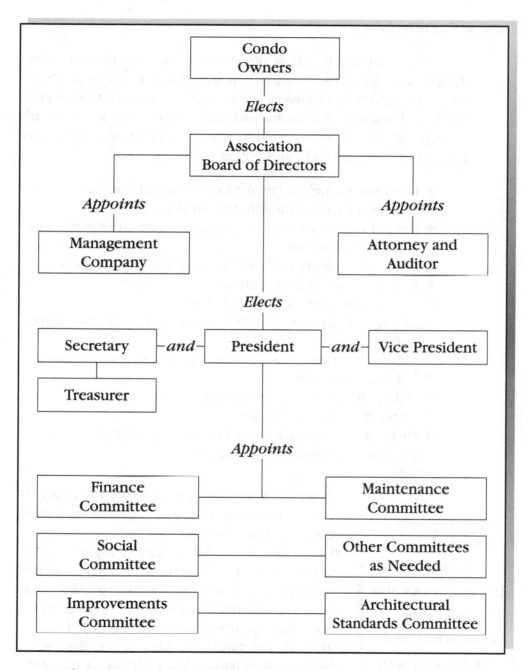

Figure 3.1 Association Organizational Chart.

The Board of Directors

Essentially, the board of directors operates as the executive, judicial, and legislative branches of the HOA government. Unlike city, state, and federal governments, HOAs concentrate power in the board without checks and balances. That's why some boards can operate like dictators until they lose an election. Boards generally have the legal right and power to:

◆ Draft the annual budget for expenses and reserves.
◆ Set the amount of the monthly HOA fees.
◆ Decide whether to levy a special assessment to pay for extraordinary charges.
◆ Charge appropriate money for capital improvements.
◆ Develop rules and regulations.
◆ Enforce the declaration and bylaws.
◆ Enforce its decisions with fines or liens against individual unit owners.
◆ Respond to unit owner concerns, request, and approvals.
◆ Publish a newsletter.
◆ Hold private meetings that exclude unit owners.
◆ Appoint governing committees.
◆ Hire and fire the management company (if the HOA employs professional management).

> **Condo boards operate with fewer checks and balances compared with the branches of government.**

As you can see, the board takes on many diverse, time-consuming, and critically important responsibilities. So you might find it amazing that most boards operate reasonably well. Naturally, as in nearly all organizations, you will find board power blocs, cliques, and private agendas. On occasion, boards will so mismanage an HOA that the upset unit owners will form an opposing electoral slate. They will campaign on the need for change. If a majority of members (unit owners) agree, they will throw out the old board and bring in a new one.

> **Beware of board members who pursue their own private agendas.**

In other words, as a unit owner, you (and your like-minded compatriots) generally cannot overturn disagreeable board decisions while the board is still sitting. But you can spearhead a drive to oust them at the next annual election.

In general, most owner-investors remain detached from the internal affairs of the HOA— as long as the board seems to be doing a decent job. Given the pettiness and belligerent nature of some unit owners, condo boards tend to overwork with little appreciation.

When things go right, too few owners say, "Thanks for doing a good job." When things go wrong, condemnation and bickering may quickly erupt.

> **Displeased HOA members can try to oust the board through an electoral campaign based on reform.**

Review the minutes. To get a good feel for board competency and HOA concerns, ask the seller to provide copies of the minutes for the past 6 to 12 months of board meetings. You might also secure a copy of the minutes for the most recent annual meeting of all homeowners in the association. As an investor, you especially want to note whether the resident owners are voicing any complaints about the tenants or the absentee investors.

> **HOA minutes and newsletters will help you assess the flavor of the condo complex.**

Review the newsletters. For more insight about pending issues and the social rapport of the development, ask the seller to provide copies of the past 6 to 12 months of the HOA newsletter. From the newsletter, you'll learn about the people who live in the complex, whether new rules or assessments are being proposed, resident births, deaths, special occasions, and other items the board may find noteworthy. In well-run HOAs, the board uses the newsletter to keep members apprised of what the board is doing and why. As in most other organizations, the newsletter also helps individual members easily communicate with all other members.

Management

Because most board members have a life to live outside of their association duties, most HOAs of more than 25 to 50 units hire management to deal with everyday issues. Such a manager might work as a full- or part-time employee of the HOA. The HOA could also hire a professional management company, such as those that supervise rental apartment complexes and single-family houses. Figure 3.2 shows you the basic split in duties between the HOA board and a hired manager. (With the consent of the board, you could employ the HOA's manager or management company to also attend to your rental unit in the complex.)

> **Most larger HOAs employ professional management.**

Managing the Managers Sometimes HOAs get into difficulty when the board fails to exercise diligent control over the management company. Generally, the HOA pays management a fixed fee or salary. At least for the term of the management contract, management gets paid regardless of how much or how little work they do. Some management staffers prefer to simply let an answering machine pick up all calls. They may not respond to complaints. They may take a laissez-faire attitude toward rules and those who break them. As a result, the quality of life within the complex deteriorates.

For one condo buyer's experience with an ineptly managed HOA, see Box 3.1. You might notice a primary cause of the problem. Too many absentee investor-owners ignored their responsibility to elect and monitor a diligent board, who in turn would supervise and control the management. Condos offer "carefree living" only to the extent that those owners in control faithfully exercise that control.

The Association	*The Management Company*
Sets policy.	Implements policy.
Establishes rules and regulations.	Enforces rules and regulations of the board.
Approves annual budget.	Recommends and implements budget.
Sets standards of maintenance.	Works and budgets according to those standards.
Establishes financial controls and re-porting requirements.	Works within these guidelines as agreed on.
Directs owner complaints to manage-ment company.	Resolves the complaint or recommends appropriate action to the board.
Approves all expenditures.	Pays all approved invoices.
Sets financial priorities.	Authorizes expenditures according to these priorities.
Sets work priorities.	Establishes work schedules according to these priorities.
Authorizes pay level for all employees.	Recommends pay levels; hires, trains, and supervises all employees.
Approves all written communications to owners.	Implements all communications from board to owners and others as directed.
Conducts board meetings as required.	Recommends and prepares agenda.
Establishes committees as appropriate.	Recommends number and type of com-mittees needed, helps committee define purpose and understand interrelation-ship of the committee to other commit-tees and board.
Approves resales and leases.	Notifies Realtor's office or owner of board's approval.

Figure 3.2   Association–Management Company Relationship.

Like many first-time homebuyers, Ann Hennig had thought off and on for years about investing in a home. But indecision and procrastination conspired to keep her renting. When her landlord gave her a 30-day notice that he wanted to move back into the house where she had been living, she decided the time was right. She would buy a home of her own.

Pushing herself to act quickly, Ann found a townhouse that was priced right, spacious, and located only five minutes from her office; it could be bought with a low-down-payment Department of Veterans Affairs (VA) mortgage assumption. Best of all, her mortgage payments (after tax deductions) would cost her less than she'd been paying in rent. Those were the good points.

After moving in, Ann discovered a few things she had overlooked: "Children screaming and riding their Hot Wheels, everyone blasting their boom boxes and car stereos, barking dogs, and late-night parties—all these things came as a big surprise to me," she said.

How did Ann get herself into this kind of situation? "First of all," she continues,

I have to explain my own ignorance. I came from the neighborhood where I had grown up. I had known my neighbors all my life, and, except for an occasional outburst, the neighbors were pretty set in their ways and were generally quiet and considerate. You could always count on peaceful afternoons and quiet evenings. Since I had never been faced with the problem of constant noise, it was not something I consciously thought about. It didn't occur to me that this place could turn into a zoo of wild kids and party animals.

Also, I moved into my townhouse in October when the children were in school, most of the neighborhood was working, the weather was cold, and not many people were outside. The few times I visited the unit before I purchased it, I didn't stay long and didn't hear any of the neighbors, or maybe I just came on relatively quiet days. Anyway, I didn't pay much attention.

But something else aggravated the problem. It seemed like we had a Gresham's law of neighborhoods. Bad residents were driving out good ones. Since I came from a neighborhood where people rarely moved, I had naively assumed that the neighbors I had when I moved in would be my neighbors for many years. At least in the beginning I did have relatively quiet neighbors beside me and in back. Within a year they were both gone. In their place came a divorced man who partied constantly, and a young single woman behind me who played her stereo from 8 A.M. to 10 P.M.—I think to accompany her barking dogs.

(continued)

Box 3.1   A Zoo of Wild Kids and Party Animals.

On top of this, parking was another problem. Each unit had an assigned parking space. When I visited the units before buying, many of the spaces were empty so it looked like parking was plentiful. But, of course, then most people had been at work. Weekends and evenings were a different story. Since most units had more than one car, parking was clearly inadequate. I also learned that residents totally disregarded the parking rules. Sometimes cars were even abandoned. Repeated calls to the police were all in vain.

Later, when some of us tried to reform our homeowners' association to develop and enforce stricter rules, we ran into a brick wall. Too many of the units were owned by absentee investors. They didn't live here and didn't care about unruly residents. And they certainly didn't want to put money into maintenance and upkeep of the property.

Box 3.1   *(Continued)*

Verify the quality of the board and the quality of the management (or look for ineptly run HOAs). Buy 6 to 10 units (or more) at steeply discounted prices. Then, form a power bloc with other concerned owners. Wrest control of the board. Turn the HOA around and profit from a quick boost in property values.

Be Wary of Self-Managed HOAs   HOAs with fewer than 25 units often manage themselves. Generally, the unit owners make this decision to save money. They also may see no need for such formality. After all, "We all know each other and get along well."

> **Self-management sometimes works. But sometimes it doesn't. Verify before you buy.**

Although that fact may be true, it does not address the issue of competency. Do the unit owners really possess expertise in budgeting for capital improvements (parking areas, roof, swimming pool), assessing the maintenance needs of the building, and contending directly with resident complaints and infractions? Do board or committee members really have the time and willingness to deal with these issues competently?

In many cases, the answer to all of these questions is yes. When time or expertise falls short, the HOA board can bring in an expert on an ad hoc basis. There's nothing wrong with this approach—when it works. But before you commit, find out precisely how the self-managed HOA carries out its managerial tasks. Occasionally, the answer to this question is, "They don't." That's an HOA that's quite likely headed for financial or operational trouble.

Committees

The types of committees shown in Figure 3.1 are pretty much self-explanatory:

- ◆ Finance committee: Runs the numbers and helps the board set fees and develop budgets.
- ◆ Social committee: Organizes community events (picnics, outings, card parties, ski trips, and so on).
- ◆ Maintenance committee: Periodically inspects the physical condition of the buildings, grounds, and recreational areas to note needed repairs or replacements.
- ◆ Improvements committee: Creates and accepts suggestions to better the quality of life within the community.
- ◆ Architectural standards committee: Develops the rules that govern the exteriors of the units and owner alterations.

In most HOAs, the committees only advise the board. Although their recommendations may carry the day, as a matter of law, condo boards typically cannot delegate actual decision-making power to the committees.

Attorney and Auditor

HOAs must comply with myriad laws that pertain to income taxes, property taxes, liability insurance, employee compensation, and employee work rules. In addition, all board actions must comply

> **The attorney and auditor keep the board legal and honest.**

with the applicable condo statutes as well as the declarations and bylaws of the association. In those unfortunate circumstances in which a board must act against a unit owner (e.g., non-payment of fees, persistent violations of rules), the board needs to follow a legally mandated procedure that guarantees due process to the HOA member in trouble.

As you can see, condo boards need an attorney on call. As to the auditor, someone's got to keep the board honest. In larger HOAs, hundreds of thousands of dollars may pass through the board's hands each year. Apart from embezzlement and self-serving insider deals, board members could let contracts go to friends or family, they might accept kickbacks, or they might just ignore paying bills or filing tax returns. The auditor is supposed to make sure all HOA monies are properly allocated and end up where they're supposed to.

This topic leads us directly to the next issue of concern for savvy buyers: How solid are the HOA's finances?

Do the HOA Finances Look Good?

Throughout the 1970s and 1980s, condominium horror stories filled the press. In those days, condo builders and developers would pull all sorts of tricks that would leave HOAs in dire financial circumstances. Apart from just plain shoddy construction, three other deceptions seemed pervasive: (1) "hidden" leases, (2) sweetheart contracts, and (3) understated HOA maintenance fees. Although developers and builders now typically avoid the most egregious tricks of the past, sleight-of-hand maneuvers still occur. So, regardless of whether you buy new construction or a condo resale, you must carefully evaluate the financial soundness of the HOA.

Undisclosed Leases

Many condo buyers have bought units for which the developer retained ownership of the land and/or recreational amenities. In turn, the developer would lease the land and facilities back to the HOA. The lease rate started low, but then skyrocketed to levels that cost the HOA members (unit owners) hundreds of dollars a month just to cover their pro rata share. Many unit owners couldn't afford to pay, which in turn forced even higher fees on those who were financially able.

> **Be wary of condos or townhouses that lease their land, recreational amenities, or other common areas.**

If that weren't bad enough, to break these leases through litigation, HOAs would often spend hundreds of thousands of dollars in legal fees and costs, only to come out on the losing end of the court's decision.

Fortunately, today the laws governing leased land have tightened. Shady developers can't rip off their buyers with impunity the same way they did several decades ago. Nevertheless, some condo and townhouse developments still sit on leased land. Also, some HOAs still lease recreational amenities, parking, or clubhouse.

Before you invest, ask whether the HOA owns all common areas, including the land under the buildings. Usually it does. But on occasion it doesn't. If leases to these areas do apply, carefully investigate how much the lease rates might increase. For example, many of the world-famous False Creek Condominiums in Vancouver, British Columbia, sit on leased land. Owners cannot predict with certainty the future amount of their HOA fees when their leases renew. You'll also want to find out if the HOA retains an option to buy the leased land (facilities) at the end of the lease term for an affordable price.

> **Can the HOA buy the land or amenities at the end of the lease. If so, at what price?**

Otherwise, as the lease termination draws closer, the value of the condo units will fall. At the end of a land lease, all buildings on the site become the property of the landowner—unless the lease renews or the lessee buys the land from the lessor.

Sweetheart Contracts

During the unit sellout period of a new condo project, the project developer maintains control of the HOA. Then, according to pro-

> **Sweetheart deals two-time members of the HOA.**

cedures set by statute and the condo documents, the developer turns the operation of the HOA over to the unit owners and their elected board. Does that mean the new condo board gets to choose who will perform condo maintenance and management? Not necessarily—at least not in the bad old days.

With many condos of yesteryear, the developer entered into long-term, effectively noncancelable sweetheart contracts to provide management and maintenance to the HOA—often at lofty prices for subpar performance. Today, thanks to changes in the condo statutes, in most states you will seldom run across the blatant types of sweetheart contracts that developers used to use. Again, though, play it safe. Ask who and how all service contracts are entered into by the HOA. Expensive prices for subpar services can break the finances of the HOA and drive down unit values.

Understated HOA Fees

The unit owners fund the expenses of the HOA through the monthly (or quarterly) maintenance and operation fees they are

> **Do the fees reflect the true costs of running the HOA? Does the HOA set aside enough money for repairs and replacements?**

required to pay. When the expenses of running the HOA and maintaining the property goes up, the fees of the unit owners go up. In the early days of condos (and still persisting today, though to a lesser degree), project developers understated this fee as a sales ploy.

The sales brochure says, "Carefree, maintenance-free living in your own oceanside penthouse for just $75 a month." A few years later the unit owners begin to learn the truth. Project maintenance requires more than $75 a month per unit just to maintain the condo seawall according to engineering specifications.

When the true costs of running the HOA are calculated realistically, they total $350 a month per unit. This is not a pleasant surprise for the unit owners.

The Budget

Most state and provincial laws now require project developers and subsequently HOA boards to periodically prepare budgets and financial reports that address all HOA financial responsibilities (see Box 4.1). As shown in Figure 4.1, budgeted expenses typically pay for such items as yard care, painting, swimming pool maintenance, waste disposal, security, insurance, and property taxes. In addition, the budget should set aside amounts for a contingency reserve fund.

- ◆ Examine HOA governing legal documents to determine whether the declarations or bylaws impose any standards that exceed those set by statute.
- ◆ Reconcile all HOA operating accounts.
- ◆ Reconcile all HOA reserve accounts.
- ◆ Compare the past year's budgeted expenses and reserve allotments to the amounts actually incurred.
- ◆ Reconcile all expenditures and balances with their corresponding bank statements.
- ◆ Identify and explain any financial discrepancies.
- ◆ Carefully estimate whether budgeted amounts for the current year will prove adequate to fund actual expenses.
- ◆ Carefully estimate all necessary capital improvements for the coming year and note any expenditures for which no funding is currently available.
- ◆ Review all delinquent owner accounts and take required enforcement action.
- ◆ Review collection procedures of delinquent accounts to recommend or implement necessary changes.
- ◆ Determine whether planned owner assessments will prove adequate to meet all upcoming expenses and capital replacements.
- ◆ Comply with all reporting deadlines.
- ◆ Critically review the total financial policies and procedures of the HOA to determine whether existing practices promote the best interests of the unit owners.

Box 4.1   A Sampling of Statutorily Designated Board Responsibilities.

Operating Expenses	Monthly ($)	Annually($)
Administration of association	200.00	2,400.00
Management fees	1,404.00	16,848.00
Building cleaning and maintenance	200.00	2,400.00
Lawn and property maintenance	1,000.00	12,000.00
Rent for recreation and other commonly used facilities	200.00	2,400.00
Expenses on association property		
Taxes	42.00	504.00
Cleaning and maintenance	20.00	240.00
Taxes on leased property	20.00	240.00
Electricity (common elements)	640.00	7,680.00
Water, sewer, and garbage service	1,800.00	21,600.00
Insurance	1,250.00	15,000.00
Miscellaneous		
Annual filing fee with Bureau of Condominiums	4.00	48.00
Professional services (legal and accounting)	200.00	2,400.00
Security provisions	0.00	0.00
Pest control	200.00	2,400.00
Total	7,180.00	86,160.00

Reserves for Replacement	Monthly ($)	Annually ($)
Building painting	768.00	2,216.00
Pavement resurfacing	150.00	1,800.00
Roof replacement	500.00	6,000.00
Swimming pool reserves	100.00	1,200.00
Total	1,518.00	18,216.00

Direct Supplementary Expenses for a Unit Owner

Rent payable for recreation lease or commonly used facilities	20.00	240.00
Expenses for limited common elements		
Parking garage maintenance	10.00	120.00
Storage locker maintenance	10.00	120.00
Total	40.00	480.00

(continued)

Figure 4.1 Annual (2003) Budget for Hollow Ridge HOA.

Budget Notes

1. The monthly expense for individual units is as follows:
   a. A-type units (0.0188 per unit) $163.52
   b. B-type units (0.0194 per unit) $168.74
   c. C-type units (0.0393 per unit) $341.84
2. The balance in the reserve accounts of the association at the beginning of the current budget year is as follows:
   a. Building painting $46,080.00
   b. Pavement resurfacing $14,400.00
   c. Roof replacement $48,000.00
   d. Swimming pool reserves $6,000.00
3. The formula for each reserve category is based on the following estimates:
   a. Exterior painting of building is scheduled every eight years and one-eighth of the total estimated cost is allocated to each fiscal year. Six of the eight years are currently on deposit.
   b. Pavement resurfacing to occur every 15 years and one-15th of the total estimated cost is allocated to each fiscal year. Nine of the 15 years are currently on deposit.
   c. Roof replacement to occur every 20 years and one-20th of the total estimated cost is allocated to each fiscal year. Eight of the 20 years are current on deposit.
   d. Swimming pool deferred maintenance to occur every six years and one-sixth of the total estimated cost is allocated to each fiscal year. Five of the six years are currently on deposit.

Figure 4.1   *(Continued)*

Once the board has set the annual HOA budget and the unit owners have approved it, the board calculates each owner's share. In some HOAs, every owner pays an equal amount. In others, owners pay according to a predetermined formula (spelled out in the legal documents). Under formula allocations, owners of larger (or more valuable) units typically pay more than those who own smaller (less valuable) units.

As you can see in Figure 4.1, the unit owners of the Hollow Ridge condos are assessed according to a formula that relates to the type of unit (size). For instance, each month, owners of A-type units pay 0.0188 of the monthly budget for expenses and reserves.

2003 Budget Amounts (Monthly)	
Operating expenses	$7,180
Reserves	$1,518
Total	$8,698
A-type @ 0.0188 (8,698) = $163.52 per month fee	

Unless the owners of larger units receive some HOA services or privileges that other owners do not, they tend to complain about paying more than their fair share. They are right. Unfortunately, for these owners, they generally don't experience much luck in getting the assessments changed in their favor.

> **One way or another, unit owners will pay for all budget shortfalls.**

Arguments such as "we should pay less, and you should pay more" seldom persuade the majority of unit owners to modify the allocations against self-interest. From your perspective as an investor, make sure you understand and accept HOA fee allocations before you buy.

Because of short-sightedness or lack of care, in the past many HOAs underfunded their contingency reserve accounts. As a result, the HOA wouldn't have the money to pay for resurfacing the parking area, installing a new boiler, or replacing a roof. In that situation, the condo board faced one of two choices:

1. Borrow the necessary funds from a bank.
2. Levy a special assessment on the unit owners.

No matter which way the board deals with the shortfall, the unit owners will end up bearing the costs.

Special Assessments

Today, well-run HOAs try to avoid the need to force unit owners to pony up hundreds (or even thousands) of dollars to cover deficits in the HOA annual budget. Many state and provincial statutes now require HOA boards to plan for capital improvements (see Box 4.2). Nevertheless, some boards still fail to fund their reserves sufficiently.

Although condominium statutes generally require HOA boards to prepare reserve studies, such statutes vary greatly in detail. Moreover, these laws exempt some HOAs, and rarely do they specify the precise amounts that HOAs must set aside.

You must always inquire to discover how the condos you are considering actually plan for and fund their reserves. California statute, for example, mandates that covered HOA boards follow the following procedures.

- Identify building components (or amenities) that will need to be replaced within 30 years.
- Estimate the remaining useful life for these components.
- Estimate the cost of repair, restoration, or replacement that such components will require.
- Calculate the yearly amounts necessary to fund these costs.
- Review the amount of monies now on hand in the reserve accounts.
- Calculate the pro rata reserve amounts that remain to be funded.

Box 4.2   Statutory Reserve Requirements of California.

> **Some HOA members object loudly to higher monthly fees— even when they are necessary to maintain the property.**

Incompetence in financial matters accounts for some board lapses. Just as often, though, board failings result because the unit owners raise too much ruckus when the board tries to increase HOA fees to fund reserves. To avoid confrontation with upset owners, some board members may adopt the view that says, "I'm not going to waste energy fighting this issue. If these cheapskates and penny pinchers can't understand the need for more reserves, that's their problem. They'll find out their error sooner or later—probably sooner."

Mandatory Payment

If and when a board levies a special assessment, unit owners *must* pay. No HOA member can say, "I never use that swimming pool any-

> **Condo law requires all HOA members to pay all fees the board assesses.**

way. Fill it in for all I care. I don't see why I should have to come up with an extra $800 this year."

As long as the board follows the procedures prescribed by state law and the condo's legal documents, unit owners can complain all they like. But neither complaining, threatening, refusing, or claiming impoverished circumstances can veto the financial liability created by a special assessment. Some HOAs allow unit owners to spread their payment burden over a period of 6 to 12 months. But the board cannot legally excuse any unit owners from paying their pro rata share (as spelled out in the condo declaration and bylaws).

"I Don't Care! I'm Not Paying"

Amazingly, on occasion, some unit owners still refuse to pay their HOA assessments, either out of some imagined principle or because they truly lack the money. That's a bad idea. Under the law, the HOA can use every collection method available to collect its unpaid assessments (special or monthly). These methods may include garnishment of wages, a lien against the title of the condo unit, and even foreclosure. In most HOAs, assessed fees count as a personal liability of the unit owner *and* a cloud against the title to the unit.

HOA Boards Must Follow Specified Procedures and Forms

You can see a sampling of forms that HOA boards use to establish, levy, collect, and satisfy their assessments in Figures 4.2 through 4.7. Briefly stated, these forms cover the following topics:

◆ *Resolution for Special Assessment (Figure 4.2).* As a first step toward levying a special assessment, the board notifies members of a financial need that lies outside of the budget. Depending on statute and the condo documents, the HOA members may have the right to reject the board's resolution.

◆ *Notice of Special Assessment (Figure 4.3).* After the resolution is adopted, the board formally assesses each unit owner. In those instances when the assessment exceeds several hundred dollars, HOAs frequently approve installment payment plans.

◆ *Declaration of Assessment (Figure 4.4).* When some unit owners owe unpaid monthly fees or assessments, all unit owners receive notice.

◆ *Satisfaction of Assessment (Figure 4.5).* Because unpaid fees and assessments become recorded liens in the public records, when eventually paid, the board must clear this title problem by filing a notice of satisfaction.

◆ *Claim of Lien (Figure 4.6).* In the given example, Mr. Waters failed to pay his monthly assessment and thereby suffers a recorded lien against his unit.

◆ *Intent to Foreclose (Figure 4.7).* Because Mr. Waters still has not paid his debt to the HOA, the HOA can put him into foreclosure.

To protect all financially responsible unit owners, condo laws give boards strong powers to enforce payment of fees and assessments. In every case, the law does give delinquent owners due process. But as long as the HOA board follows proper procedures, it can forcefully pursue collection. Because HOA boards do possess such strong powers to assess and collect, you really need to review closely the soundness of the HOA finances before you irrevocably commit to buying.

A Resolution of the Board of Administration Adopting a Special Assessment for Building and Ground Maintenance; Establishing a Due Date for Payment; Establishing Method for Payment

THAT WHEREAS, the Board has determined that the buildings of the condominium are in need of painting and repair, and that the plants and shrubs on the condominium property have been damaged by the winter freezes, and

WHEREAS, the reserve funds of the Association are insufficient to provide for the needed maintenance, repair, and replacement.

NOW, THEREFORE, BE IT RESOLVED by the Board of Administration of Hollow Ridge Condominium Association, Inc., as follows:

Section 1. THAT there is hereby levied a special assessment in the total sum of $11,000.00 for the purposes of painting and repairing the condominium building and for the replacement of plants and damaged shrubbery on the common elements of the condominium. All funds not expended for such purposes shall be deposited in the reserve account for building painting.

Section 2. THAT the assessment shall be allocated among the condominium units in the same percentage that each unit shares ownership of the common elements.

Section 3. THAT the assessment shall be due on June 1, 2004, and shall be delinquent thereafter. The assessment may be paid in full on or before the due date without penalty, or may be satisfied by paying $200.00 on or before June 1, 2004, and $100.00 on the 1st day of each month thereafter, together with interest at the rate of 12% per annum, until the special assessment is fully paid.

ADOPTED by the Board of Administration this 10th day of January, 2004.

(CORPORATE SEAL)   HOLLOW RIDGE HOMEOWNERS
                                           ASSOCIATION, INC.
ATTEST

_____   By _____
Secretary   President

Figure 4.2   Resolution for Special Assessment.

HOLLOW RIDGE HOMEOWNERS ASSOCIATION, INC.
A Corporation Not-for-Profit

SPECIAL ASSESSMENT NOTICE

NOTICE IS HEREBY GIVEN that the Board of Administration has adopted a special assessment to be used for the painting and exterior repair of the building and the replacement of freeze-damaged shrubbery. The assessment has been allocated among the unit owners based upon each unit's allocated share of the common elements as follows:

Unit	*Assessment Amount*
#101	$1,100.00
#102	$1,100.00
#103	$1,100.00
#104	$1,100.00
#105	$1,100.00
#106	$1,100.00

DUE DATE for the special assessment is June 1, 2004, and the Board has authorized alternative methods for payment as follows:

1. The owner may pay the full assessment on or before March 1, 2004, or;

2. The owner may pay $200.00 on or before June 1, 2004, and $100.00 on or before the first of each month thereafter, together with interest at the rate of 12% per annum, until the special assessment is paid in full.

DONE AND ORDERED by the Board of Administration on January 10, 2004.

HOLLOW RIDGE HOMEOWNERS
ASSOCIATION, INC.

By _____
                 Secretary

Figure 4.3 Special Notice of Assessment.

HOLLOW RIDGE HOMEOWNERS ASSOCIATION, INC., hereby gives notice that, by action of the Board of Administration on January 10, 2004, after notice of its intention to consider an assessment at a meeting on said date, a special assessment was levied against each unit in the condominium. At the option of the unit owner, the assessment was payable in full on or before June 1, 2004, or by paying $200.00 on or before June 1, 2004, and $100.00 the first of each month thereafter, together with interest at the rate of 12% per annum, until the assessment is paid in full. The owners of the units electing to pay by installment are set forth below, and the Association does hereby declare that the assessments are outstanding and payable as described above.

Owner	Unit Number, Hollow Ridge, pursuant to the Declaration of Condominium Recorded in O.R. Book 800, Page 100, Public Records of Pinellas County, Florida	Principal Amount of Assessment
Matthew Marshall	Unit #102	$1,100.00
Joseph A. Jones and Ann Marie Jones	Unit #105	$1,100.00
ABP Corporation	Unit #106	$1,100.00

DONE AND EXECUTED this 30th day of January 2004

(CORPORATE SEAL)   HOLLOW RIDGE HOMEOWNERS ASSOCIATION, INC.

ATTEST

_____   By_____

Secretary   President

Figure 4.4   Declaration of Assessment.

THIS SATISFACTION OF ASSESSMENT made this 30th day of September 2006, by Hollow Ridge Homeowners Association, Inc., is hereby given as evidence that the Declaration of Assessment levied against the units described herein below on January 30, 2004, and recorded in O.R. Book 1001 at Page 101, Public Records of Pinellas County, Florida, has been paid in full and is duly satisfied as to said units, to wit:

Owner	Unit Number, Hollow Ridge, pursuant to the Declaration of Condominium Recorded in O.R. Book 800, Page 100, Public Records of Pinellas County, Florida	Principal Amount of Assessment
Joseph A. Jones and Ann Marie Jones	Unit #101	$1,100.00
Matthew Marshall	Unit #102	$1,100.00
ABP Corporation	Unit #106	$1,100.00

DONE AND EXECUTED this 30th day of September 2006.

(CORPORATE SEAL)   HOLLOW RIDGE HOMEOWNERS
                        ASSOCIATION, INC.

ATTEST

_____   By _____
Secretary   President

Figure 4.5   Satisfaction of Assessment.

CLAIM OF LIEN

BY

HOLLOW RIDGE HOMEOWNERS ASSOCIATION, INC.

A Corporation Not-for-Profit

STATE OF FLORIDA
COUNTY OF PINELLAS

In accordance with the authority of the Declaration of Condominium and chapter 718, Florida Statutes, HOLLOW RIDGE HOMEOWNERS ASSOCIATION, INC., hereby claims a lien for all unpaid assessments now delinquent and hereafter accrued against the condominium unit and owner described below, in the initial amount and from the date stated, together with interest and reasonable attorney's fees and costs incident to the collection hereof, as follows:

Owner	Due Date	Assessment
Fred Waters	June 15, 2004	$200.00

PROPERTY DESCRIPTION

Unit 105, HOLLOW RIDGE, A CONDOMINIUM, according to the Declaration of Condominium recorded in O.R. Book 800, Page 100, and Condominium Plat Book 8, Page 10, Public Records of Pinellas County, Florida, together with an undivided 2.5375 of the common elements appurtenant thereto.

EXECUTED this 15th day of July 2004.

(CORPORATE SEAL)   HOLLOW RIDGE HOMEOWNERS
                     ASSOCIATION, INC.

ATTEST

_____   By _____
Secretary   President

Figure 4.6   Claim of Lien.

HOLLOW RIDGE HOMEOWNERS ASSOCIATION, INC.
100 Waterfront Drive
Waterfront, FL 33444

July 20, 2004

Mr. Fred Waters
105 Waterfront Drive
Waterfront, Florida 33444

Re: Claim of Lien
        Unit 105, HOLLOW RIDGE CONDOMINIUMS

Dear Mr. Waters:

This is to advise you that Hollow Ridge Homeowners Association, Inc., has filed its Claim of Lien on July 15, 2004, a copy of which is enclosed, against the unit owned by you. You are further notified that the Association intends to foreclose the Claim of Lien pursuant to Section 718.116, Florida Statutes.

To satisfy the Claim of Lien and avoid foreclosure, the following must be remitted:

Delinquent Assessment(s)	$ 200.00
Interest through August 1, 2004	2.25
Clerk of the Court—Recording	9.00
Certified Postage	1.55
Attorney's Fee	100.00
TOTAL (AUGUST 1, 2004)	$ 312.80

Please be further advised that the delinquent assessment is accruing interest at the rate of 4.9 cents per day subsequent to August 1, 2004.

                          HOLLOW RIDGE HOMEOWNERS
                          ASSOCIATION, INC.

                          By _____
                                 President

Enclosure: Certified Copy of Claim of Lien

Figure 4.7   Intent to Foreclose.

Your Financial Due Diligence: Summing Up

Far too many condo buyers focus on the unit itself. They only casually inquire about the HOA and its finances. Don't make this mistake. Although the condo statutes have improved the financial operations of HOAs, errors, shortfalls, and unpleasant surprises still occur.

> **Carefully review the financial condition of the HOA.**

Even worse, some buyers purchase their units without even understanding their obligations to pay whatever amounts of fees and special assessments the HOA board levies. For you to make money with a condo, you must factor these monthly costs and special assessments into your investment calculations. Study the annual budget.

More important, gather up copies of the annual HOA financial reports dating back five years or so (see Figure 4.8). Among other things, reviewing multiple years of financial reports will help you judge the stability and predictability of the HOA board's financial responsibility. Specifically, be sure to answer these questions: How accurately has the board budgeted? Does it hit its numbers fairly closely or are they all over the map? Closely check the balances in the reserve accounts. Do these amounts seem adequate? Ask whether the board expects to levy any special assessments within the foreseeable future.

Prior to closing on your unit, verify that the seller owes no unpaid assessments. If not paid by the seller, you will have to pay them. All unpaid HOA charges accrue against the unit owner—regardless of when that person took ownership. If the HOA can't or won't collect from the seller, it will collect from you.

How Much Insurance?

Every HOA and every unit owner needs to carry two types of coverage:

Expenses for the HOA	Expenditures ($)	
	Budgeted	Actual
Administrative	2,400.00	2,400.00
Management	16,848.00	16,848.00
Building cleaning and maintenance	2,400.00	2,400.00
Lawn and property maintenance	12,000.00	12,000.00
Rent for recreation and other facilities	2,400.00	2,400.00
Expenses on association owned property		
Taxes	504.00	504.00
Cleaning and maintenance	240.00	500.00
Taxes on leased property	240.00	240.00
Electricity (common elements)	7,680.00	5,820.00
Water, sewer, and garbage service	21,600.00	22,600.00
Insurance	15,000.00	14,978.00
Miscellaneous		
Annual filing Fee with Bureau of Condominiums	48.00	48.00
Professional Services (legal and accounting)	2,400.00	2,600.00
Security provisions	0.00	300.00
Pest control	2,400.00	2,000.00
Total	86,160.00	85,438.00
Income		
Assessment collections		104,376.00
Interest income from operation account		372.32
2003 surplus		420.24
Total		105,168.56
Summary		
Total Income		105,168.56
Total Expenses for Operations		−85,438.00
Sub-total		19,730.56
Total reserve collections (2003)		−18,216.00
Common surplus		1,514.56
		(continued)

Figure 4.8   Financial Report (2003) for Hollow Ridge HOA.

	Reserves ($)			
	Building Painting	Paving Resurfacing	Roof Replacement	Pool Reserves
Beginning balance	33,992	11,670	50,400	4,440
2003 collections	9,216	1,800	6,000	1,200
Interest earned	2,872	930	3,600	360
Subtotal	46,080	14,400	60,000	6,000
2003 expenditures	0	0	12,000	0
Total reserves at 2003 year end	46,080	14,400	48,000	6,000

Figure 4.8   *(Continued)*

◆ *Liability insurance.* This coverage should protect the HOA, the board, and the unit owners against liability for personal injury lawsuits. Such lawsuits could involve slips and falls, swimming pool drownings, or other types of accidents.

◆ *Property damage.* This type of coverage may reimburse the HOA and unit owners for covered damages caused by fires, hurricanes, tornadoes, mudslides, earthquakes, and other such disasters.

> **Learn the coverage of your HOA, your tenant, and yourself.**

As a member of an HOA, you will need to examine closely the insurance policy that the HOA carries and the policy that protects you personally. In addition, advise (or require) your tenants to buy a renters' policy to cover their personal belongings and risks of liability. Neither your policy nor the insurance policy of the HOA will extend any direct protection to tenants.

The Lesson of the Oakland-Berkeley Firestorm

When fire swept through the Oakland-Berkeley, California, hills, Ron and Betty Bugaj lost their $500,000 home and all their personal belongings. The Bugajes were not alone. In one of the worst residential firestorms in U.S. history, more than 3,300 homeowners suffered total losses. The entire 600-unit Hiller Highlands condo development was razed by the firestorm. As tragic as the fire was, for many of the property owners their troubles were just beginning. "The damage we really suffered," said Betty, "was in our negotiations with the insurance company."

Like more than 1,000 other firestorm victims, the Bugajes learned after the fire that their homeowners' insurance policy would pay much less than they expected. To get the amounts they thought they were entitled to, the Bugajes wrangled back and forth with their insurance company for more than 10 months. Adding to their hassle was the $75,000 in lawyer bills and consulting fees their negotiations with the insurance company cost them.

> **Even upper-income, well-educated property owners can fail to pay close attention to their insurance until it's too late.**

In the end, the Bugajes and most of the other firestorm victims settled with their insurers—but only after the California Department of Insurance, various consumer advocacy groups, and widespread unfavorable publicity pressured the insurance companies to give in. To some extent several insurers had tried to lowball their policyholders, but most of the settlement problems resulted because homeowners had not purchased the insurance coverage they actually needed (or thought they had).

Review Specific Coverage The important lesson of the Oakland-Berkeley firestorm was not that most insurance companies are bad guys. Rather, it's that far too many condo and single-family homeowners don't understand their insurance coverage.

They buy a homeowners' policy and assume (incorrectly) they have all the protection they need.

To make sure your condo coverage adequately protects your unit, your belongings, and common property, ask your insurance agent or check your policy and the HOA policy to answer the following questions.

> **Your insurance policy only covers certain types of disasters. Make sure you know the exceptions.**

What Perils Are Covered? In insurance language, perils cause losses. Yet no insurance policy covers every contingency. Some policies exclude hurricanes, floods, mudslides, sink holes, earthquakes, and riots. Sometimes frozen water pipes or roof collapse due to a buildup of snow and ice are not covered. After you learn what your basic coverage omits, you and the HOA can usually buy endorsements to secure extra protection.

What Property Is Covered? With millions of Americans now working from home, recognize that business property or sales inventories may not be covered under the condo policy. Nor are pets, a golf cart, or a snowmobile. Similarly, expensive antiques, jewelry, furs, artwork, or a collection of stamps, coins, or baseball cards may lack sufficient coverage. When pertinent, find out whether these kinds of things are protected, and, if so, for how much. More

> **All insurance polices exclude (or limit) coverage for certain types of property.**

than likely, you'll have to pay extra to secure adequate protection. If you (or your tenants) are writers, store an extra copy of each manuscript in a safety deposit box. (Dozens of writers in the Oakland-Berkeley fire lost computer disks and partially completed books and articles.) A homeowners' policy won't pay for the value of work to date. Even if someone has completed a manuscript, the insurer will only reimburse for the paper (materials), not the work product. This also holds true for artwork and other such items.

As a condo or townhouse owner, distinguish clearly between property covered by the HOA's insurance and the property that remains your responsibility. For example, if a water pipe bursts within a wall and causes water and plumbing damages, who pays for what? Check with the board.

How Much Will the Company Pay?   This issue causes the most problems between property owners and insurers. That's because there's lots of wiggle room for confusion and ambiguity.

First, consider the buildings. Generally, you or the HOA choose replacement cost or actual cash value coverage. With a *replacement cost* policy, the insurer agrees to pay enough to repair or rebuild the buildings at today's prices. Under *actual cash value* coverage, the company subtracts a figure for depreciation from the costs of replacement. It's better to buy replacement cost coverage. Otherwise, the older the buildings and the greater the wear and tear, the less you will collect.

> **All policies include multiple types of coverage limits.**

Regardless of what type of coverage you and the HOA select, here are eight areas in which misunderstandings frequently occur (as they did in the Oakland-Berkeley firestorm):

1. How much will you be able to collect if you choose not to rebuild?
2. What happens if government regulations prevent repairs or rebuilding? (For example, some houses and condo developments are now located in coastal areas, floodplains, wetlands, or hillsides and cannot be rebuilt because of new safety or environmental regulations.)
3. What if new government regulations (safety codes, environmental laws, building regulations) significantly increase the costs to rebuild the property?
4. In the Oakland-Berkeley firestorm, many destroyed buildings were 20 to 40 years old. According to current building codes, they couldn't be rebuilt as they were. Extra

regulations added as much as $50,000 per unit to their rebuilding costs. Yet insurance policies often exclude these types of new regulatory costs. This fact came as a big surprise to many property owners when they learned that to rebuild they must pay large amounts from their own pockets. (A *guaranteed* replacement cost policy is one way to meet this problem.)

5. How much will your policy reimburse you for a property's unique architectural or historical value? (Usually nothing unless you or the HOA has requested special coverage.)

6. If your insurer drags its feet while settling a claim, are you entitled to interest payments on the proceeds when the company finally does pay?

7. How much are the various policy limits? No matter how much it costs to rebuild or repair a property, reimbursement won't exceed the policy limits. Make sure you and the HOA periodically increase the limits of coverage to keep up with rising costs of construction. Note, too, that most policies apply lower "internal" limits for certain types of property or perils.

8. If coverage is set by an actual cash value policy, how does the insurance company calculate depreciation?

Discuss these questions with an insurance agent and the HOA board (or finance committee). Don't wait to sort out shortfalls in coverage until after you suffer a loss.

> **You must insure your unit's appliances, fixtures, finishings, and furnishings.**

Give attention to household furniture and personal belongings. To collect as much as possible for the contents of your property, choose a guaranteed replacement cost policy. Keep a list and photographic (or video) inventory of all property. To collect, you must prove loss. Photos or videos stored in a safe place can serve as proof of what personal property was in the unit. Without a detailed inventory of your pos-

sessions, chances are you'll forget some items for which you're entitled to collect.

How Much Liability Protection?   In addition to protecting your unit and its contents, your unit owners' policy will protect you against liability lawsuits. Typically, this covers negligence
claims when someone is injured on your property.

As a member of an HOA, I again encourage you to examine
the type of liability coverage and the policy limits that the HOA
carries. In some states, you can be held liable (along with other
homeowners) when someone is negligently injured on the common areas of the property (swimming pool, bike trails, tennis
courts, clubhouse, hallways).

> **How much will
> the HOA's
> insurance pay to
> those who win a
> lawsuit against
> the HOA?**

Attorney Benny Kass, a specialist in condo
and HOA law, warns that too many community
associations "are pitifully underinsured and represent a significant risk to HOA members." Do
not ignore the HOA coverage on the assumption
that all HOA insurance policies will adequate
protect you for negligence lawsuits against the
HOA. Learn the details of your state's laws. Make
sure your liability coverage will pick up wherever the HOA policy leaves off.

> **Insurers have
> lost billions and
> are now raising
> premiums and
> restricting
> coverage.**

How Much Are the Premiums?   Apart
from fully understanding your insurance coverage, before you invest in a specific condo unit,
determine how much insurance protection will
cost you. Over the past 10 years, property insurance companies and homeowners have suffered billions of dollars in losses (Hurricane
Andrew, the Oakland-Berkeley firestorm, the
San Francisco earthquake, the Los Angeles riots,
Midwest floods, Los Angeles–Malibu fires).

Toxic mold claims have also caused large, unexpected losses
for insurers. In response, some companies have raised premiums

and tightened underwriting in geographic areas with high loss potential. For example, after Hurricane Andrew, many major insurance companies canceled tens of thousands of Florida property insurance policies, and several insurers tried to withdraw completely from writing policies in hurricane areas. In California, insurers have tried to eliminate or severely limit the coverages they offer for earthquake losses. For these and other reasons, prior to buying a condo (or house), check coverage and premiums very closely. In some higher-risk areas, you may not be able to get the coverage you need at a price you're willing to pay.

Any Lawsuits?

As one last part of your financial due diligence, find out if the HOA is suing or being sued—or if any legal cause of action appears imminent but suit has not yet been filed. Chiefly, you're interested in lawsuits that could materially damage the finances of the HOA (or you personally as a unit owner).

HOA as Plaintiff

For example, as plaintiff, the HOA could be suing the builder of the development for some type of construction defects. If the HOA loses (or if the builder is judgment-proof), the members of the HOA could be assessed high fees to cover the legal costs as well as remedy whatever construction deficiencies need attention.

> **HOAs sometimes sue the builder of the project for construction defects.**

The HOA might also sue a unit owner for nonpayment of fees. Normally, these suits are not material to the big-picture HOA finances unless large numbers of owners are in default—as occurred in Massachusetts in the late 1980s. (Such a disaster would not likely occur again because HOAs have lobbied for much improved HOA protective legislation.)

HOA as Defendant

Sometimes disgruntled unit owners sue the HOA because the HOA has (in the eyes of the unit owner) unduly imposed its power against the owner. ("No, you can't enclose your patio." "Yes I can! I'll see you in court.") In other instances, a lawsuit could prove more dangerous. Say that a child was killed by a car on a community street because (allegedly) the HOA failed to put in speed bumps and a stop sign.

If the victim's parents win a large award for damages, the court could require the HOA, and possibly the unit owners, to pay several million dollars in damages. Absent sufficient insurance, such a judgement could wreck the finances of the HOA.

Be Wary of HOAs in Litigation

As a practical matter, I never lose sleep over worry that I could lose money because my HOA is being sued. Most owners don't because the probability of an uninsured loss is very slight.

> **Plaintiff or defendant, investigate HOA litigation.**

Nevertheless, if you find a desirable unit where the HOA stands to lose (or gain) a substantive sum from litigation, consider it a warning sign. Ask a competent HOA lawyer to explain all potential outcomes. Then ask, "What do these implications mean for owners who now plan to enter the community?"

CHAPTER 5

What Do Condo Residents Say?

How can you learn the relative pros and cons of various condominium and townhouse developments? What features do residents like? What features do they dislike? What would they improve? To answer these questions, ask the people who live in condos and townhouses. When you learn what residents like and dislike about everyday living in a multifamily community, you can make a wise investment decision.

You won't necessarily choose the absolute best condo, but you will choose the one that seems to offer the best value.

> **Learn the pros and cons of condo developments and you will invest wisely and profitably.**

What Residents Say about Their Condos/Townhouses

In this chapter, I relay a sampling of comments that I and others have turned up in consulting work and market research conducted for condo/townhouse developers. In addition, I relate my personal experiences. Not only have I invested in condos, I have lived in three different condo projects—two in Williamsburg, Virginia, and one in Champaign, Illinois. I can testify that overall I and nearly all other residents were pleased with each of these communities—in terms of their individual units, the developments, and the homeowners' associations.

Overall Satisfaction

My experiences represent the norm. Upwards of 85 percent of condo/townhouse residents express satisfaction with the overall living conditions and the investment value of their condo buildings and developments.

From your standpoint as an investor, learning about resident likes and dislikes will add to the money you can make from your condo investments for two overriding reasons:

◆ Communities with desirable (versus undesirable) features will help you attract better tenants.
◆ Communities (or buildings) that appeal to most residential (or potential buyers) will help boost the resale value of your investment units.

Surveys show that tenants who live in well-run condo/townhouse properties stay longer and are willing to pay higher rents vis-à-vis apartment rentals in buildings with similar features and amenities. Indeed, my own eight-month stay at the Columbus Plaza rental apartments in Chicago convinced me that I would never again live in a rental apartment building—even though (should a short-term need arise again), I would consider renting a comparable unit located in a condo/townhouse community. Why? The quality of life ranks superior in the condo.

> **Condos and townhouses offer a higher quality of life.**

Overall, in addition to quality of life issues, owner residents say they've chosen condo life over rental apartments because they are tired of paying rent and want to build equity. They also report that they feel more secure, have a sense

> **Condo buyers are tired of wasting money on rent. They want to build equity.**

of more privacy, and appreciate having friends and neighbors close by when needed.

Compared with owning a single-family house, owners of condos/townhouses typically cite security, low maintenance, affordability, and better location (generally meaning that they can buy a condo in an area where houses are either unavailable or, if available, unaffordable). For a sampling of comments from satisfied owners, see Box 5.1.

"I see townhouse ownership as a real alternative to a single-family dwelling because of lower costs and a chance to get an earlier return on our investment."

"For the first time, I'm able to put my money into a home investment instead of rent, and it gives me a tax break. I've been here only three weeks. The price for my unit has jumped $5,000. That appreciation is exciting."

"For the price we paid, we really got good value. We have good neighbors and feel secure here."

"A comparable single-family home would prove prohibitive on our income."

"For four years my children and I lived in our single-family home, but the problems were too great. For a divorcée with three children, a townhouse is ideal. Maintenance is simple."

"We are very impressed. We have as much privacy here as with any house we have owned. People are very friendly. The association keeps everything in top condition. We love it."

"Due to high density here, the quality of neighbors can make a tremendous difference. Our neighbors are young and friendly. We have much in common. Fantastic community spirit that has made our life here very enjoyable."

"I appreciate living on one floor. I am slightly handicapped. The close parking and lawn care are especially great for my needs."

"I was tired of having to get in my car to go anywhere. With the location of my condo, I can walk to my office as well as dozens of restaurants, cafes, bookstores—you name it—it's sure to be somewhere close by."

Box 5.1   Comments from Satisfied Owners.

Wise Investors Pay Attention to the Negatives (and Positives) of Condo Buildings and Developments

Notwithstanding overall satisfaction, many residents do voice complaints and comments that point out features that they would like to see improved. Satisfaction doesn't imply perfection.

Do not misunderstand, however. The complaints that I have turned up in surveys and report in this chapter and in Chapter 6 do not represent the norm. I selected such comments to help you better identify the features that residents prefer and those that annoy them. When you see a project where these negatives pile up, you will know to steer clear of it—unless perhaps you can buy it for a steal of a price or you see strong potential for turnaround.

> **Avoid condo projects where the negatives pile up—unless you can buy at a steep discount.**

Not all of the issues we discuss will apply to every type of condo and townhouse. Yet in familiarizing yourself with a broad variety of topics, you will better prepare yourself to wisely size up any situation that you happen to run into.

What Features Rank Most Important?

When asked open-ended questions about their units and developments, residents tend to comment or complain about the following issues:

- Poor construction/workmanship
- Misleading sales presentations
- Noise
- Neighbors
- Pets
- Children
- Renters
- Density
- Privacy
- Unit location
- Affordability
- Security
- Recreation facilities
- Maintenance
- Parking
- Elevators

- ◆ Site planning
- ◆ Environmental features
- ◆ Unit features/design

- ◆ Rules and regulations
- ◆ HOAs

Develop and refine your perceptions about each of these issues and you will sharpen your ability to invest profitably.

Poor Construction, Careless Workmanship, and Unexpected Repairs and Replacements

"Christine Estep is weary—weary of paying for a home she can't live in," opened a front-page article in the *Miami Herald*. Estep is

Construction defects plague many old and new condo buildings.

one of the tens of thousands of people whose homes were damaged by Hurricane Andrew. But instead of having her property repaired, Christine and the other 343 homeowners in her Village Homes condo complex are about to see their homes demolished. The relatively new complex was "so riddled with construction defects" that engineers have recommended tearing down all the units and rebuilding from scratch.

To make matters worse, the developer of the complex was the well-known Florida development company Arvida. And at the time of the first phase of construction, Arvida was a subsidiary of the Walt Disney Company. After Disney, JMB Realty, another company of high standing, became Arvida's parent. In a multimillion-

Even well-known companies may construct shoddy buildings.

dollar case like this, accusations fly among homeowners, architects, lawyers, engineers, and contractors. Yet no one disputes the engineers' basic conclusion that the construction quality of the units in the Village Homes complex failed to meet even minimum standards of safety.

Engineers, as well as government investigators, say the condo buildings had undersized foundations, inadequately designed roof trusses, masonry walls without necessary steel reinforcement, unanchored support posts, and missing hurricane straps. Now you might wonder, aren't newly constructed buildings inspected and approved by government building inspectors? How could major defects slip by? A lot of other people asked the same questions. But it's not the first time.

Government Inspectors Sometimes Fail to Do Their Jobs

Over the years, many cities throughout the United States have been rocked by permits-for-sale bribery and payoff scandals. Janet Reno, former attorney general of the United States, previously worked as Florida's prosecuting attorney for Dade County (Miami). In that capacity she spearheaded a drive to investigate the government building inspection process. Reno never prosecuted anyone for a crime, but her office did file charges for lax enforcement of building codes.

An undercover investigator discovered that one county building inspector inspected and approved seven newly built houses in five minutes. A former building inspector in Dade County was quoted by the *Miami Herald* as saying, "It was a farce. The building and zoning department for years pushed quantity, not quality." (Remember, all of those new buildings add millions of dollars to property tax collections. Construction projects bring thousands of jobs to an area. Cities and counties that push economic growth definitely do not want to upset development and construction companies.)

> **Don't place blind faith in the government permit and construction approval process.**

Although it will be years (if ever) before a complete accounting of errors and responsibilities are tallied up and assigned to the various parties involved in Estep's case, the construction defects and lax inspection practices that brought about her losses are all too common. Just because a building is new (or nearly new) does not mean it's defect-free. A few builders and developers are crooks; others are careless; some need to cut corners "temporarily" to stay solvent; and others simply make mistakes. Any way you look at it, *new* does not necessarily mean *perfect.* (For more comments on disappointing workmanship, see Box 5.2.)

The following quotations have been chosen from survey research only to illustrate the types of problems with workmanship that seem most common—not to indict the majority of condo builders or buildings.

"I am particularly concerned about the miserable, shoddy construction and the use of cheap appliances and fixtures. When our toilet is flushed, it sounds like an avalanche. Because of the noisy furnace fan and air conditioner, we cannot hear each other and spend a good part of the day shouting, 'What? I can't hear you.'"

"We'd be happy here if the construction were of better quality. Walls and woodwork are crooked and poorly finished. Plywood floors are loose and squeak. Insulation is not adequate. Plumbing repeatedly leaks or is stopped up."

"It's obvious the workmen didn't care. Cabinets, cupboards, and vanity are scarred with scrapes and gouges. Our neighbors upstairs can be heard plainly— just like in apartment living. The cheapest of everything was used."

"Construction here is very poor. You can hear toilet flushing from both sides. My basement leaks in a heavy rain. The rear fence is so poorly built that it falls over in a high wind. The gate won't close without being wired shut. Bedroom furniture can't be moved upstairs without damaging walls and ceilings."

"I would think the builder would insist on better workmanship instead of having callbacks. Our fiberglass tub and shower had to be repaired numerous times. . . . Someone got playful and tossed wood chips into the plumbing and we're still having problems."

"Our townhouse is not yet three years old and its features are a disgrace . . . bathtub leaks, air conditioning won't cool the upstairs, no insulation between the roof and cheap plasterboard ceilings."

"There isn't a square or straight wall in the entire unit. Townhouse living *should* be more pleasurable if they would build quality instead of slapping them up overnight."

"Studs are not at legal distances. Carpets are so thin that carpet nails on the stairs hurt our feet. Medicine cabinets are cheap and don't fit right."

"Floors are bouncy. Drywall is poorly installed. Many seams and cracks are beginning to show."

Box 5.2   Sharpen Your Vision to Notice Poor Workmanship.

Avoid unpleasant surprises. Employ a professional inspector even when you're buying a new or recently built house or condo.

When Buying an Existing Unit, Check the Resale Package

In a recent letter to a Q&A newspaper columnist (and real estate attorney) who addresses reader concerns about condos, an upset new owner queried, "I just closed on my condo three weeks ago and I'm being hit with a $1,500 assessment which will go toward paying for a new roof. Can the board do this? Why wasn't I told this roof replacement was on the agenda?"

The columnist answered:

> From what you have written, I can only conclude that you failed to read the resale package that was given to you at the time you were negotiating to buy the unit. You also must have failed to obtain (or read) the seller's disclosure statement. I know that many of these legal and financial documents might seem quite impenetrable to the inexperienced buyer. But the law does not permit you to ignore this responsibility.

| Learn the good, the bad, and the ugly before you invest. |

When you invest in an existing condo or townhouse, you buy the good, the bad, and the ugly. If the building needs repair work or its major components need to be replaced, the HOA must pay for these improvements. If the reserve monies prove inadequate for the job, the board will call on the unit owners to cover the shortfall (one way or another).

Resale Package Corrects Former Abuses   As you recall from Chapter 4, in the early years of condos, neither builders nor sellers warned their buyers when the HOA for the development was woefully underfunded. New condo buyers routinely suffered

	payment shock as they were forced to pay un-expected (and unbudgeted) repairs and expenses. To solve that problem, most states now mandate buyer resale packages—sometimes an inch or two thick.

> **Condo residents and HOAs speak most authoritatively through the resale package.**

payment shock as they were forced to pay un-expected (and unbudgeted) repairs and expenses. To solve that problem, most states now mandate buyer resale packages—sometimes an inch or two thick.

To avoid unpleasant surprises about building defects, underfunded HOAs, and pertinent rules and regulations, read these resale documents and financial reports.

The condo residents speak most authoritatively through their association's resale package (and the seller's written disclosure statement).

What Does the Resale Package Include?   The basic resale package includes many of the documents that are discussed in Chapters 4, 7, 8, and 9. In addition, you are certainly permitted to ask for any other document or type of information discussed throughout this book. You can view a sample foreword to a resale package in Figure 5.1. To really learn your rights, responsibilities, regulations, and restrictions, do as most buyers do not and read the resale package. Look for the issues raised throughout all of our discussions of HOAs and community living.

Seller Disclosures

As another precaution against investing in a condo that suffers construction defects, poor workmanship, or needed repairs, ask the seller to complete and sign a disclosure statement. But be aware that one of the most misunderstood topics in real estate is the legal concept of disclosure. Because the laws and practices of disclosure are constantly changing, many home sellers, buyers, investors, and even real estate sales agents have become confused.

From the early 1900s up to the 1960s, real estate agents represented sellers. Legally, agents worked for the interests of property owners. With respect to homebuyers, the rule was caveat

---

Common Interest Community Resale Document

Pursuant to Section 172-198 of the Common Interest Ownership Act Illinois Statutes—Public Act 109-77

Forest Glen Condominium Association

106 Meridian Street
Des Plaines, IL

Address of Unit

Unit No. 222   160 Meridian Street
Des Plaines, IL

Name of Unit Owner(s) Bricker Johnson

The undersigned Virginia Evans being duly authorized by the Association hereby certifies that as of the 15th day of June 2003 the following statements accurately to the best of my knowledge and belief reflect the state of the records of my Association.

---

1. A set of declaration, bylaws, and any amended regulations is enclosed.

2. The Association does have a right of first refusal for sale or lease of a unit.

3. The common charges are presently $139.00 per month and are paid through see statement. The special service district charges are presently $95.00 per month and are paid through see statement. See statement following. The "flip charge" of $250.00 (has) been paid. See #14.

Note: This Resale Certificate is valid only thirty (30) days from date of issue. After that date this documents must be updated.

(continued)

Figure 5.1 Composite Foreword to Resale Package.

Forest Glen Condominium Association

Page 2

4. Capital expenditures for current year are estimated at ___$0___. Capital expenditures for the next fiscal year are yet to be determined. However, it must be understood that unforeseen incidents can occur which could cause common expenses to rise above that which has been budgeted. In accordance to the Declaration and Bylaws of the Association, the Board of Directors has the responsibility to declare a special assessment in these cases. Capital expenditure for the tax district is ___$2,000.00___.

5. There are other fees for:

<u>Parking</u>	None
<u>Garage parking</u>	See owner
<u>Automatic door opener</u>	See owner
<u>Dog fee</u>	None
<u>Storage</u>	Seller's responsibility to show where storage bin is located and pass on the key.
<u>Pool key</u>	Seller should give pool tag to purchaser for pool season May–Sept. New tag each season.

6. There is approximately $187,000 in the Association reserve fund at present. Reserve funds for the special service district are $11,000.

7. A copy of the current operating budget is attached.

8. There are no unsatisfied judgments pending at present. No suits are pending.

9. A copy of the insurance coverage is enclosed.

(continued)

Figure 5.1   *(Continued)*

Forest Glen Condominium Association
Page 3

10. There are no restrictions in the Declaration affecting the amount to be received by a unit owner on the sale, condemnation, or casualty loss to a unit or the community or the termination of the community. [*Author note:* Some condos that are developed and originally sold at below market price under certain affordable housing programs do include such limitations on seller/owner proceeds from unit disposition or destruction.]

11. The charge for preparation of the certificate is $75.00.

12. The monthly common fees are due and payable by the first of the month. If the common fee is not received by the 10th of the month, a late charge of $50.00 is automatically added to your account.

NO MONTHLY STATEMENTS/BILLS ARE MAILED
A statement is mailed only if the account is in arrears.

13. If the unit is used as a rental unit, an Illinois sales/service tax is automatically added to the account.

14. The "buyer" will be responsible for the payment of the $250.00 "flip charge" if the "seller" of the unit has not paid it at the closing.

15. The blue recycling bin should be transferred to the new owner. A new bin would have to be purchased for $5.00.

16. This is not a cooperative.

17. The Association is incorporated and the name of the statutory agent for service filed with the Secretary of State is Virginia Evans.

(continued)

Figure 5.1   *(Continued)*

Forest Glen Condominium Association

Page 4

18. There is no pending sale or encumbrance of the common elements.

19. The use and occupancy restrictions in the Declaration or Bylaws appear as follows on: Pages 4, 5, 6, & 7; Article 9, Use, Purposes, & Restrictions.

Figure 5.1   *(Continued)*

> **Caveat emptor no longer rules the law of disclosure.**

emptor, "let the buyer beware." In most property purchases, the law required neither sellers nor their agents to reveal a home's defects. If you didn't discover a home's crumbling foundation or inadequate wiring, that was your tough luck. You had little recourse against the sellers or the agent. Unless the sellers or their agent gave explicitly false warranties or representations—"That roof never leaks"—you were assumed to have bought the home in as-is condition.

Today, the doctrine of caveat emptor is dead. From the late 1960s and still evolving up through the present, innumerable court decisions, federal and state laws and regulations, and real estate licensing standards have sealed the coffin on "let the buyer beware." The general rule has become "let the sellers and their agents beware."

Today the law gives little comfort to sellers or realty agents who fail to disclose any serious defects of a property. Whether you're working with a seller's agent, a buyer's agent, or a dual agent, anyone who fails to reveal serious defects can be held liable for that omission. Yet even with the death of caveat emptor, plenty of room still exists for confusion, misunderstanding, and deception.

Serious Defects   First, consider the term *serious.* What kinds of defects qualify as serious? At one extreme is a Massachusetts case. A house had a dangerously defective gas heater. On several occasions the heater had malfunctioned. The home's owner and soon-to-be seller was told by a repairman that the heater could easily start a fire. Even with this warning, the seller did not replace or correctly repair the heater. Nor did he inform the eventual buyers of the home.

> **Some sellers still try to cover up or hide defects.**

Shortly after the buyers took possession, the heater exploded. The results were fatal: Two members of the family died. The court held the seller criminally liable. He was convicted of involuntary manslaughter and sentenced to 15 years in prison.

Defects in a home that could likely lead to extensive property damage, injury, or death are serious. Both sellers and agents must disclose them or suffer the consequences. But what about, say, substandard wiring that is nevertheless in good condition and has never been a problem? That's a gray area. What about several light switches and electrical outlets that don't work? Those are probably not serious.

Due to these gray areas of liability and uncertainties—not to mention potential injury or loss of life—insist that sellers tell you *all* of a property's problems. Many sellers and some agents have not adjusted to the demise of caveat emptor.

> **Insist that the sellers give you a full written disclosure on the property and HOA.**

To illustrate: Consider this question from a would-be seller. In a letter to Q&A newspaper columnist Nina Groskind, a homeowner writes that he knows his home has "several flaws, some minor, some more significant." He then asks (fully prepared to hide as much as possible), "What obligation do I have to 'tell all' to people interested in purchasing my home?"

Ms. Groskind answers that the homeowner might be able to get away with "nondisclosure." But (1) he'd better not tell his real estate agent, because the agent would have to pass the information along to the buyer; and (2) the owner should not make any explicit false statement that could mislead any prospective new owners of the home.

It's sellers like these that you must guard against.

"Known" or "Suspected" Defects   As you try to get as much information as you can about a prospective condo, HOA, and neighborhood, another type of problem arises. What if the seller or the agent doesn't know about the termites in the foundation or the wood rot under the roof? What if they don't "know" but only "suspect" a defect might exist? In the case of no knowledge, courts generally rule that sellers or agents can't be expected to disclose what they don't know. However, ignorance doesn't offer an airtight defense.

Laws in many states require owners or agents to make certain kinds of property investigations. In Massachusetts sellers must test their properties for urea formaldehyde foam insulation. In California real estate agents must visually inspect most properties they list for sale. Even further, some judges and juries have held sellers or agents liable for not disclosing defects they should have known about or reasonably suspected might exist—even though they claimed no direct knowledge.

In a far-reaching California case, a realty firm was held liable for not disclosing that a home's hillside location made it susceptible to damage from mudslides. The agent claimed no knowledge or expertise on the topic of mudslides. The court essentially said "too bad." Even if the agent didn't know, he should have reasonably suspected there might be a problem.

> **Disclosure means different things to different people.**

As you can see, the entire area of inspections and disclosures can confuse everyone involved in a property transaction. In so many ways the law is ambiguous or simply not well understood. That's why disclosure and nondisclosure contribute to so many homebuying mistakes. The traditional tendency and practice of sellers to hide or understate defects adds to the potential for error.

But there's also another long-standing practice in real estate sales that can divert you from getting the information you need to make a good decision. It's called puffery.

Beware of Puffery   "This is a great neighborhood. You're really getting a bargain. This unit's in superb condition. You'll just love the people here. Oh yes, it's very quiet." Often homebuyers who don't get the information they need fail because they unconsciously accept puffery in lieu of facts. None of these statements actually includes any factual content.

> **Sellers and agents often puff up the positives of a property.**

Some unethical agents (or sellers) deliberately use puffery to mask their lack of knowledge—or as an explicit attempt to avoid disclosure. These agents have learned to couch their comments in terms of platitudes or opinions because these permit them to escape liability for misleading you.

"You said this was a great neighborhood," complain the angry homebuyers to the agent who sold them their home.

"Well, it *is* a great neighborhood," responds the agent. "Sure there's a crack house several doors down, and I know the drive-by shootings can be annoying. But the neighborhood association is working hard to turn things around. All this community spirit really does make this a great neighborhood. You just can't find that spirit and feeling of togetherness in many neighborhoods these days."

By the agent's definition, the neighborhood is great. Can you prove that your definition of *great* outweighs the agent's? Did the agent misrepresent the neighborhood? Were his or her comments

> **Insist on facts, not rose-colored opinions.**

merely sales puffery and a matter of opinion? If you took a case like this to court, you would probably stand a better chance of winning today than in the past. But in most states you'd do just as well spend your money on lottery tickets as on lawyers.

Exceptions to the Laws of Disclosure   Although society is moving away from the doctrine of caveat emptor, the evolving laws still omit some types of sellers, properties, and transactions. Government agencies, financial institutions, auctioneers, and court-appointed trustees may be excluded from some disclosure laws. Buyers of commercial and investment real estate receive less protection than homebuyers. If you're buying at a foreclosure sale or through probate, you will probably be buying as is. In some states, homes that are for sale by owner (without an agent) need not meet the same high standards of disclosure required of real estate agents.

> **Not all sales of real estate are subject to mandatory disclosure laws.**

Rules to Follow   Today's laws of disclosure make buying real estate less risky than in the past. Yet disclosure laws aren't the entire answer to the difficult task of information gathering. They scatter into many gray areas; they may be circumvented by puffery; they may not be understood adequately by agents or sellers; and such laws frequently carve out exceptions for certain types of persons, properties, or transactions.

> **Never assume that disclosures tell the full story about a property.**

As a result, you must buy proactively. Don't expect others to automatically reveal all they know or should know about a property and its neighborhood. Take the initiative and follow these guidelines:

◆ Ask your real estate agent (or lawyer) to explain fully the laws of disclosure that apply to homebuying in your area. Learn how disclosure laws may not apply; learn the types of nondisclosure problems that are prone to arise in the homes or neighborhoods where you're looking.
◆ Ask your agent (or the sellers) questions that require factual answers. Don't accept opinions. Probe for details.

◆ Ask the sellers to prepare a written list of every defect, problem, or shortcoming of their home and neighborhood. If anything is not 100 percent perfect, tell them you want to know about it.

◆ Stay alert for agent or seller evasions such as, "I believe," "I think," or "As far as we know." If the sellers or their agent don't know, then follow up with further inquiry or investigation. Many buyers mistakenly accept these kinds of seller or agent hedges.

◆ Hire professional inspectors to examine the condition of the property, its component systems (heating, air conditioning, electrical, ventilation), and built-in appliances.

◆ Closely inspect the property and neighborhood yourself. In the end, it's going to be your investment. Successful investors take charge of the inspection process.

◆ Assume everyone you're working with acts in good faith. But take precautions as if they aren't.

Unethical Builders and Sales Reps

Whether buying new or resale, verify what the Realtor, the sales rep, or the builder's promotions tell you about a condo project. If you're buying direct from the sellers, the same cautions apply. In the field of real estate sales, you will run into more than your share of the ethically challenged.

Sales Rep Disconnect

In most instances, when you buy from a builder's sales rep, you are really buying from a traveling salesperson. These sales reps move from project to project, from builder to builder. "Make the sale" becomes their all-encompassing battle cry.

One embittered condo buyer says,

> Our main complaint is about the false advertising and selling. Salesmen here have little connection with the builder. They told us anything to make a sale. We were promised ownership of the park land right across from the sales office, but now it's being built on. Behind us, on land that was promised to be kept open, fourplexes have been built. The sales brochures showed green space, playgrounds, and walking paths. You don't see any of these, do you?

> **Never assume woods, green spaces, farmland, or park areas will remain as they appear today.**

How can builders and sales reps mislead with reckless abandon? Read the fine print. (See Box 5.3.) You'll see why.

Seller has not made and does not make any representations as to the physical condition, expense, operation, or any other matter or thing affecting or relating to the Condominium, except such representations as may be specifically set forth in this Agreement. This Agreement represents the entire understanding and agreement of the parties hereto, and Seller and Purchaser acknowledge that neither is relying on any statement or representation, written or oral, which has not been embodied in this Agreement. Purchaser represents that he has read and is familiar with this Agreement, and the Declaration of Condominium, a true copy of which is attached hereto as Exhibit "2."

The acceptance of the Condominium Warranty Deed by Purchaser shall be deemed full performance and discharge of every agreement, obligation, and representation made on the part of Seller in accordance with the terms and provisions hereof, and the only agreements or representations which shall survive the delivery and acceptance of such Deed shall be those which may be herein specifically stated to survive the delivery and acceptance thereof.

Box 5.3 Builder Sales Contracts Disavow Promotional Misrepresentations.

The Documents Control

The marketing folks develop the ads and sales presentations. The crafty lawyers write the fine print of the legal documents that disavow sales and promotional misrepresentations and exaggerations.

When buyers complain, "We were told—" they are promptly shown the fine print that likely includes wording such as:

- "All plans subject to change."
- "Actual floor plans may vary from those shown in renderings and sales brochures."
- "Builder retains the right to adapt project to changing market conditions."
- "No representations or promises made outside the four corners of these documents shall apply."
- "Sales reps may not bind the company."

Are Such Tactics Legal?   Will courts uphold such misleading tactics? Sometimes yes, sometimes no. It depends on the exact nature of any oral or promotional promises. It depends on how clearly the builder conveyed the exculpatory language to the buyers. Most of all, it depends on what evidence gets admitted at trial—and, in the contest of "he said, she said," who the judge or jury believes.

How to Prevent Unpleasant Surprises   To avoid getting far less than you thought you bargained for, study the fine print of the sales brochures—which may in fact be written in difficult-to-read four-point type with either a 60 percent screen or reverse print (like the nearly invisible warnings about cancer in most print ads for cigarettes). Naturally, too, closely watch for exculpatory and limiting language in every document you sign.

Most critically, develop an offense. Write down every promise or representation that is made to you. Then type it out. When signing your purchase agreement, attach this list of promises to your

> **Write down and type out all sales promises and representations. Then attach them to your purchase contract.**

contract and require the builder's *authorized* representative to sign it. If the representative won't sign, either withdraw from the purchase or go forward with your eyes wide open. You know the risks that you're taking. (For a sampling of unfulfilled promises and representations, see Box 5.4).

"Display models are shown with many extras such as wallpaper and covered patio. Not only did we not get these features, the covenants won't let us cover the patio."

"Our homeowners' association had to take our builder to court to make good his promise to build a swimming pool."

"The salesman didn't tell us about the association rules. We wanted to add some pizzazz to our blah exterior. Now we find we can't."

"We were all told that there would be at least 50 feet of trees between us and that cluster of buildings over there. This was a selling feature. All of those lovely trees were cut down and the new units almost put in our back yard."

"We were promised many things that the builder never delivered, such as storage sheds, and more attractive light fixtures in the hallways. Some room measurements are a foot shorter all around than shown in the brochure."

"The sales staff was untruthful. We paid $5,000 extra for an end unit. We were told we could plant a garden. After we moved in, we found that no vegetables were allowed. Golf was promised without a charge. Now we must pay to play."

"I think it unfair that developers do not tell you all of the charges when they sell you a unit. Our HOA just got dumped for a $10,000 turnover fee."

"A builder who doesn't finish his build out for 10 or 15 years shouldn't be allowed to promise schools, parks, and playgrounds when those won't be built for a decade or more. Our five-year-old will be almost ready for college by then."

Box 5.4   A Sampling of Misrepresentation and Unfulfilled Promises.

Children: Little Monsters or Little Darlings

Since 1988, federal law requires condo, townhouse, and single-family home developments to accept parents with children. Except for eligible, age-restricted senior citizen complexes, parents with children can move into any home (or apartment) that they're willing and able to pay for. Although some housing complexes (and local laws) limit the number of persons per unit (usually two per bedroom), no complex can declare any unit or grouping of units as off-limits to all kids. Federal edict stamps out reasonable accommodation.

> **Only eligible seniors' projects may exclude children.**

Consequently, before you invest in a condo/townhouse project, learn whether the HOA, nonparents, and the parents themselves manage to foster harmony and avoid discord throughout the community.

Potential Problems

One condo resident pretty much sums up how many nonparent community residents feel. She complains, "If children are going to be forced on us, someone should have better planned the design. It's very annoying to have your property and possessions destroyed by children who have no place to play safely. I feel the whole lifestyle concept of condominiums is better suited for adults."

> **Federal law prohibits sensible compromise.**

Another condo resident remarks, "My complaint is that adults should be separated from families with small children. There is nothing more irksome than kids screaming and yelling, especially at the pool." (Unfortunately, federal law prohibits this sensible solution. How is it that only persons over age 55 are entitled to a kid-free environment?)

But it's not just screaming small children that can annoy. One married resident in her 40s doesn't particularly care for the behavior of teenagers who live in (or visit) her

<table>
<tr><td>**Do teenagers loiter and create problems?**</td></tr>
</table>

complex. "Teenage girls—tramps you might say—and older boys from the outside hang out, throw wine bottles and beer cans on lawns, swear, and carry on in cars. Townhouse living would be great if parents would control their teenagers."

A Parent Speaks

When Juanita Maertz bought her townhouse, she knew civil rights laws forced the development to accept her sons, ages four and six. Except for housing developments restricted to seniors, neither rental companies nor HOAs may exclude children. But accepting children because of the law and making them welcome are two different issues.

<table>
<tr><td>**HOA members can work to change the rules.**</td></tr>
</table>

After Juanita moved into the condo community, she discovered that HOA rules forbid children to play on the grounds of the development. Parents were supposed to take their kids to a nearby park. "Sure, we accept kids here," Juanita remembers one disgruntled resident telling her. Then he added, "We just don't tolerate them."

To make her new home livable, Juanita joined her HOA's board, formed a political coalition with other parents, and eventually got the rules changed to try to create a more child-friendly environment. "It was a lot of time and effort," she recalled. "But we had no choice. It's our home, too, and our kids should have the right to play here." Of course, from her viewpoint, Juanita is right. But those without children may feel they have a right to peace and quiet.

(I am pleased to report that none of the three condo/townhouse developments where I have lived incurred any problem with children. In well-managed projects with responsible parents, children need not create problems.)

Pets

As do children, pets tend to create a dividing line between irresponsible owners and other residents. You can easily recognize the types of complaints that pets generate:

- ◆ "We have a problem with dogs and children using the same area."
- ◆ "Some dog owners think that everyone enjoys free fertilizer."
- ◆ "In spite of the rules, many pets are allowed to run loose."
- ◆ "If that yapping poodle doesn't shut up, I'm gonna wring its neck."

In my experience, most condo/townhouse developments and even a majority of high-rise condos do permit pets. Again, like parents, pet owners must maintain control over their animals to promote community peace, quiet, and respect for persons and property.

Problems with Renters

> **Investors typically prefer that fewer than 20 percent of all units in a complex are occupied by tenants.**

With few exceptions, a relatively high percentage of renters in a condo building will drag down property values in terms of other similar projects where owner-residents occupy more than 80 percent of the units. Generally, the tipping point for a condo/townhouse development falls somewhere between 60 and 80 percent occupancy by owner-residents.

When a building ends up with less than 60 percent owner-residents (more than 40 percent renters), many lenders will even refuse to offer mortgage financing for the entire project—or they may insist on higher down payments and higher interest rates. Why do large numbers of renters tend to lower the rate of appreciation in a development? It's partly due to the tenants themselves and partly due to the investors who own the units. Some typical complaints:

◆ "We suffer heavy turnover here. Realtors scoop up bargain-priced units and rent to people who just don't care about taking care of the property."
◆ "The typical renter never considers the effects of their rude behaviors. They race their cars, play loud music, and allow their dogs to run loose."
◆ "Most problems of parking, maintenance, and noise seem to come from renters who are not interested in the community."
◆ "As long as their tenants pay the rent, absentee investors don't care about the property."

> **"Absentee owners don't care enough about the property."**

These types of complaints raise two issues for condo investors who want to make money over the long run.

Should You Buy into a Project That's Heavy with Renters?

As implied before, I advise you to stay away from renter-heavy projects unless the cash flow will pour in so freely that you can make money even if the units fail to hold their value. Or, alternatively, if you see turnaround potential. (Also, in college towns, some condo complexes succeed as rental units for students.)

Say, for instance, you find a troubled, renter-dominant building. The units are selling for just $85,000 and can be rented for $900 a month. Moreover, comparable units in nearby owner-resident buildings sell for $110,000 to $125,000. The few rentals in those predominantly owner-occupied buildings lease for around

$1,200 per month. If the cheaper, renter-occupied building were structurally sound in physical design and condition, I would consider buying. The strong current cash flow with upside potential in value and rent collections look pretty good. With such a large difference in price, the renter-occupied property might also start appealing to owner-occupants who aren't willing or able to pay the higher priced owner-dominant project.

> **Renter-heavy communities often sell at lower prices.**

Exercise Investor Responsibility

When you do invest in a condo project—especially one that's predominantly owner-occupied—exercise your responsibilities to the other members of the HOA. Show respect. Carefully screen your tenants. Make sure your rental applicants understand all rules of the HOA. Secure a large enough deposit to guarantee compliance.

> **To preserve the value of the community, closely screen prospective tenants.**

Investors who neglect their properties and fail to enforce tenant discipline invite HOA retaliation. (Heavy fines and greater restrictions on rental units are two common responses.) Just as foolishly, irresponsible investors run down the value of their own investments. Casual indifference does not contribute to long-term wealth building.

CHAPTER 6

More Likes and Dislikes of Community Living

Perhaps more than any other feature of community living, density determines resident satisfaction. People don't want to feel crowded. As a result, the skill with which the developer blends site planning into building construction will affect resident lives for decades. Once the buildings are up and the streets are paved, the livability of the project is to a large degree predetermined.

Density

"What density can we get?" When developers spy a site that they believe would work well for condominiums or townhouses, they try to figure out how many units the zoning authorities will permit the developer to build. In the minds of most developers, more units per acre equals more profits. Unfortunately for some condo/townhouse developments, this drive for greater density conflicts with livability.

Although it would be easy to say that low density per se always beats high density, such a simple rule does not reflect reality. Some developments of 12 units per acre live better than those with only 8 units per acre. Many big-city high-rise condos sell for price tags of

> **High density need not provoke feelings of being crowded.**

$1 million and up (way up). Yet these buildings may include more than 200 units per acre.

What really counts toward resident satisfaction is how crowded the project *feels*. Well-designed construction and site planning can greatly alleviate the crowded feeling of high-density developments.

People per Unit

In fact, rather than units per acre, you might well measure density by the number of people who live in the development. A 60-unit development with an average of 3 persons per unit can easily feel more crowded than a 90-unit development with an average of 1.5 persons per unit. When you judge density of a community, inquire about the size of the resident population, not just the number of units within the complex. (See Box 6.1 for some resident comments about crowding.)

"The builder created a good product, but he's packed too many people into this area. He has not been careful to discourage large households from squeezing into small units."

"The most serious problem here is overcrowding. Planning for this development was done strictly to maximize density and short-term profits. Streets are narrow, and buildings are too close together. Most units have two cars but only one assigned parking space. The pool is too small. We were promised an Olympic-size pool but didn't get it."

"The builder planned and sold more three-bedroom units than smaller sizes. He knew he would have a lot of children, yet there is little provision for play areas—only a small sandbox and a set of swings."

"Put buildings back to back as little as possible and increase the common green space between rows so that backs are further apart. Try to leave trees along the buffer strip to absorb sounds and block vision. Our present back yards are so close together that I feel I'm eavesdropping on half the neighborhood in spite of the patio fences. It works the other way, too. I feel imposed on."

Box 6.1   Watch out for Projects that Seem Overcrowded.

Project Density versus Unit Crowding

In some developments, government planners force condo/townhouse developers to set aside a large number of acres for environmental reasons. Overall, when you divide the total number of acres into the number of units in the development, you get a pretty low number. "Just 6.1 units to the acre," the sales brochure proudly announces. Although all of that green space at the south end of the development looks good, it frequently contributes little to resident satisfaction.

> **How closely has the developer packed in the buildings?**

What Surrounds the Unit? For many residents, the area closest to their unit counts the most. Residents want pleasant views from inside their homes. They don't like staring out into a parking lot or another building. Open spaces, wooded areas, and water may not typically add much value to a unit—unless these views enhance the everyday lives of the building's residents. Taking a Sunday walk on a tree-lined path doesn't offset the hemmed-in feeling that's created by unit crowding and unaesthetic site planning.

As another personal aside, two of my townhouses looked out to wooded areas through huge windows. Although both of these developments were constructed with high density, pleasant views from inside the units eliminated the feelings of being crowded.

> **Developments with long rows of buildings displease most condo buyers and residents.**

Clusters or Rows? As a rule, residents do not like developments with long linear rows. Long rows look even worse when HOA regulations require sterile conformity of exterior appearance and landscaping. Instead, residents prefer variations in setbacks, winding streets, staggered roof lines, small clusters of units, and short rows.

> **Place the buildings in perspective. Do they work well together?**

Although clusters beat long, monotonous rows of buildings, not all clusters are created equally. When clusters or short rows are jammed together, residents lose what they like most: privacy, quiet, and open space. The buildings need room to breathe. As one resident observed,

The architecture here is good—but it wouldn't win any prizes. . . . What makes our project successful is the idea—the land plan, itself. The important attribute here is the layout, the way the different types of buildings relate to each other.

We have low-rise, medium-rise, and high-rise buildings, all relating well to each other. It is the way they are arranged, and the spaces between them that makes for a good environment.

High-Rise Density   Most residents of a high-rise condo care little about the number of units in the building per se. A 20-story building doesn't necessarily feel any more crowded than a 60-story building. However, narrow hallways and long corridors typically provoke distaste, just as do narrow streets and long rows in low- and mid-rise projects. As for lobby areas, neat, clean, and well-kept count for more than size itself. Above all, a high-rise condo development needs an adequate number of high-speed elevators. Any building that requires a 5- or 10-minute wait for an elevator will generate resident dissatisfaction.

> **When investing in a high-rise building, test the speed of the elevators during rush hours.**

Multiple Visits/Curb Appeal

To best judge the density of a building or development, visit at different times of the day and the week. A project that seems quiet

> **Be wary of projects that give the feeling of a tenement.**

and people-free at 10 A.M. on Wednesday can change its character completely in the evenings or on weekends. (Recall Ann's experience in Box 3.1.) Ideally, walk the complex and talk with residents. Focus, too, on the details of how people relate to their buildings, how the buildings are sited with respect to each other, and how the buildings, parking areas, lawns, and open spaces create a pleasant layout effect—or a jumble of encroachments and aesthetic eyesores.

Overall, does the project provide curb appeal? When driving by—or pulling into the project—do you see well-kept buildings and lawns, landscaped yards, and plentiful parking, with a subdued view of asphalt or concrete? Or does the development come close to reminding you of a New York Lower East Side tenement as depicted in the Bowery Boys movies of the 1930s?

Unit Location

Whether townhouse, low-rise, or high-rise, the specific location of a unit within a building and within the development counts heavily toward the quality of life and overall satisfaction of the homeowner or tenant. Just as executives prize the corner office, so, too,

> **Unit location can add thousands to market value.**

do condo owners value corner and end units. With only one common wall, more lights, and a greater sense of privacy, end units generally rent or sell faster and at higher prices. Many potential unit buyers and tenants (especially those with a bias toward single-family houses) prefer to avoid interior units.

Perimeter or Interior Building Site

Because of less traffic, privacy, and frequently better views, homebuyers (and tenants) generally prefer units that are located on the

> **Look for new construction with underpriced units in favored locations within the building.**

back perimeter of a development. As with end units, homes located in buildings along a rear perimeter sell or rent faster and at a higher price.

As a side note, on occasion, you can buy into a new development and pick up units in preferred locations at what turns out to be a bargain price relative to other units in the project. I've seen builders sell these more desirable units at a $2,000 premium. Shortly thereafter, the resale market ups the premium to $20,000.

This same type of underpricing for the most desirable unit locations also can occur in high-rise buildings. How much is a corner view unit on the 45th floor worth vis-à-vis the same style unit on the 9th floor that looks directly into an office building? Probably more than $50,000. In high-rises, always try to place a value on the view. (But do determine first whether the view is permanently *protected*. If not, it's not worth much of a price premium.)

Why Underprice Preferred Locations?

In past years, builders unintentionally underpriced choice units because they did not have enough experience with condos and townhouses to judge market price premiums accurately. Today, some builders still make this mistake.

> **Occasionally, a builder who wants fast, early sales may promote the best units at a modest premium.**

Another reason, though intentional, also contributes to underpricing. Sometimes builders want to generate fast early sales so they can tout the strong market acceptance of their product. By underpricing the most desirable units (relative to other less desirable units), builders can stimulate sales. "Buy now. Choice units available. Price increase in 30 days." This type of promotion will motivate potential buyers sitting on the fence to commit before they lose the chance of a lifetime.

Downhill or Uphill?

When units (or buildings) sit at street level on sloping lots, most townhouse buyers prefer the downhill side. Such sites typically provide a better view to the rear of the unit. Plus, because the unit is built on a downward sloping lot, builders can add a lower level for relatively little more in construction costs. Such units also bring in more light than homes built into the upslope part of a hill.

However, when the entrance to the building (or unit) actually sits significantly below grade, the unit loses much of its downslope premium. People do not like walking or driving down (or up) to enter their units. Of course, that disadvantage is sometimes more than offset by other desirable features, such as a panoramic view (as is afforded many homes located in the hills of Portland, West Vancouver, or La Jolla, California).

> **Townhouse residents like walk-out lower levels.**

Sight, Sound, and Smell

You also need to identify whether the location of a unit exposes it to any unique disadvantages of sight, sound, or smell. As already pointed out, the views from the interior of a unit will vary significantly. Some units face trash dumpsters, parking lots, or the backs of buildings, and others enjoy the serenity of woods, water, or green spaces.

In terms of noise, notice whether the unit is positioned to suffer from loud traffic flow, the screaming and shouting of kids at play, or noisy equipment (building HVAC fans, elevators, or even air traffic). One condo resident voiced a strong complaint because his unit was located directly above the entrance to the parking garage of his building. Each time the garage door opened and closed, he was disturbed by the loud door opener motor as well as the door movement itself. Repeated pleas to the HOA failed to bring relief.

As to odors, most foul smells emanate from cooking or smoking by neighbors. Perhaps any unit could suffer this liability if HOA

> **Does the neighbor next door love to cook cabbage and liver?**

rules don't regulate it tightly—as they should. Seek seller disclosure on this point. Buyers frequently overlook the possibility of foul odors. If the neighbor's favorite foods are cabbage and liver, you might want to shop for a different unit. In some areas, wind patterns can bring in odors from dumps, stables, or waste treatment facilities.

Unit Features and Design

"The HOA planted grass and some shrubs in front," reports one unit owner,

> but almost nothing on the side. I wanted my yard to look better, so I bought some low ground cover. I was putting it in one morning when a passing car screeched to an abrupt stop. The driver rushed out of his car and nearly shouted at me, "All of these plants have to go—take them out."
>
> I shot back, "Who the hell are you?" He announced that he was president of the HOA, and said "We want everything uniform." I said that I, too, wanted everything uniform—uniformly beautiful—and that's exactly why I'm planting this ground cover and these flowers.

Uniform versus Uniformly Beautiful

That resident captured perfectly one of the transcending issues within all well-kept condo/townhouse projects. When does uniformity morph into monotony? When do owner improvements provide beauty for all, rather than obnoxious idiosyncrasy? The

> **Does project uniformity create monotony or beauty?**

> **Residents love to personalize their front entrances.**

most desirable developments somehow manage to operate with a beneficial flexibility. They steer between a mentality of authoritarian rigidity and anything goes.

Front Doors and Landscaping Most resident owners especially like to personalize their front doors and landscaping. They want the front of their houses to announce their individuality, pride of ownership, and artistic flair. An HOA that stamps out improvements that achieve these goals will soon appear drab and boring. Contrary to the wishes of some dictatorial HOA presidents (and architectural review boards), owners should enjoy the right to modify and improve their units subject primarily to standards of good taste, not government issue.

Rear of the Unit Does the rear area of the unit offer a balcony, terrace, or patio? Where possible, is fencing permitted or required? If so, what colors and materials? Can the unit owner enclose the rear area of the unit? If so, in what prescribed manner?

As with front entries, do these rear (or side) areas complement the aesthetics of the development yet reserve a degree of choice to the unit owner? Excessive rules about patios, balconies, decks, and terraces raise many complaints among resident owners. On the other hand, if not policed, at least to a certain degree, such rear (side) areas end up a mishmash of ad hoc storage areas, sun rooms, makeshift greenhouses, and barbecue grills. When buildings are sited back to back, the rear areas of the units can turn into an eyesore for the neighbors who must view them.

Unit Size

In terms of unit size, you can take the measure of units in three different ways: square footage, room count, and ceiling height.

Square Footage Especially in low- to moderate-priced units, residents often complain that they wish their units were larger. "Room sizes here are too small—a bedroom of 10' × 10' just is not large enough. Cupboards are too small for pots and pans. Our bathrooms need to be more spacious. You have to step outside just to have enough room to change your mind."

Empty units/builder tricks. Investors and homebuyers sometimes misjudge the spaciousness (or lack thereof) of a unit because they view the unit when it's empty of furnishings. Once they try to move furniture into the unit—or around within the unit—they discover that the small space severely limits its usability.

> **Builders create illusions and false perceptions to make the units look larger.**

When marketing new units, builders can create false perceptions about size. Sometimes they furnish their sales model units with under-sized furniture, increase a feeling of light and spaciousness through their selective placement of mirrors, or they remove interior doors, thus permitting the placement of furniture in areas where it otherwise would not fit.

In their written floor plan diagrams and sales brochures, builders may:

◆ Include closet space within the dimensions of a room without specifically indicating that they have done so.
◆ Report interior room dimensions to include outside roof overhangs, such as those on garages, patios, and porches.
◆ Simply omit room dimensions (like super-small bedrooms and bathrooms) in cases for which the dimensions would alert buyers to their woefully inadequate size.
◆ Mark off as rooms living areas that in fact will only be separated by room dividers.
◆ Deliver completed units with room sizes measurably smaller than those of the model sales units.
◆ Play the semantics game. Liberally use terms such as *den, study, atrium, garden,* and *sun room.* But in reality, the

areas so designated turn out much smaller (or less usable) than those pictured in the mind's eye when such words are employed as room descriptions. More than a few surprised purchasers have shouted, "You call this a den?"

◆ Reverse the actual floor plans in the completed units from those shown in the models—even though this switch diminishes the livability of the units.

> **Is a sun room really a sun room—or merely ill-usable space?**

Builders (and sellers of existing units) naturally want to make their units appear as large as possible. All other things being equal, the bigger the unit, the higher its value. That's why you need to verify precisely how a builder or seller has actually measured the square footage figures they quote you.

> **Not all similar square footages live equally well.**

How square footage quotes can go wrong. "In my building, a vintage condo conversion that was originally built in the 1920s," says one resident-owner, "I've seen units exactly like ours for sale with advertised square footages as low as 1,700 square feet up to a high of 2,300 square feet. Six hundred square feet is an entire apartment in New York!" This owner is making the point that although the size of a condo (or house) directly affects its value, you must interpret square-footage figures with caution. To avoid mistakes, use the following guidelines to check the figures.

1. Watch out for measurement errors. One of my previous homes was listed on the property tax rolls as 2,460 square feet. In fact, it was closer to 3,200 square feet. Errors happen.

2. Take note of inferior quality space. The square footage of an attic that's been converted into a spare bedroom isn't worth as much as the square footage of the original living area. A finished basement of 800 square feet isn't the

equivalent of an 800-square-foot second story that's fully integrated into the home. Don't just compare units in size, also compare the quality and livability of their finished space.

3. Be wary of inconsistent size comparisons. The sellers of one house may describe it as 1,600 square feet and include a converted garage that's now a den in that square-footage figure. Another owner of a similar unit may describe it as 1,300 square feet and simply footnote the makeshift den as an extra, but not include its size in the quoted square footage of the unit. Also, some owners include square footage that may lack heating, cooling, or both.

> **Never trust a measure of square footage until you've measured it yourself.**

When used carefully, square footage comparisons can give you a good idea of relative unit values in a project. Used naively, they can mislead you into believing you're getting a bargain when you're actually overpaying. Watch out for measurement errors. Watch out for those converted garages, finished attics, enclosed patios, and basement dens. Figure them as nice extras. But keep in mind that they're often not worth as much as many sellers think they are.

Room Count   In every market some types of units sell (or rent) faster than other types. Maybe 2-BRs/2-Bths are hot; maybe buyers or renters are snapping up 1-BR/1-Bth and efficiencies. As an investor, you will want to monitor the market to determine which room counts show the most promise.

Ideally, most people would like to find a unit with square footage and room count that suffers from excess supply in the sales market but shows up as a shortage in the rental market. The surplus inventory of units for sale will help you negotiate a bargain price with a motivated seller. The shortage in the rental market will help you fill the unit quickly at a favorable rental rate.

Verify tenant demand by room count.	*Surplus/surplus, shortage/surplus.* Beware, though, of a surplus/surplus market situation. Or what could prove more difficult in the short run, a unit size and room count that is getting high bids from buyers but suffering excess supply as a rental. In other words, investors

must keep tabs on the prices in the sale market, as well as the rental rates that tenants are willing and able to pay.

Market strategy counts. Robert Griswald tells of buying a 12-unit apartment building consisting of all two-bedroom, one-bath units. Because the building was located just 1.5 miles from a college campus, he originally thought he would attract two students (roommates) to the units. To his surprise, that strategy failed. He reports:

> Although many prospective tenants looked at the units, our actual rents were very slow and our vacancies remained unacceptable. Clearly, I was trying to define and force the rental market and prospective renters to adapt to my perception of their needs. [When it dawned on me that I would have to change my plan] I began to carefully review the comments of prospective tenants and actually listen to their needs. I found that there was a strong market for faculty and graduate students but they preferred to live alone.[1]

Listen carefully to tenant feedback.	Griswald then further discovered that faculty and graduate students primarily wanted quiet and a place to work or study without noise or interruptions from roommates. With this more accurate picture of needs, he says, "I quickly realized that I could market these very same

2-bedroom, 1-bath units to this new target market . . . . [So] I

---

1. Robert Griswald, *Property Management for Dummies* (Hoboken, NJ: John Wiley & Sons, 2001), 70.

> **Market the unit in a way that highlights the features tenants want.**

revised my marketing effort and changed my ads in the college newspaper to read, "1-Bedroom plus Den."

With that change in advertised room count, Griswald says that he was still able to reach his originally intended market, but only after changing the product to better fit what that market wanted. Griswald then provides advice that matches perfectly a theme of this book: "Look at your rental condo/townhouse unit from the perspective of the most likely tenants. Then promote and accentuate the features of your rental unit that will prove of greatest interest to that market."

This example shows that when it comes to finding tenants, not only does room count (and size) matter, but how you market that room count can also prove important.

Ceiling Height   Nearly every market-savvy homebuyer and investor knows to compare unit values and livability by square footage and room count. Increasingly, though, height also counts significantly. Cathedral ceilings, vaulted ceilings, 10- or 12-foot ceilings—all of these unit features enhance the feeling of spaciousness within a unit. Even better, when ceiling height is accented with skylights or clerestory windows, the unit appears brighter as well as more spacious.

> **Adjust your estimates of market value to account for ceiling height.**

If you learn that a supposedly comparable 1,100-square-foot, two-bedroom, two-bath unit recently sold for $185,000, don't immediately conclude that you know the market value of the unit that you're inspecting. Before you move to that step, verify (among other things) the respective ceiling heights of the units. High ceilings can command large price premiums.

Livability

What features contribute most to the livability of a unit? In addition to square footage, room count, and ceiling height, condo/townhouse residents like pretty much the same kinds of internal features as people who live in single-family houses:

- Storage areas
- Convenient laundry
- Quiet/soundproofing within units and between units
- Views
- Knockout kitchens and baths
- Attractive, durable floor coverings
- Easy room-to-room traffic flow
- Foyer
- Fewer stairs
- Natural light
- Private spaces
- Quality fixtures and appliances
- Central HVAC
- Fireplace/bookshelves

Unfortunately, if homebuilders incorporated every feature that buyers want into their projects, few prospects could financially qualify to buy the units. Builders face a task that involves dozens of compromises. They must strive to design and construct a unit that gives buyers what they want most, but at a price they can afford to pay.

> **Closely evaluate the relative livability of the unit. Your tenants will call this place home.**

Some builders succeed. Others do not. What do residents say about their units? See Box 6.2 for a sampling of comments. As you look at units, keep comments like these in mind. They should stimulate your critical insights and help you better compare the strengths and weaknesses of competing apartments and townhomes.

"The laundry should be closer to where dirty clothes originate. I'm tired of carrying baskets up and down two flights of stairs."

"Our sliding glass door off the living room should not give us a view into other houses or next-door patio fences. We should be able to look out to plants or attractive fencing that we could landscape. This would give units more privacy— which all of us want."

"Our rooms make us feel too closed in. Fewer interior walls and fewer ground-floor rooms would give a more spacious look."

"The exterior design makes me feel like I'm inside an apartment building, because my roof line just extends from my neighbor's. I'd like to see offsets and staggered fronts to give a more individual look."

"The greatest inconvenience we contend with is lack of storage. We need a large ground-floor storage area for skis, tents, and bicycles. Also, we need a larger kitchen with a pantry. Bathrooms need more storage."

"This unit is poorly planned in terms of the little things. The laundry room lacks a floor drain. I can't buy bicycles because there's no place to put them. And sometimes I must walk a half block carrying groceries because the parking's too far away."

"The only thing we don't like here are the 26 steps in our three-floor unit."

"I would like a window in the master bath. And there is no good place to store vacuum cleaners and brooms. We need a pantry, too."

"I long for a private outdoor area where I could eat or read in nice weather."

"Our outside architecture is acceptable, but insides are humdrum little boxes in a big box with no visually interesting or attractive features."

"The exhaust fan from my neighbor's kitchen blows cooking odors into my patio. They cook with foul odors that are quite offensive. When my fan's not running, the odors even waft into my kitchen."

"We need a foyer. The front door drops everyone directly into the living room. All traffic everywhere in our apartment crisscrosses the living room."

"We were used to having a dining room. We miss it."

"We can't keep an eye on our children when they're outside playing."

"Late at night I hear my neighbor snoring. Thin walls have inhibited my sex life and our feeling of privacy."

"Our bathroom and kitchen fixtures, cabinets, and appliances reek with shoddy, low-quality work."

"Salesmen should warn people buying close to a pool that they will hear a lot of noise and yelling."

"I don't appreciate all of the restrictions. It's just too socialistic for me."

Box 6.2   Features Residents Love to Hate.

Recreational Amenities

Where else but in a condo development can you buy a home for one-half the median price of a single-family house—yet still get walking trails around a lake, 2 Olympic-sized swimming pools, 12 tennis courts, and a fitness center? For many owner-residents, a condo complex offers a great way to live: no maintenance work *and* great recreational activities.

Will Tenants Pay Higher Rents?

Although many condo/townhouse projects include a delightful variety of recreational amenities, these facilities do come with a price tag. As an investor, you need to decide whether you can recover enough extra revenue in rents to warrant the additional unit price and the extra costs of monthly maintenance fees.

Also, it turns out that for many resident tenants, grand plans for relaxing by the pool or getting in shape with those 6 A.M. workouts never materialize. Consequently, like many unit owners, these tenants begin to feel that they've made a bad bargain. They resent paying higher rent for facilities they rarely (if ever) use. When their lease renewal comes up, they decide to move.

What If Tenants Pay and Play?

In contrast, some tenants specifically choose high-amenity developments. They don't mind paying for these facilities because every weekend they're going to invite 10 or 12 of their closest friends over to swim, play tennis, and then party down with a barbecue on their patio (or balcony).

When tenants pay and play, resident-owners often feel like some tenants overuse and abuse the facilities. Aggrieved residents complain to the board. The board complains to you. Your otherwise carefree investment begins to require some attention.

What to Do?

By pointing out problematic issues here (and elsewhere), I'm not trying to discourage you from any particular type of condo investing. Units that appeal strongly to owners (more so than to investors and their tenants) may prove to give you higher cash flows and greater price appreciation.

Nevertheless, do realize that projects with high levels of recreational amenities require you to sharpen your pencil (or turn on your calculator). Run the numbers carefully. How much more revenues will the units pull in? How much more per month will you need to pay for HOA fees? What's the purchase price premium for units located within high amenity developments? If your extra revenues outweigh your extra costs, go for it.

> **High-amenity projects do not always charge higher monthly fees.**

Security

Condo and townhouse living typically offers its residents a relatively safe and secure environment. Indeed, I have never heard of a "high-crime" condo development in the same sense that we hear about high-crime neighborhoods. As a result, people who travel frequently or are otherwise away from home enjoy the "lock and leave without worry" feeling that goes with condo living.

> **Lock and leave is becoming a very attractive feature of community living.**

I Love "Lock and Leave"

During the time I lived in my Williamsburg townhouse, I left it unattended for six weeks while I was traveling in Australia. Not once did I ever fear a break-in. As the U.S. population ages and more retirees consider condos, they voice high praise for lock and leave.

Play It Safe: Ask!

Nevertheless, err on the side of caution. As you evaluate condo/townhouse buildings and developments, inquire about break-ins, thefts, burglaries, and assaults. Check with the police. Check with the condo security force, if the HOA employs one.

Moreover, when you inspect individual units, notice the internal security. Does the unit include a smoke alarm and burglar alarm? Are entry doors protected with deadbolt locks and peepholes? Do window locks appear solid and firm? Are the sliding glass doors equipped with burglar pins?

> **Verify the crime-free nature of the community. But also check the security of the unit(s) you buy.**

Before you buy and place a tenant in the unit, remedy any vulnerabilities that you discover. (Howard Johnson's was found liable to the tune of $2 million when an attacker entered the room of singer Connie Francis through a feebly locked sliding glass door.) In these times, take precautions, even when precautions seem unnecessary.

Summing Up: Likes and Dislikes

What is true for security stands true for your condo investing generally: Exercise care even when caution seems unnecessary.

The great majority of residents who live in condos and townhouses think highly of their HOAs, buildings, and developments. The great majority of buildings and developments have appreciated in value and will continue to do so. The great majority of condo/townhouse investors have profited from their rentals—even without the traditional hassles of landlording.

> **Shop carefully, even when special care seems unnecessary.**

With such a history of success, let me again emphasize why I liberally quote residents and owners who critique and complain. I want to push your odds of making money from, say, 80 percent, up to 99 percent. Remain alert to potentially troubling areas of mistake, and you lift your odds for success. But just as important, you can lift your returns far above the average— even though the average, in real estate already outdistance stocks, bonds, annuities, and the much chancier financial products that Wall Street is now trying to sell, such as derivatives and hedge funds.

Alert and wise, savvy condo/townhouse investors can enjoy the best of all worlds—high returns, low risk, and limited personal effort.

CHAPTER 7

Understand the Bylaws

A disgruntled homeowner recently wrote an opinion piece for a local newspaper under the title, "Trapped by homeowners' associations—Make sure you aren't signing into one, because you can't get out." This complaining writer went on at length to detail all of the ways that she felt her HOA was violating her constitutional rights.

> They dictate the type of grass you can plant, the type of flowers you can grow, the type of vehicle you can drive, and the type of pet you can own. There are residents with home-based businesses who perpetually fear that they will be discovered. We have residents who are livid because they were fined for leaving an upscale boat in the parking lot.

Before you invest, investigate the rules.

Fortunately, this writer's lament does not reflect the views of most residents who live within the bounds of an HOA. It does, however, emphasize the point that I cover in this and the following two chapters. Before you invest in a condominium or townhouse, first understand the HOA's rules.

Rules Create Value

Mainly, rules create value for all properties covered by an HOA. Otherwise, HOA developments (buildings) would abolish them. Imagine that a builder puts up a new 40-story, 100-unit condo building with unit prices ranging from $450,000 up to $1.5 million. A prospective buyer comes in to inspect the project. The buyer asks, "May I see a copy of the rules and regulations that will apply?"

The sales rep responds, "Rules! We don't have no stinking rules! Residents who live in our building won't be pestered by some socialistic regime. This is the good ol' U.S. of A.—not the defunct Soviet Union. Around here, we believe that your home is your castle. All of our buyers are free to treat their units as they please."

No Supply Because There's No Demand

How many of these upscale units do you think this imaginary builder would sell? Absolutely none. Right? If there were a market for non-HOA condo buildings and developments—either multifamily or single-family—some enterprising builder would create them. No builder has created them because no one really wants them. Even first-time homebuyers who choose entry-level condos and low-priced, new single-family houses expect to gain the benefit of HOA rules and regulations (or at least tightly written deed restrictions). (Visit any well-kept mobile home park. What will you find? Rules. If you would like to

> **Developers know that most buyers want tight rules.**

see the effects of very loose—almost nonexistent—zoning and HOA restrictions, visit Anchorage, Alaska. For my taste, at least, this city lacks even minimal aesthetic and land-use standards.)

Choose the Right HOA for You

The writer of the previously cited newspaper opinion missed the key issue. She spreads her complaint too broadly. She indicts all

> **The right rules enhance livability.**

HOAs. Instead, she should look in the mirror and indict herself. She obviously chose a home in the wrong HOA. That's the *real* issue. Moreover, although she may not care for her own HOA, evidently the majority of homeowners in her association do support the board. Otherwise, they would pitch out the board members at the next election.

Elsewhere in her op-ed piece, this writer admits that at the time she bought her townhouse, she "wasn't even aware of most of these petty rules." So, once more, who's to blame for her chagrin? The HOA or this writer? Time and time again, I hear complaints about HOA rules and regulations. I ask the disgruntled soul, "Why did you buy a unit there if you detest the rules?"

Nine times out of ten, the complainer confesses to negligence. "Uh, I guess I should have read the resale package more carefully."

What Will You Find in the Resale Package?

As we've previously discussed (Chapter 5), the resale package includes most of the legal and financial documents that will help determine the profitability of your condo investment. You've looked at the budget, the annual financial report, reserves, and assessments. Now, in this chapter and the following chapters, we will look at the rules and regulations that govern the HOA, the board, and the unit owners.

You can find these rules in three different legal documents.

◆ Bylaws
◆ Declarations of covenants, conditions, and restrictions
◆ Board-issued rules and regulations

In addition, throughout the United States and Canada, every state and province has enacted condo (or strata title) legislation. These laws set the framework for an HOA's legal documents, and in some

> **HOA legal documents must fit within the state's condo statutes.**

cases actually prescribe detailed rules that HOA members and the board must follow. Likewise, condo legislation tries to set forth some basic legal rights and responsibilities of HOAs vis-à-vis unit owners.

Naturally, courts get into the action as well. When disputes arise within an HOA, courts resolve ambiguities or enforce the terms of the HOA's legal documents where those documents don't conflict with statute. (For example, an HOA rule that prohibited a unit owner from modifying his front entry to permit wheelchair access of a spouse would probably violate the Americans with Disabilities Act. If so held, the courts wouldn't enforce the rule against that unit owner.)

Creating Value within a Context of Fairness

> **Investors need to assess HOA rules from two perspectives.**

Overall, condo legislation and court decisions support HOAs. Experience has proven that for the most part HOAs do serve the best interests of unit owners. They enhance the quality of life within the development. They boost property values.

Nevertheless, HOAs do not offer a one-size-fits-all set of rules and living conditions. What's right for you in one development may be wrong for someone else.

In fact, investors face a twin impact: The HOA will govern you, and it will govern your tenants. Therefore, you will want to judge the HOA rules from both the perspective of an investor and from the perspective of your target market.

The Condo Bylaws

For the most part, condo bylaws spell out the operational rules of the HOA. Such rules itemize the procedures that govern

- ◆ Member meetings
- ◆ Board make-up
- ◆ Board elections
- ◆ Board meetings
- ◆ Board powers and duties
- ◆ Association officers and duties
- ◆ Association committees
- ◆ Books and records
- ◆ Assessments (authority and procedure)
- ◆ Amendment process

You can see a copy of the bylaws for Pine Valley Community Association in Box 7.1. As is typical of HOA bylaws, Article I describes the HOA and Article II defines the principal terms used throughout this document. You will note that HOA bylaws are always written under the authority of the HOA's corresponding declaration (see Chapter 8). The two documents work together.

Meetings of Members (Article III)

All HOAs operate democratically in the sense that members meet periodically, discuss issues, and vote. However, when members meet, what they can discuss, and the specific issues that are put up to vote vary according to the terms of the HOA declaration and bylaws. As with all organizations, HOA bylaws detail procedural items, such as notice, quorum, and voting (secret ballot, proxies, absentee members.)

> **The bylaws set procedures for member meetings, quorum, and voting.**

Condo legal documents seldom (if ever) require members (owner-residents or investors) to attend HOA meetings or cast votes. But if you want to voice an opinion or suggest improvements, member meetings give you that right and opportunity.

ARTICLE I

NAME AND LOCATION, The name of the corporation is Pine Valley Community Association, Inc., hereinafter referred to as the "Association." The principal office of the corporation shall be located at _____ but meetings of members and directors may be held at such places within the State of Ohio, County of Sumter, as may be designated by the Board of Directors.

ARTICLE II

DEFINITIONS

Section 1. "Association" shall mean and refer to Pine Valley Community Association, Inc., its successors and assigns.

Section 2. "Properties" shall mean and refer to that certain real property described in the Declaration of Covenants, Conditions, and Restrictions, and such additions thereto as may hereafter be brought within the jurisdiction of the Association.

Section 3. "Common Area" shall mean all real property owned by the Association for the common use and enjoyment of the Owners.

Section 4. "Lot" shall mean and refer to any plot of land shown upon any recorded subdivision map of the Properties with the exception of the Common Area.

Section 5. "Owner" shall mean and refer to the record owner, whether one or more persons or entities, of the fee simple title to any Lot which is a part of the Properties, including contract sellers, but excluding those having such interest merely as security for the performance of an obligation.

Section 6. "Declarant" shall mean and refer to _____, his successors and assigns if such successors or assigns should acquire more than one undeveloped Lot from the Declarant for the purpose of development.

Section 7. "Declaration" shall mean and refer to the Declaration of Covenants, Conditions and Restrictions applicable to the Properties recorded in the Office of *Clerk of the Court of Sumter County, Ohio.*

Section 8. "Member" shall mean and refer to those persons entitled to membership as provided in the Declaration.

(continued)

Box 7.1   Bylaws of Pine Valley Community Association.

ARTICLE III

MEETING OF MEMBERS

Section 1. Annual Meetings. The first annual meeting of the members shall be held within one year from the date of incorporation of the Association, and each subsequent regular annual meeting of the members shall be held on the same day of the same month of each year thereafter, at the hour of *7:30* o'clock, P.M. If the day for the annual meeting of the members is a legal holiday, the meeting will be held at the same hour on the first day following which is not a legal holiday.

Section 2. Special Meetings. Special meetings of the members may be called at any time by the president or by the Board of directors, or upon written request of the members who are entitled to vote one-fourth (1/4) of all of the votes of the Class A membership.

Section 3. Notice of Meetings. Written notice of each meeting of the members shall be given by, or at the direction of, the secretary or person authorized to call the meeting, by mailing a copy of such notice, postage prepaid, at least 15 days before such meeting to each member entitled to vote thereat, addressed to the member's address last appearing on the books of the Association, or supplied by such member to the Association for the purpose of notice. Such notice shall specify the place, day, and hour of the meeting, and, in the case of a special meeting, the purpose of the meeting.

Section 4. Quorum. the presence at the meeting of members entitled to cast, or of proxies entitled to cast, one-third (1/3) of the votes of each class of membership shall constitute a quorum for any action except as otherwise provided in the Articles of Incorporation, the Declaration, or these Bylaws. If, however, such quorum shall not be present or represented at any meeting, the members entitled to vote thereat shall have power to adjourn the meeting from time to time, without notice other than announcement at the meeting, until a quorum as aforesaid shall be present or be represented.

Section 5. Proxies. At all meetings of members, each member may vote in person or by proxy. All proxies shall be in writing and filed with the secretary. Every proxy shall be revocable and shall automatically cease upon conveyance by the member of his Lot.

(continued)

Box 7.1 *(Continued)*

ARTICLE IV

BOARD OF DIRECTORS: SELECTION:TERM OF OFFICE

Section 1. Number. The affairs of this Association shall be managed by a Board of nine (9) directors, who need not be members of the Association.

Section 2. Term of Office. At the first annual meeting the members shall elect three directors for a term of one year, three directors for a term of two years and three directors for a term of three years; and at each annual meeting thereafter the members shall elect three directors for a term of three years.

Section 3. Removal. Any director may be removed from the Board, with or without cause, by a majority vote of the members of the Association. In the event of death, resignation, or removal of a director, his successor shall be selected by the remaining members of the Board and shall serve for the unexpired term of his predecessor.

Section 4. Compensation. No director shall receive compensation for any service he may render to the Association. However, any director may be reimbursed for his actual expenses incurred in the performance of his duties.

Section 5. Action Taken without a Meeting. The directors shall have the right to take any action in the absence of a meeting which they could take at a meeting by obtaining the written approval of all the directors. Any action so approved shall have the same effect as though taken at a meeting of the directors.

ARTICLE V

NOMINATION AND ELECTION OF DIRECTORS

Section 1. Nomination. Nomination for election to the Board of Directors shall be made by a Nominating Committee. Nominations may also be made from the floor at the annual meeting. The Nominating Committee shall consist of a Chairman, who shall be a member of the Board of directors, and two or more members of the Association. The Nominating Committee shall be appointed by the Board of Directors prior to each annual meeting of the members, to serve from the close of such annual meeting until the close of the next annual meeting and such appointment shall be announced at each annual meeting. The Nominating Committee shall make as many nominations for election to the Board of Directors as it shall in its discretion determine, but not less than the number of vacancies that are to be filled. Such nominations may be made from among members or nonmembers.

(continued)

Box 7.1 *(Continued)*

Section 2. Election. Election to the Board of Directors shall be by secret written ballot. At such election the members or their proxies may cast, in respect to each vacancy, as many votes as they are entitled to exercise under the provisions of the Declaration. The persons receiving the largest number of votes shall be elected. Cumulative voting is not permitted.

ARTICLE VI

MEETING OF DIRECTORS

Section 1. Regular Meetings. Regular meetings of the Board of Directors shall be held monthly without notice, at such place and hour as may be fixed from time to time by resolution of the Board. Should said meeting fall upon a legal holiday, then that meeting shall be held at the same time on the next day which is not a legal holiday.

Section 2. Special Meetings. Special meetings of the Board of Directors shall be held when called by the president of the Association, or by any two directors, after not less than three (3) days notice to each director.

Section 3. Quorum. A majority of the number of directors shall constitute a quorum for the transaction of business. Every act or decision done or made by a majority of the directors present at a duly held meeting at which a quorum is present shall be regarded as the act of the Board.

ARTICLE VIII

POWERS AND DUTIES OF THE BOARD OF DIRECTORS

Section 1. Powers. The Board of Directors shall have power to:

(a) adopt and publish rules and regulations governing the use of the Common Area and facilities, and the personal conduct of the members and their guests thereon, and to establish penalties for the infraction thereof;

(b) suspend the voting rights and right to the use of the recreational facilities of a member during any period in which such member shall be in default in the payment of any assessment levied by the Association. Such rights may also be suspended after notice and hearing, for a period not to exceed 60 days, for infraction of published rules and regulations;

(c) exercise for the Association all powers, duties and authority vested in or delegated to this Association and not reserved to the membership by other provisions of these Bylaws, the Articles of Incorporation, or the Declaration;

(continued)

Box 7.1 *(Continued)*

(d) declare the office of a member of the Board of Directors to be vacant in the event such member shall be absent from three (3) consecutive regular meetings of the Board of Directors; and

(e) employ a manager, an independent contractor, or such other employees as they deem necessary, and to prescribe their duties.

Section 2. Duties. It shall be the duty of the Board of Directors to:

(a) cause to be kept a complete record of all its acts and corporate affairs and to present a statement thereof to the members at the annual meeting of the members, or at any special meeting when such statement is requested in writing by one-fourth (1/4) of the Class A members who are entitled to vote;

(b) supervise all officers, agents, and employees of this Association, and see that their duties are properly performed;

(c) provide fully as otherwise specified in the Declaration, to:

(1) fix the amount of the annual assessment against each Lot at least thirty (30) days in advance of each annual assessment period;

(2) send written notice of each assessment to every Owner subject thereto at least thirty (30) days in advance of each annual assessment period; and

(3) foreclose the lien against any property for which assessments are not paid within thirty (30) days after due date or to bring an action at law against the owner personally obligated to pay the same.

(d) issue, or cause an appropriate officer to issue, upon demand by any person, a certificate setting forth whether or not any assessment has been paid. A reasonable charge may be made by the board for the issuance of these certificates. If a certificate states an assessment has been paid, such certificate shall be conclusive evidence of such payment;

(e) procure and maintain adequate liability and hazard insurance on property owned by the Association;

(f) cause all officers or employees having fiscal responsibilities to be bonded, as it may deem appropriate;

(g) cause the Common Area to be maintained.

ARTICLE VIII

OFFICERS AND THEIR DUTIES

Section 1. Enumeration of Officers. The officers of this Association shall be a president and vice-president, who shall at all times be members of the Board of Directors, a secretary, and a treasurer, and such other officers as the Board may from time to time by resolution create.

(continued)

Box 7.1   *(Continued)*

Section 2. Election of Officers. The election of officers shall take place at the first meeting of the Board of Directors following each annual meeting of the members.

Section 3. Term. The officers of this Association shall be elected annually by the Board and each shall hold office for one (1) year unless he shall sooner resign, or shall be removed, or otherwise disqualified to serve.

Section 4. Special Appointments. The Board may elect such other officers as the affairs of the Association may require, each of whom shall hold office for such period, have such authority, and perform such duties as the Board may, from time to time, determine.

Section 5. Resignation and Removal. Any officer may be removed from office with or without cause by the Board. Any officer may resign at any time giving written notice to the Board, the president, or the secretary. Such resignation shall take effect on the date of receipt of such notice or at any later time specified therein, and unless otherwise specified therein, the acceptance of such resignation shall not be necessary to make it effective.

Section 6. Vacancies. A vacancy in any office may be filled by appointment by the Board. The officer appointed to such vacancy shall serve for the remainder of the term of the officer he or she replaces.

Section 7. Multiple Offices. The offices of the secretary and treasurer may be held by the same person. No person shall simultaneously hold more than one of any of the other offices except in the case of special offices created pursuant to Section 4 of this Article.

Section 8. Duties. The duties of the officers are as follows.

President

(a) The president shall preside at all meetings of the Board of Directors; shall see that orders and resolutions of the Board are carried out; shall sign all leases, mortgages, deeds, and other written instruments and shall co-sign all checks and promissory notes.

Vice-President

(b) The vice-president shall act in the place and stead of the president in the event of the president's absence, inability, or refusal to act, and shall exercise and discharge such other duties as may be required by the Board.

(continued)

Box 7.1 *(Continued)*

Secretary

(c) The secretary shall record the votes and keep the minutes of all meetings and proceedings of the Board and of the members; keep the corporate seal of the Association and affix it on all papers requiring said seal; serve notice of meetings of the Board and of the members; keep appropriate current records showing the members of the Association together with their addresses, and shall perform such other duties as required by the Board.

Treasurer

(d) The treasurer shall receive and deposit in appropriate bank accounts all monies of the Association and shall disburse such funds as directed by resolution of the Board of Directors; shall sign all checks and promissory notes of the Association; keep proper books of account; cause an annual audit of the Association books to be made by a public accountant at the completion of each fiscal year; and shall prepare an annual budget and a statement of income and expenditures to be presented to the membership at its regular annual meeting, and deliver a copy to each of the members.

ARTICLE IX

COMMITTEES

The Association shall appoint an Architectural Control Committee, as provided in the Declarations, and a Nominating Committee, as provided in these Bylaws. In addition, the Board of Directors shall appoint other committees as deemed appropriate in carrying out its purpose.

ARTICLE X

BOOKS AND RECORDS

The books, records, and papers of the Association shall at all times, during reasonable business hours, be subject to inspection by any member. The Declaration, the Articles of Incorporation, and the Bylaws of the Association shall be available for inspection by any member at the principal office of the Association, where copies may be purchased at reasonable cost.

(continued)

Box 7.1   *(Continued)*

ARTICLE XI

ASSESSMENTS

As more fully provided in the Declaration, each member is obligated to pay to the Association annual and special assessments which are secured by a continuing lien upon the property against which the assessment is made. Any assessments which are not paid when due shall be delinquent. If the assessment is not paid within thirty (30) days after the due date, the assessment shall bear interest from the date of delinquency at the highest allowable rate by Ohio law, and the Association may bring an action at law against the Owner personally obligated to pay the same or foreclose the lien against the property, and interest, costs, and reasonable attorney's fees of any such action shall be added to the amount of such assessment. No Owner may waiver or otherwise escape liability for the assessments provided for herein by nonuse of the Common Area or abandonment of his lot.

ARTICLE XII

CORPORATE SEAL

The Association shall have a seal in circular form having within its circumference the words: PINE VALLEY COMMUNITY ASSOCIATION, INC.

ARTICLE XIII

AMENDMENTS

Section 1. These Bylaws may be amended, at a regular or special meeting of the members, by a vote of a majority of a quorum of members present in person or by proxy, except that the Federal Housing Administration (FHA) or the Veterans Administration (VA) shall have the right to veto amendments while there is Class B membership.

Section 2. In the case of any conflict between the Articles of Incorporation and these Bylaws, the Articles shall control; and in the case of any conflict between the Declarations and these Bylaws, the Declarations shall control.

Box 7.1 *(Continued)*

Board of Directors (Articles IV–VI)

In most HOAs, members elect a governing board (usually made up of three to nine directors). Typically, during the time the board holds office, it exercises great discretionary power over HOA operations. The board serves as a legislature, court, and executive all rolled into one.

When unit owners first join an HOA, some believe that the members themselves will be making operational decisions and association rules by voting on issues as they arise. Not true. If that were the case, everyone would spend much of their time in meetings and debate. On some critical issues (e.g., large budget increases), the condo statutes may give members the power to override a board; however, such an authorized reversal proves the rare exception.

> **HOA members rarely vote to directly decide operational issues.**

In nearly all of its decisions, the board reigns. As long as it complies with HOA documents (and applicable law), its decisions will stand. If a board does make an unpopular choice, dissenting members of the HOA can't call a member vote to bring up the issue again. Dissenters, though, can:

> **Unit owners can pursue various methods to influence board decisions.**

◆ Try to persuade the board to change its decision (or practices).

◆ Campaign against the offending board member(s) at the next general or special election. (Article III, Section 2, gives the HOA board and HOA members permission to call special meetings at any time. Article IV, Section 3, gives the members the right to remove any board member at any time—with or without cause.)

◆ Object that the decision (or practice) violates the condo declaration, bylaws, or applicable statutes or court decisions.

◆ Sell out and find another place to live or invest.

Power and Duties (Article VII)

When you read through the powers and duties of the board, you will see what I am talking about. Among other powers, these bylaws delegate to the board the right to:

- Adopt rules and regulations for the common areas; adopt codes of conduct for members and guests; and levy penalties for violations.
- Exclude noncompliant members from voting or using the HOA's recreation facilities.
- Hire and fire property managers.
- Levy annual and special assessments.
- Foreclose a lien for unpaid assessments.
- Spend HOA funds to maintain the common areas.

> **Courts will rarely second-guess condo boards.**

Presumed Competent In carrying out their duties, boards are presumed to promote the best interests of the HOA and its members. Absent egregious decisions that bear no rational relationship to community interest, no member can reject board rules because he or she believes the rule to be "stupid," "petty," or "ridiculous."

No Authorized Selective Enforcement However, boards must not arbitrarily enforce HOA rules. The board must treat all members impartially.

Frieda Johnson may suffer financial hardship because her husband recently died, but she still must pay her HOA assessments or face the same penalties as any other homeowner. Jamael Jones may have beautifully painted his front door and window shutters. But if his artistry violates the rules, then the board can't selectively issue Jamael a waiver unless it is prepared to do so for all other members.

An HOA board that favors some and penalizes others will stir up disharmony throughout the HOA. Boards may exercise

> **Unit owners must force the board to enforce rules evenhandedly.**

considerable power, but members must never permit the board to grant exceptions (with or without good cause) unless the exception applies to everyone in similar circumstances. Moreover, the board should draft clearly written rules that define when it will issue exceptions.

In no instance can a board legitimately waive a rule incorporated within the HOA declaration or bylaws. Only a member vote to amend can legally modify rules spelled out in these documents.

Association Officers and Duties (Article VIII)

Again, contrary to the expectations of many new owners, HOA members in full do not elect the officers of the association. The board elects the officers. In addition, most condo bylaws require that only board members may stand for election as president or vice-president of the HOA.

You might also notice that under the Pine Valley bylaws, the board can fire any officer at any time with or without cause.

In contrast, the bylaws require a vote of unit owners to oust a board member. But as noted, Article IV, Section 3 (along with Article III, Section 2) means that upset homeowners need not endure an unpopular director for the remainder of his or her term. Call a meeting, hold an election, throw the scalawag out.

> **The condo board elects and removes all officers of the HOA.**

Although the officers and board members hold considerable power while in office, they hold office only to the extent that a majority of unit owners accept their service. Board members can't draft and enforce absurd, petty, or ridiculous rules unless members of the HOA acquiesce ultimate control to the board.

Committees, Records, Assessments, and Seal (Articles IX–XII)

Because I've already discussed committees, records, and assessments at length, I won't repeat those discussions here. For purposes of example, though, read through Articles IX–XI to see how the Pine Valley bylaws handles these issues. Article XII, which authorizes the HOA to use a corporate seal, rarely offends even the most individualistic HOA member.

The Amendment Process (Article XIII)

The developer drafts the first set of bylaws, declaration, and ordinary rules and regulations. Thereafter, the HOA can change any rule or procedure it chooses by a vote of the membership. To modify its bylaws, the Pine Valley HOA need only muster a majority vote in an announced meeting that satisfies a quorum. Bylaws that govern other HOAs may require super majorities (such as two-thirds).

> **The developer creates the original condo bylaws. The members may modify the bylaws through a special vote.**

The Class B membership refers to units owned by the developer during the period that he or she is trying to sell the units. Evidently, the FHA and the VA had approved this project for their loan programs. As a condition of this approval, the agencies wanted to be able to prevent any changes to the bylaws that would (in their opinion) diminish the value of the units.

Summing Up

How do HOA members elect the board? How can they get rid of board members? What notices must the board issue? What powers can the board exercise? How do members call for a special meet-

The bylaws seldom make good bedtime reading (unless you're trying to fall asleep). But they do give you critical info about the operations of the HOA.

ing or special election? How easy (or difficult) is it to modify or amend the bylaws? The HOA bylaws will answer these questions and many others.

All HOAs operate according to the democratic principle that allows members to vote. But the HOA bylaws spell out the who, what, where, why, and how of these elections. Unlike the constitutions of the federal and state governments, the governing legal documents of an HOA authorize the board to act administratively, legislatively, and judicially. To protect your interests and your investment, cast your vote for HOA board members with full knowledge of who you're voting for and where they stand on the issues that concern you.

CHAPTER 8

Understand the Declaration

Known formally as the Declaration of Protective Covenants and Restrictions, the developer's attorney drafts this document to establish the condominium regime. Once drafted and recorded in the county land records office, the document legally binds the developer and eventual buyers of the condo or townhouse units that the developer builds.

The Declaration Creates and Governs the HOA

In Exhibit 8.1 you can see the basic terms of the declaration that created the Villa Belle regime. Although Exhibit 8.1 does not include the entire document, the excerpts shown highlight some of the more important issues that you need to look for when you obtain a resale package for a unit that you're considering.

Don't Rely on the Legal Opinions of a Real Estate Agent

You should never rely on what a real estate agent tells you about a condo's legal restrictions. My own experience with Villa Belle

THIS DECLARATION OF PROTECTIVE COVENANTS AND RESTRICTIONS OF VILLA BELLE (hereinafter referred to as "Declaration"), made this 28th day of May, 1997, by MILNER CONSTRUCTION COMPANY, a Florida General Partnership, Developer.

WITNESSETH:

WHEREAS, Developer is the owner of the real property described in Exhibit "A" attached hereto and desires to create thereon a residential community with common facilities for the benefit of said community, and

WHEREAS, Developer desires to provide for the preservation of the values and amenities in said community and for the maintenance of said common facilities; and, to this end, desires to subject the real property described in Exhibit "A" to the covenants, restrictions, easements, charges, and liens hereinafter set forth, each and all of which is and are for the benefit of said property and each owner thereof; and,

WHEREAS, Developer has deemed it desirable, for the efficient preservation of the values and amenities of said community, to create an agency to which should be delegated and assigned the powers of maintaining and administering and enforcing the covenants and restrictions, and collecting and disbursing the assessments and charges hereinafter created; and,

WHEREAS, Developer has incorporated under the laws of the State of Florida, as a nonprofit corporation, VILLA BELLE COMMUNITY ASSOCIATION, INC., for the purpose of exercising the functions aforesaid;

NOW, THEREFORE, the Developer declares that the real property described in Exhibit "A" is and shall be held, transferred, sold, conveyed, and occupied subject to the covenants, restrictions, easements, charges, and liens (sometimes referred to as "Covenants and Restrictions") hereinafter set forth, all of which shall be binding upon, and enforceable by, the Developer and subsequent owners of lots, parcels, or units in the property, and which shall run with the land.

1. NAME AND ADDRESS
    The name by which the Condominium shall be known and identified is VILLA BELLE, a condominium, and its address shall be 3800 Beach Road, Sarasota, Florida.
2. THE CONDOMINIUM ACT
    Chapter 718, Florida Statutes, as amended, 1996, is incorporated herein by reference, and all provisions thereof shall apply to this condominium to the extent that said Statute is not inconsistent with the provisions contained in this Declaration.

(continued)

Exhibit 8.1   Declaration of Protective Covenants and Restrictions for Villa Belle.

3. SURVEY AND FLOOR PLAN

A survey of this condominium, a graphic description of the improvements in which the units are located and of the units themselves, a plot plan locating such improvements and the land leased to the condominium Association, and a floor plan identifying each unit and the common elements, and the approximate dimensions of each, appear on that certain Condominium Plat of the condominium being recorded herewith in Condominium Book 22, at Page 44 of the Public Records of Sarasota County, Florida, and are incorporated herein by reference. A copy of said survey and plot plan is attached herein as Exhibit "B."

4. PLAN OF DEVELOPMENT

This condominium shall consist of two (2) separate buildings, each containing two (2) apartment units, numbered as Units "1" and "2," whose street address shall be 3818–3820 Beach Road, Sarasota, Florida, and "3" and "4," whose street address shall be 3824–3826 Beach Road, Sarasota, Florida, and as more particularly shown on Exhibit "B." Title to each unit shall be conveyed by warranty deed by the Developer in substantially the same form as the sample deed attached hereto as Exhibit "C."

5. DEFINITIONS

The terms used herein shall have the meanings stated in the Condominium Act, Chapter 718, Florida Statutes, 1996, hereinafter called the "Act," and all provisions thereof shall apply to this condominium to the extent that they are not inconsistent with the provisions contained herein, and shall include the following:

(a)   "Unit" means a condominium unit as defined by the Act, and as used herein shall refer to those units shown on Exhibit "B" attached hereto.

(b)   "Owner" means a unit owner as defined by the Act.

(c)   "Association" means VILLA BELLE ASSOCIATION, INC., a nonprofit corporation organized under the laws of Florida, and its successors.

(d)   "Member" means an owner of a unit who is a member of the Association.

(e)   "Common elements" means all portions of the condominium property other than a unit and shall include the items stated in the Act as well as those set forth in Paragraph 8 hereof.

(f)   "Condominium parcel" means a condominium unit together with an undivided share in the common elements appurtenant thereto.

(continued)

Exhibit 8.1   *(Continued)*

6.   UNIT BOUNDARIES AND OWNERSHIP

A unit shall consist of the space bounded as follows:

(a)   *Upper and Lower Boundaries.* The upper and lower boundaries of a unit shall be the following boundaries extended to an intersection with the perimetrical boundaries:

   1.   *Upper Boundary.* The horizontal plane of the undecorated finished ceiling of the upper living level, extended to its intersection with the perimetrical boundaries.

   2.   *Lower Boundary.* The horizontal plane of the undecorated finished floor of the lower living level, extended to its intersection with the perimetrical boundaries.

(b)   *Perimetrical Boundaries.* The perimetrical boundaries are the vertical planes of the undecorated finished interior of the walls bounding the unit extended to intersections with each other and with the upper and lower boundaries.

7.   PERCENTAGE OF OWNERSHIP OF COMMON ELEMENTS

There shall be appurtenant to each of the units an equal one-fourth (1/4) ownership of the common elements. The common expenses and common surplus of the condominium shall be divided and apportioned equally among the units.

8.   COMMON ELEMENTS

The common elements shall include, in addition to the items set forth in the Act, the following:

(a)   The land described in Exhibit "A" and shown on the survey and plot plan attached hereto as Exhibit "B," and all improvements thereon, except for units as shown on said plot plan and as hereinabove described.

(b)   An undivided share of the condominium surplus.

(c)   Installations for furnishing of utility services to more than one unit or to the common elements or to a unit owner other than the unit containing the installations.

(d)   The property and installations in connection therewith acquired for the furnishing of services to more than one unit or to the common elements.

(e)   Easements for maintenance of common elements.

(f)   All outside surfaces of walls except for entrance doors to each unit, windows, screen doors, screening, porches, air conditioning units, stairways, and storage rooms designed for the exclusive use of a particular unit. Any covering replacement or modification of stairways, glass, or

(continued)

Exhibit 8.1   *(Continued)*

screened surfaces must be approved in advance by the Association (and the Developer so long as it is managing the affairs of the Association).

(g)   All roofs, overhangs, foundations, exterior structures, and surfaces of lower level of each unit; walkways, landscaping, driveways, parking areas, lawns, and fences.

(h)   The common wall between adjoining units "1" and "2" and between adjoining units "3" and "4" extending laterally to the unfinished face of the stud wall (on the second and third stories) and to the unfinished face of the masonry wall (on the first story), and extending vertically upward to the outer extremity of the exterior surface of the roof and downward to the bottom of the footing shall be common elements with respect to repair or replacement thereof.

9.   LIMITED COMMON ELEMENTS

The following structures shown on Exhibit "B" shall be deemed Limited Common Elements, the use of which shall be limited to the unit owner to whom such use has been assigned by means of this declaration or by the Association:

(a)   Carports located under the buildings;

(b)   Assigned parking spaces outside the buildings.

The cost of maintaining and repairing the limited common elements set forth above shall be a common expense of the Association except where damage to such elements has been caused by a particular unit owner or his tenant or guest, in which event the unit owner shall reimburse the Association for the cost of repairing such damage.

10.   PARKING

There are a total of eight (8) parking spaces on the condominium property. Each unit owner shall be assigned the use of one (1) exclusive parking space either underneath his unit or elsewhere on the common elements. No unit owner (or his tenant or guest) may occupy more than a total of two (2) parking spaces at any one time.

11.   EASEMENTS

Owners of units shall have a perpetual easement for ingress and egress to and from their units over stairs, drives, walks, and other common elements; an exclusive easement for the use of the air space occupied by the condominium unit; cross easements for support, maintenance, repair, and replacement of ceilings, floors, and walls constituting common party walls, ceilings, and floors of adjacent units; easements to and from the parking areas; and to all utility meters, lines, or conduits wherever attached to the exterior walls or units.

(continued)

Exhibit 8.1   *(Continued)*

The common elements and all units shall also be subject to:

(a)   Easements, as may be necessary, through units for conduits, ducts, plumbing, wiring, and other facilities for the furnishing of utility services to other units or common elements.

(b)   Easements for the installation and maintenance of public utility lines, equipment, and services along, under, or over roads, streets, and walkways, installed or provided in or on said common elements for public travel or for the benefit of this Condominium.

(c)   Easements for encroachments presently existing or which may hereafter be caused by settlement or movement of the building or minor inaccuracies in construction, which encroachment shall be permitted until such encroachment no longer exists.

12.   COMMON EXPENSES

The common expenses shall include:

(a)   Expenses of administration, expenses of maintenance, operation, repair, or replacement of the common elements, and of the portions of units to be maintained by the Association.

(b)   Expenses declared common expenses by provisions of the Declaration or by the Bylaws.

(c)   Any valid charge against the Condominium property as a whole.

(d)   Charges for utility services except such services as are metered separately to each unit.

(e)   Expenses of maintaining the grounds, driveways, water and sewer lines, parking areas, walkways, and taxes assessed against the common elements.

(f)   Fire and other casualty and liability insurance as provided herein.

(g)   Costs of management of the Condominium and administrative costs of the Association, including professional fees and expenses.

(h)   Labor, materials, and supplies used in conjunction with the common elements.

(i)   Damages to the Condominium property in excess of insurance coverage.

(j)   All other costs and expenses that may be duly incurred by the Condominium Association through its Board of Directors from time to time in operating, protecting, managing and conserving the Condominium property and in carrying out its duties and responsibilities as provided by the Condominium Act, this Declaration or the Bylaws.

(continued)

Exhibit 8.1   *(Continued)*

13. ASSOCIATION

(a)   The affairs of the Condominium shall be conducted by VILLA BELLE ASSOCIATION, INC., a corporation not for profit, heretofore organized under the laws of the State of Florida. A copy of the Articles of Incorporation of the Association is attached hereto as Exhibit "D." All persons owning a vested present interest in the fee title to any of the condominium units, which interest is evidenced by a duly recorded instrument in the Public Records of Sarasota County, Florida, shall automatically be members of the Association, and their respective memberships shall automatically terminate as their vested interest in the fee title terminates. The Condominium will be operated pursuant to the Bylaws of the Association, a copy of which is attached hereto as Exhibit "E."

(b)   No unit owner, except as an officer of the Association, shall have any authority to act for the Association.

(c)   The powers and duties of the Association shall include those set forth in the Bylaws referred to herein, but in addition thereto the Association shall:

1.   Have the irrevocable right to have access to each unit from time to time during reasonable hours as may be necessary for maintenance, repair, or replacement of any common elements therein, or for making emergency repairs therein necessary to prevent damage to the common elements or to other unit or units.

2.   Have the power to adopt budgets, to levy and collect assessments, and to maintain, repair, and replace the common elements.

3.   Maintain accounting records according to good accounting practice, which shall be open to inspection by unit owners at all times.

4.   Prescribe such "reasonable house rules" as it shall, from time to time, consider essential.

14. VOTING RIGHTS

Each of the units shall be entitled to one (1) vote at meetings of the Condominium Association. In the event of joint ownership of a unit, the vote to which that unit is entitled shall be apportioned among the owners as their interest may appear, or may be exercised by one of the joint owners by written agreement of the remaining joint owners of such unit provided such agreement is filed with the secretary of the Association prior to the meeting at which such vote is to be cast.

(continued)

Exhibit 8.1   *(Continued)*

15. AMENDMENTS

Developer reserves the right to amend this Declaration and the exhibits attached hereto for the purpose of reflecting minor changes in the plans and specifications of the buildings and improvements or more accurate location of boundaries between units, or as may be required by lending institutions, title insurance companies, government agencies or officials, or for the purpose of correcting clerical errors in this declaration or attached exhibits, prior to the recording of a deed to any of the original purchasers of condominium units herein, but no such amendment shall be made which shall materially affect the rights of any such purchaser or the value of any unit therein without obtaining the written consent of the purchaser of any such unit so affected. Such amendments shall be executed by Developer and the joinder or further consent of individual unit owners or holders of recorded liens or other interests in the condominium property shall not be required. Amendments shall take effect immediately upon recordation in the Public Records of Sarasota County.

(a) This Declaration may be amended at any time by affirmative vote of three (3) of the four (4) units, provided that until the initial conveyance of all four (4) units, no amendment shall be made without the written consent of Developer, its successors or assigns, and provided further that no change in percentage ownership as set forth in Paragraph 7 shall be effective until 100% of the unit owners agree. No amendment to this Declaration shall be effective unless in writing, executed with the formalities required of a conveyance of real property, and recorded in the Public Records of Sarasota County, Florida.

(b) Notwithstanding anything contained in this Declaration or any of the Exhibits annexed hereto, to the contrary, the written consent of each institutional lender holding a first mortgage upon any condominium parcel or parcels shall first be obtained before this Declaration may be amended or the Condominium terminated, which said consent shall not be unreasonably withheld.

16. SALE, TRANSFER, LEASE, OR OCCUPANCY OF A UNIT

In order to assure a community of congenial residents and protect the value of the units and the common elements, the sale, rental, leasing, mortgaging, and other transfer of a unit by an owner other than a Developer shall be subject to the following provisions:

(a) *Sale or Lease.* No condominium unit owner may dispose of his unit by sale or lease without prior written approval of the Board of Directors of the Association and no lease shall be for a term less than one (1) month.

(continued)

Exhibit 8.1   *(Continued)*

(b) *Gifts and Inheritance.* If any condominium unit owner shall acquire his title by gift or inheritance, the continuance of his ownership of his condominium unit shall be subject to the approval of the Board of Directors of the Association.

(c) *Other Transfers.* All sales and leases shall be approved in writing by the Board of Directors of the Association, or its duly authorized committee or authorized agent before same shall be effective, and before someone other than a member of the unit owner's immediate family may occupy such unit. Such approval shall not be unreasonably withheld but shall be based upon good moral character, social compatibility, and financial responsibility of the proposed purchaser, transferee, lessee, or occupant. A waiver of this provision or the failure to enforce it in any particular instances shall not constitute a waiver or estop the Association from enforcing this provision in any other instance. A lessee shall not assign his lease or sublet his unit without the prior written approval of the Board of Directors.

(d) If the purchaser or lessee is a corporation, approval may be conditioned upon a requirement that all persons occupying the unit be approved by the Board. In no event shall a unit be occupied other than by a single family.

(e) *Exception for Mortgagees and Developer.* Notwithstanding anything to the contrary herein, the provisions of this paragraph shall not be applicable to transfer to mortgagees, whether in foreclosure or by judicial sale, or by a voluntary conveyance in lieu of foreclosure, whereby such mortgagee becomes an owner, nor to the Developer until after Developer has initially conveyed or disposed of all interest in the property, nor to any sale or lease by such mortgagee or Developer.

(f) *Developer's Units and Privileges.* Notwithstanding anything herein to the contrary, Developer is irrevocably empowered to sell, lease, or rent units to any persons approved by it. Developer shall have the right to transact on the condominium property any business necessary to consummate sale of units in VILLA BELLE including, but not limited to, the right to maintain a sales office, signs, and models of the premises, to have employees in the office, and to use the common elements to show apartments. The sales office signs, and all other personalty pertaining to sales shall not be considered common elements and shall remain the property of Developer. In the event there are unsold units, Developer retains the right to be the owner thereof under the same terms and conditions as other owners, save for the right to sell, rent, or lease as contained in this paragraph.

(continued)

Exhibit 8.1   *(Continued)*

17. **RESTRAINT UPON PARTITION**

Any transfer of a condominium unit must include all elements thereof as afore-described and appurtenances thereto, whether or not specifically described, including, but not limited to, the condominium unit owner's share in the common elements and his Association membership.

18. **MANAGEMENT**

Developer hereby reserves to itself the right to manage the affairs of the condominium and of the Association until it has initially conveyed title to all four (4) units or one (1) year from the date hereof, whichever first occurs, but such management privilege may be relinquished prior thereto at the option of the Developer by written waiver addressed to the Association. During the period when management is reserved to Developer, it shall have the sole and exclusive right to take all actions and do all things on behalf of the Association, including, but not limited to, the right to enter into leases, to make contracts and agreements on behalf of the Association for the operation of the condominium property, draft rules, and to levy assessments.

19. **MAINTENANCE AND REPAIRS**

The responsibility for maintenance and repairs of the Condominium shall be as follows:

(a) *By the Association.* The Association shall maintain and repair and replace at its expense the following:

    1. The exterior surfaces of the buildings including the roofs and walls, but excluding windows, entrance doors, and screens; the foundations and supporting structures under each building; also, the common wall between units "1" and "2" and between units "3" and "4" extended upwards to the exterior surface of the roof and downwards to the bottom of the footing shall be the responsibility of the Association.

    2. All conduits, ducts contributing to the support of the building or within interior boundary walls, and all such facilities contained within a unit which services part or parts of the condominium other than the unit within which it is contained.

    3. Grounds, landscaping, recreation areas, roads, parking areas, walkways, and stairways.

    4. Common elements, as defined in Paragraph 8, and limited common elements.

    5. Exterior lighting.

(b) *By the Unit Owner.* Each condominium unit owner shall maintain, repair, and replace at his own expense:

(continued)

Exhibit 8.1 *(Continued)*

1.   The interior surfaces within or surrounding his unit, including walls, floors, ceilings, interior doors, air conditioning units, heating system, screen enclosures, entrance doors (except the Association shall paint the exterior surface of entrance doors), windows and glass surfaces, exterior stairway leading to the unit, and balconies and porches.

2.   All appliances, plumbing and electrical systems within units, television and telephone outlets and equipment, switches, wires, pipes, and conduits serving that unit. The phrase "electric" system in this paragraph shall be construed as referring to those items of electrical conduit, wire switches, fixtures, and equipment, located within the unit or on the unit side of the electric meter servicing said unit but not including the meter itself. The phrase "plumbing" system in this paragraph shall be construed to mean all plumbing items from the trunk line connection to the unit or in the unit itself, including sanitary facilities, fixtures, and equipment.

(c)   The Association shall have the right to assume part or all of the maintenance of any one or more units as the Board of Directors may determine from time to time. No condominium owner shall make any alterations or structural additions to his unit or to the common elements or remove any portion thereof, nor modify the exterior appearance of his unit, nor do anything that would jeopardize the safety or soundness of the building containing his unit, or impair any easement, without first obtaining the written approval of the Board of Directors. Until all four (4) units have been initially conveyed by the Developer, the written consent of the Developer shall also be required for any structural change within a unit.

(d)   Each owner shall promptly report to the Association any defects or need for repairs, the responsibility for which is that of the Association. Each unit owner shall allow the Board of Directors or their authorized agents or employees to enter any unit for the purpose of inspection, maintenance, repair, or replacement within units or the common elements, or in case of emergency threatening the units or the common elements, or to determine compliance with this Declaration or the Bylaws, but such right of entry shall be exercised at reasonable times and upon reasonable notice to the unit owner.

(e)   Each unit owner shall pay for all utilities which are separately metered to his unit, and his pro rata share of utilities furnished to more than one unit.

(f)   Enforcement of Maintenance. In the event the owner of the unit fails to maintain it as required above, the Association or any other unit shall have the right to proceed in a court of competent jurisdiction to

(continued)

Exhibit 8.1   *(Continued)*

seek compliance with the foregoing provisions, or the Association shall have the right to assess the unit owner and the unit for the necessary sums to put the improvements within the unit in good condition. After such assessment, the Association shall have the right to have its employees or agents enter the unit and do the necessary work to enforce compliance with the above provisions. In the event the Association fails to comply with its obligations by virtue of this paragraph, any owner or institutional lender may apply to a court of competent jurisdiction for the appointment of a Receiver for the purpose of carrying out the terms and conditions required to be performed by the Association.

20.   ASSESSMENTS AND LIENS

The Board of Directors of the Association shall adopt an annual budget of anticipated income and estimated expenses for each fiscal year, and each unit will be responsible for its proportionate share of such annual assessment based upon its pro rata liability for common expenses. One-twelfth (1/12) of each unit's annual assessment shall be due and payable in advance to the Association on the first day of each month of each fiscal year. In addition, the Board of Directors shall have the power to levy special assessments against all units, if necessary, to cover unanticipated expenditures which may be incurred during the fiscal year. Any assessments which are not paid when due shall bear interest from the due date until paid at the rate of ten percent (10%) per annum, and the Association shall have the remedies and liens provided by the Condominium Act with respect to unpaid assessments, which shall include accrued interest and reasonable attorneys' fees incurred by the Association incident to the collection of such assessment or enforcement of such lien. The Board of Directors may require each unit owner to maintain a minimum balance on deposit with the Association for working capital and to cover contingent expenses from time to time.

Except as hereinafter provided with respect to lending institutions acquiring title, a unit owner, regardless of how title is acquired, shall be liable for all assessments coming due while he is the owner of the unit. In a voluntary conveyance, the grantees shall be jointly and severally liable with the grantors for all unpaid assessments against the latter for the unit share of unpaid common expenses up to the time of such voluntary conveyance.

(a)   The Association shall have a lien on each condominium unit and against the record owner thereof for any unpaid common expenses, and interest thereon. Such lien shall include reasonable attorney's fees

(continued)

Exhibit 8.1   *(Continued)*

incurred by the Association incident to the collection of such common expenses or enforcement of such lien. Such lien shall be executed and recorded in the Public Records of Sarasota County, Florida, in the manner provided by law, but such lien shall be subordinate to the lien of any mortgage or other liens recorded prior to the time of the recording of the lien by the Association.

(b)   Liens for the unit share of common expenses may be foreclosed by suit brought in the name of the Association in a like manner as a foreclosure of mortgage on real property as more fully set forth in Chapter 718, Florida Statutes.

(c)   Lending institutions acquiring title to condominium units by virtue of foreclosing a mortgage shall, while the title to such unit remains in the name of such institution and the unit is not occupied or leased, be relieved of the obligation to pay a pro rata share of the common expenses, including the portion attributable to any rent due the Developer or its assigns pursuant to the terms of the lease between Developer and the Association as hereinafter more specifically mentioned. This provision shall not preclude such an assessment against an occupant of any apartment owned by such institution for services voluntarily accepted by the occupant.

21.   USE RESTRICTIONS

The following restrictions shall apply to and bind the condominium property, all units, and the common elements:

(a)   Each condominium unit shall be used exclusively as a one-family residential dwelling and no business or trade shall be permitted to be conducted thereon or therein.

(b)   The occupants and owners of each unit shall keep and obey all laws, ordinances, regulations, requirements, and rules of all governmental bodies, divisions, or subdivisions insofar as the same pertain to the control or use of such unit.

(c)   No condominium parcel or unit shall be divided or subdivided or severed from the realty and no structural alterations or changes shall be made within said unit without prior approval of the Board of Directors of the Association.

(d)   No unit shall be the subject of partition in kind and all unit owners do, by their acceptance of a conveyance of such unit, waive any right to a partition in kind.

(e)   No unit owner shall permit or suffer anything to be done or kept in his unit which will increase insurance rates on his unit or on the common property.

(continued)

Exhibit 8.1   *(Continued)*

(f)   No unit owner shall commit or permit any nuisance, immoral, or illegal act in his unit or in or on the common elements.

(g)   The occupants of units shall abide by all Bylaws and all Rules and Regulations promulgated by the Association concerning occupancy and use of the condominium units and common elements and areas.

(h)   Should any of the foregoing restrictions or any other provision of this Declaration or the Bylaws be violated, any unit owner or the Association acting on behalf of the unit owners as a class, shall have the right to institute suit in any court of competent jurisdiction to enjoin further violations and to obtain money damages for past violations, and the prevailing party shall be entitled to court costs and reasonable attorney's fees for enforcing this Declaration or Bylaws.

22.   INSURANCE

Casualty and liability insurance upon the condominium property and the property of the condominium unit owners shall be governed by the following provisions: [Provisions not included here.]

23.   COVENANTS

All provisions of the Declaration shall be construed to be covenants running with the land and with every part thereof and therein and every unit owner and claimant of the land or any part thereof or interest therein in his heirs, successors, executors, administrators, and assigns shall be bound by all of the provisions of the Declaration.

24.   INVALIDATION

Invalidation of any portion of this Declaration or of any provision contained in a conveyance of a condominium unit whether by judgment, court order, or law, shall in no way affect any of the other provisions which shall remain in full force and effect.

In the event any court should hereafter determine that any provision as originally drafted herein violates the rule against perpetuities, or any other rule of law because of declaration shall not thereby become invalid, but instead shall be reduced to the maximum period allowed under such rule of law and for such purpose measuring lives shall be those of the incorporators of the Association.

Exhibit 8.1   *(Continued)*

> **Agents often misrepresent HOA CC&Rs (covenants, conditions, and restrictions).**

serves as a case in point. I viewed this property as a potential investment, and as you might expect, prior to entering serious negotiations, I peppered the sales agent with questions about the units and their associated legal documents.

However, the answers the agent gave me were quite wrong about the rental restrictions, the voting procedures, and the division of the limited common elements.

Not an Indictment

I don't mean to indict this agent, for, in fact, he did hedge the answers he gave me. "I believe," "I think," "If I recall correctly," "the owner told me," and so it goes.

> **Beware when sellers or sales agents hedge their answers.**

Unfortunately, too many condo buyers and investors accept hedged answers as fact and then forget to verify. As I repeatedly advise, *read the language of the document itself.* Whenever you hear an agent or seller use language such as "I think" or "As I recall," train yourself to hear whistles and see flashing lights.

The Purpose and Terms of the Declaration

The declaration not only creates the homeowners association, it also attempts to provide for the preservation of the values and amenities in the community. The covenants, conditions, and restrictions (frequently referred to as CC&Rs) intend to prevent members of the HOA from doing things to or on the condo property that will diminish its value.

> **The declaration is designed to enhance the values of the units.**

Look at the last sentence of the opening section of the declaration, where it says that the covenants and restrictions "run with the land." Because of that statement, today's buyers of Villa Belle units can rest assured that this declaration will continue to bind all future buyers.

One Drawback

When members of an HOA wish to change their association *bylaws,* all they need to do is win a majority vote in a member meeting that satisfies the quorum requirement. When members of an HOA want to change the *rules issued* by their board, they merely need to persuade the board to act (or they can elect a new board). However, when unit owners wish to change their declarations, they must convince anywhere from *63.6 percent up to 100 percent of all unit owners* (a super majority) to vote for the change. (The declaration itself spells out the precise percentage.)

As if that weren't difficult enough, every lender who holds a first mortgage on a unit within the project also must sign off on

> **An HOA cannot easily amend its declaration.**

the change in the declaration. Although lenders may not unreasonably withhold their consent, the task of getting their signatures does present another hurdle. A large condo building or development could include 50 (or more) separate mortgage lenders.

Generalities or Details?

Because modifying the declaration requires a major effort, some developers try to limit CC&Rs to the more general and less contentious issues (e.g., no partitioning or subdividing of units). Other developers, however, include detailed dos and don'ts about such issues as parking, pets, architectural standards, and, most important from the investor perspective, rules about renting.

> **Many declarations incorporate rules for everyday living. Others rely on HOA boards to draft such detailed rules.**

So, it's not enough to know that an HOA has prescribed a certain rule or restriction; you also want to discover whether that rule derives it power from the board-issued regulations, the association's bylaws, or the declaration. If it's in the declaration, more than likely it's there for the long haul.

"More than likely," though doesn't necessarily mean "never." As Exhibit 9.4 will show, members of the Pine Valley HOA successfully amended their declaration to exclude the use of dens as bedrooms. This rule change reduced the potential density of the development. Among other things, this rule prohibited parents with one small child from living in one-bedroom/den units.

The Terms of the Declaration

In the following narrative, I key my discussions to the enumerated excerpts from the Villa Belle declaration. When you know

> **Look for HOAs with rules that investors can live with and profit by.**

what issues, terms, covenants, and restrictions to look for when you read through various condo declarations, you'll be able to better sort out the condos you want to consider versus those you will prefer to avoid. Remember, the actual terms of an HOA's declaration can put that development at a disadvantage vis-à-vis other condo projects (buildings). Or, the terms of the declaration could give an HOA a competitive edge.

Most important, you will want to invest only in those HOAs that give you the benefits and protections you want. In sum, these HOAs do not make leasing units too difficult, nor do they unfairly allocate common area expenses and voting rights.

Name and Address (1)   What's in a name? Marketing power. Although relatively few condo developments change their names, if the name of a project lacks market appeal, just changing its name can add thousands of dollars to the values of the units. Changing the name changes buyer perceptions. Should you invest in a condo or townhouse project that requires a makeover, definitely encourage a name change in the HOA's turnaround plans.

> **What's in a name? Marketing power.**

The Condominium Act (2)   As it is written, the clarity of this paragraph leaves much to be desired. When a statute conflicts with a term within the declaration, that statute takes precedence—unless it merely fills in as a default option for the HOA. Sometimes, that statute provides minimums (e.g., insurance coverage, voting procedures, reserve policies) that the HOA may exceed. In most states, you can buy a community association handbook that will fully describe the intersection of condo law and HOA documents, policies, and practices.

For example, in California the Piedmont Press annually publishes the *Condominium Bluebook*. Similarly, in Florida, Suncoast Professional Publishing brings out yearly editions of the *Condominium Concept: A Practical Guide for Officers, Owners, and Directors of Florida Condominiums*. Check with a condo director or your public library to see what similar kinds of publications are available in your state (or province, e.g., *The Condominium Manual* for British Columbia).

> **When HOA declarations conflict with statute, the statute rules.**

Survey and Floor Plan (3)   All declarations fully describe the physical common area property and the units themselves via plot plans, surveys, and building descriptions. It's very important for you to understand what property unit owners own and what property the HOA owns. In some condo/townhouse developments, units sit on commonly owned HOA property. In others, individuals own their lots (as described in the survey and plot plan). Sometimes the buildings sit on leased land.

As you can see here, the declaration refers to "land leased to the condominium association." I first learned about this clause when I read this declaration. The agent never mentioned it.

Plan of Development (4)   When you buy into a new development or a development where the builder plans to add phases, try to learn as much as you can about the fully completed project in terms of number of units, price ranges, amenity package, and recreational facilities. How will additional units add to the density of the total project? Will different phases involve separate HOAs? Or will multiple associations exist? If so, how will this fact affect the use, maintenance, and expense of the common areas, including streets and parking?

As a savvy buyer, always anticipate the future. Those beautiful woods could end up as a site for another 60 units.

> **Get the details on future phases.**

> **No standard definitions rule. Look to the declaration itself for how it defines the terms it uses.**

Definitions (5)   Although most condo declarations define terms such as *member, association, common elements,* and so forth in a similar manner, take notice of the definitions in any document you examine. You can never tell for sure when some lawyer or developer might throw you a curve ball.

Unit Boundaries and Ownership (6) You can see the boundaries of your unit on the survey and building plans. This verbal description here, though, gives you a more definitive understanding. It's commonly said that with a condo, you own all that's within the air space of your unit. You do not typically own the exterior walls, ceiling, or floor—these are common elements. But you do own the paint on the walls, the carpet on the floors, and the paint on the ceiling.

> **Not all condo "units" are defined in the same way.**

This definition of your unit becomes especially important in allocating the responsibility for maintenance, repair, and replacement between you and the HOA.

Percentage Ownership of Common Elements (7)   In this condo building, all unit owners own equal shares of the common elements and therefore pay equal contributions toward HOA expenses. In some HOAs, ownership of the common elements relates directly to the type or size of unit that you own. These types of allocations often force owners of larger units to pay more for common area maintenance—yet they derive no significant benefit for doing so. They don't get more time on the tennis courts, an extra parking space, or special pool time. They just pay more.

> **Some HOAs unjustly assess owners of larger units larger monthly fees.**

(General) Common Elements (8)   Typically, HOAs divide their common elements into two categories, general and limited (see item 9). By closely reading the descriptions of the common elements, you gain further specific knowledge abut the areas and components of the property for which the HOA carries responsibility. Naturally, you might assume that all property that doesn't fall within the definition of a "unit" is common property. That's true. But an explicit statement of common elements helps further clarify this division.

Limited Common Elements (9)   The declaration usually sets aside certain common elements for the exclusive use of a unit owner. Limited common elements may include patios, decks, balconies, assigned parking spaces, storage lockers, and yard space. The HOA normally pays to maintain, repair, and replace limited common elements—except in those cases in which the owner has caused excessive or unusual damage.

> **Unit owners may reserve limited common elements for their individual exclusive use. But HOAs often pay the maintenance for these areas.**

Parking (10)   Most HOA boards develop very detailed rules about parking (as you will see in Chapter 9), but they must do so within the confines of the declaration. Generally, HOAs deal with parking in terms of open parking, assigned spaces, or deeded spaces. As you can see here, Villa Belle assigns one space to each unit and prohibits any unit owner from occupying more than two spaces at any one time.

Given that parking can become a concern in many condo projects, you should closely review the declaration and board-issued rules about where, when, and what types of vehicles unit owners (tenants, guests) may park within the condo development.

> **Parking may be open, assigned, or deeded.**

Easements (11)   An easement gives one person the right to use or cross through the property of someone else. Because all condo owners must enter their units from common area property, technically they require an easement (or some other permissive agreement) to make it legal. Otherwise, the HOA board could erect NO TRESPASSING signs on all HOA common areas.

> **The declarations grant easements to unit owners but also reserve easements for the HOA to enter individual units.**

Interestingly, one condo association used the absence of an easement to essentially terminate an onerous lease of their recreational facilities (pool, tennis courts, clubhouse). The developer had locked the HOA into a lease at a low rate (to get the units sold). After five years, the lease came up for renewal. The developer tripled the rental. The HOA didn't want to submit to extortion. But neither did members want to give up their use of these facilities.

The developer played hardball. "Pay the rental I demand, or lose your lease. I'll then open the facilities as a recreational club to the general public."

Oops. The developer forgot one critical fact. Neither he nor any member of the public could walk or drive to the recreation area—except by crossing through HOA property. In the original condo documents, the developer (and his attorney) had failed to reserve an easement (right of access) to the recreation facilities that he continued to own. If he didn't lease (or sell) the facilities to the HOA, the recreation facilities would sit idle. No one other than a member of the HOA could legally gain access to them across HOA property.

Subsequently, having lost this gambit, the developer sold to the HOA on their terms, not his. He had tried to play hardball without a glove.

Common Expenses (12)   The common expenses section of a declaration spells out the purposes for which the HOA board can spend the association's monies. As is typical, this broad language gives the board authority to pay for any expense or capital improvement that will "protect, conserve, and maintain" condo property.

Association (13)   In addition to the responsibilities previously discussed (bylaws, budgets, bookkeeping, rule making), this section of a declaration also gives the HOA board the right to access any unit to make necessary repairs or replacements. This right of access also extends to inspections to make sure unit owners continue to comply with all house rules and CC&Rs (see Section 19, item f). No warrant is necessary, just reasonable notice.

> **Does the association follow the "one unit, one vote" principle?**

Voting Rights (14)   One unit, one vote has become the standard declaration of HOA voting rights. However, some HOAs allocate voting rights pro rata with the assessment of common expenses. If larger units pay more, then their owners should enjoy more say in determining who serves on the HOA board. This sounds reasonable. But most HOAs follow the principle of the U.S. Constitution. No matter how much you pay in taxes, you only get one vote.

Amendments (15)   The amendments clause gives the developer special rights during the time that he or she controls the HOA. Otherwise, to amend the declaration requires a 75 percent vote of unit owners—except in matters of determining the allocation of common expense changes, which require a 100 percent vote. Without this exception, 75 percent of the unit owners could vote to impose all common area expenses on the remaining 25 percent. This declaration also gives mortgage lenders the right to approve (or disapprove) amendments before they can take legal effect.

> **To amend the declaration requires a super majority vote by all unit owners.**

Sales, Transfer, Lease, or Occupancy of a Unit (16) These paragraphs of the declaration place extensive (and possibly severe) restraints on the unit owners (although it exempts the developer). The HOA board must approve in writing all transferees for their "good moral characters, social compatibility, and financial responsibility." The board could even prevent relatives who inherit the property from taking up residence.

> **Declarations may limit the right to lease, sell, or occupy a unit.**

Because the Villa Belle units sit directly across the street from Siesta Beach (Gulf of Mexico), I considered using one or more units as a rental for short-term vacationers (as is common in that area and within many of the investor-owned/second-home types of condo units. The agent reported no problems that he could see. My reading of the declaration, though, revealed a much different picture. Besides board approval in writing, no rentals of less than 30 days were permitted. The declaration clearly scrapped my plans.

Restraint upon Partition (17)   Nearly all condo declarations prevent partitioning a condo parcel. Imagine that you bought a unit in a development with fantastic recreation facilities. But you travel so much that you never get a chance to use them. You get a bright idea! Sell your member rights to use the pool and tennis courts to someone else.

Nope, you can't do it. There is no right of partition. Nor could you sell your storage locker, deeded parking space, or patio. If you own a three-bedroom, three-bathroom unit, you couldn't remodel it into a two-bedroom, two-bath and one-bedroom, one-bath unit. Quite reasonably, the rule against partitioning preserves the integrity of the whole development. Without this restriction, some unit owners might slice and dice their parcels to the detriment of the whole community.

> **No unit owner may subdivide his or her interests in condo property.**

Management (18)   Again, the developer through this paragraph extends to himself special rights and privileges to unilaterally manage the HOA for a period up to one year after the date of the declaration. This prerogative as written here seems reasonable. In some declarations the developer establishes and retains privileges that disadvantage the HOA and increases their costs (exorbitant leases, sweetheart deals, no common area assessments applied to developer-owned units). Before buying, investigate the perks, prerogatives, and privileges that the developer retains exclusive of all other unit owners.

> **Declarations always grant the developer special rights, privileges, and prerogatives.**

Maintenance and Repairs (19)   The maintenance and repair section again attempts to clarify who pays for what. Read closely the similar clauses that you will find in the declarations you review. They typically will precisely

> **The declaration defines who pays how much.**

detail and describe an extensive list of maintenance items on both the interior and the exterior of the unit.

Ask the sellers to give you a narrated walk-through of the unit to delineate owner responsibilities from those of the HOA. As a "lazy" investor, you should prefer those units where the HOA does almost everything except dust the furniture.

Assessments and Liens (20)   The paragraph explores in legal detail the assessment, levy, and lien procedures discussed in Chapter 4.

Use Restrictions (21)   All condo declarations spell out how unit owners, tenants, and guests may or may not use condo property. The usage paragraph in the Villa Belle declaration includes fairly standard language in that it:

- Excludes any use but residential.
- Prohibits home offices or businesses.
- Prohibits any activity that increases the insurance rates for the HOA.
- Requires unit occupants to obey all government laws that relate to the use or occupancy of the unit. (Speeding or robbing a bank doesn't violate the declaration. Leaving a garbage pile in the kitchen in violation of health codes would.)
- Requires occupants to obey all HOA rules and CC&Rs.
- Prohibits occupants from becoming a nuisance or acting immorally (at one time a common restriction, less so today).

Most important, notice that this paragraph gives every unit owner the right to enforce the declaration and other HOA rules against any other unit owners. If a complaint to the board doesn't bring relief, you can take that saxophone-playing neighbor to

| | court. The judge will then enforce the declarations against the offensive resident(s). Judges may award damages, issue an injunction, or both. |

Who can enforce HOA rules?

Verify the types of insurance coverage and policy limitations of the HOA.

Insurance (22) The declaration will mandate certain *minimum* insurance coverage for the association. These minimums should never substitute for a thorough analysis of HOA insurance needs by a condo insurance specialist and the HOA's attorney.

Covenants (23) This section restates the fact that these enumerated CC&Rs "run with the land." However, because of the common law "rule against perpetuities," many condo declarations omit "run with the land." Instead, they limit the running of the CC&Rs to a period of, say, 25 or 50 years. The Sabal Point Condominium in Miami, Florida, for example, was built in 1965. Its original declaration expired on January 1, 2000.

Be wary of expiration dates. The HOA could turn sour.

Don't assume the declaration lasts forever. If the complex is more than 20 years old, the HOA members may need to begin drafting a new declaration (or reinstating the existing one). Under no circumstances (that I can think of) should an HOA actually permit its declaration to lapse. That result could provoke a litigious free-for-all as dissident unit owners begin to alter, modify, decorate, and use their properties in ways that otherwise have been prohibited.

Invalidation (24) An invalidation clause remains a standard part of many contracts and agreements. It generally means that if for some reason a court rules against (or refuses to enforce) one part of the declaration, all other CC&Rs continue to operate.

> **The declaration will survive even though a court refuses to enforce a particular rule or paragraph.**

For example, say an unmarried couple decides to buy one of the units at Villa Belle. The HOA board disapproves the couple from buying because the declaration prohibits immoral conduct. The couple takes the board to court.

The relativist judge believes in a so-called right of privacy and throws out the board's decision. "Immorality," says the judge, "provides too much ambiguity and subjectivity. The board needs more modern, objective standards before this court will enforce them." That ruling would in no way affect the voting rights or common expense paragraphs of the declaration. The immorality clause is severed. The remainder of the document stands.

Summing Up

I hope that now you realize why all condo experts urge investors and homebuyers to closely inspect the declaration before buying a condo. The declaration (in rather permanent form) spells out the detailed rights, responsibilities, and expenses attached to your ownership of condo property.

CHAPTER 9

Understand the Rules and Regulations

In our trilogy of legal documents, we now turn to the board-issued rules and regulations. Remember, the developer sets the basic framework for the homeowners' association through the original declaration and bylaws filed to establish the condominium regime and the HOA. These documents then give the HOA board the authority to draft, implement, and enforce any other rules that will preserve the values of the units and enhance the quality of life for all residents of the HOA community.

Board-Issued Rules: Community Values or Dictatorship

You can see from the Pine Valley HOA rules (Exhibit 9.1) that condo boards can and do write rules that govern nearly anything you can think of where the behavior of one person might adversely affect the condo property, the board, or another resident.

Although some people complain about socialistic or even dictatorial boards, my experience (and my conversations with other current and past HOA residents) tells me that such complaints for the most part vastly overstate the case against board-issued regulations. If you closely review the long list of rules of

We, the Board of Directors, have consolidated the Rules and Requirements in brief, so that everyone will be informed. Remember, it is the responsibility of the unit owner to be sure his/her tenants abide by the Rules and Requirements of Pine Valley.

1. ***Maintenance of Unit***
   You, the owner, are responsible for all repairs and maintenance within your unit, including windows, screens, plumbing pipes, washing machine hoses, heating air valves, electrical, etc.

2. ***Unit Occupancy and Use***
   Only two (2) persons per bedroom can occupy a unit. IMPORTANT: The Den CANNOT be made into a second bedroom. No use other than residential permitted. No professional offices or home businesses shall be conducted from any unit.

3. ***Balcony/Terrace***
   Must be kept neat with no drying or airing of towels or storage of boxes, etc., visible over the railing. Note: Balcony/terrace must be kept clean of snow by unit owner.

4. ***Security System***
   It is important that residents call 911 IMMEDIATELY if they hear a loud buzzing sound day or night in the hallway. After you call 911, please call Consolidated Management Services at 765-4321.

5. ***Adults/Children***
   Any activities that are harmful to buildings, hallways, common areas, shrubs, and trees are prohibited.

6. ***Charcoal Grills***
   Charcoal grills are not permitted; only GAS or ELECTRIC.

7. ***Sunscreens***
   Sunscreens are permitted on balconies if you purchase one the color of the dark brown wood trim, but it must fit properly and be attractive. NOTE: Awnings are not approved. Full screening is not permitted; however, you may screen up to the railing, and paint it the same color as the balcony/terrace.

8. ***Blocked Drains***
   It is important that the lint trap on your washer be cleaned frequently. Also, that you DO NOT throw food solids or items such as bacon grease into the kitchen drain or allow hair to go down the bathroom drains. It is also important that every few months you pour LIQUID drain cleaner, such as Liquid Plumber, down all your drains. The Association CANNOT be responsible for cleaning your unit drains when blockage is caused by the residents' negligence. It will be the responsibility of the unit owner to correct the problem.

(continued)

Exhibit 9.1   Pine Valley Condominium Rules and Regulations.

9. ***Parking***

All vehicles must be confined to clearly outlined parking spaces. All unlicensed vehicles, vehicles parked in fire lanes, in front of trash bins, or in grandfathered designated Senior Citizen or Handicapped parking spaces may be towed away at the owner's expense.

NOTE: No liability is assumed by the Association for any property damage or theft resulting to the vehicles during towing or storage due to illegal parking. Cars must NOT be "stored" on property. No boats, trailers, or other recreational vehicle may be kept anywhere on the grounds, nor any vans with printing on the sides or back. *No trucks are allowed.* No signs of any kind may be placed on any vehicles, i.e., FOR SALE. Passenger cars may only be parked in front of units. Bumper of car should not extend over the sidewalk. Vans must be parked on the perimeter ONLY. All vans must be for transportation use only. No commercial use is allowed. IMPORTANT: Reserved parking can be obtained if resident has a *handicapped permit from the State of Ohio with a one-time charge of $100.00 for painting/handling.* If you require a handicapped reserved space, send a letter to the Board of Directors, Pine Valley Management Office, with a copy of your State handicapped permit and a check for $100.00 made payable to Pine Valley Condominium Association. All vehicles must have a numbered RR parking permit sticker.

10. ***Common Charges***

Common charges are due and payable on the first of each month. There is a 10-day grace period, after which a late charge of $50.00 is added to your account. If payment is not received by the 30th of the month, a 1.5% interest charge is automatically placed on your account.

11. ***Pool/Pond Rules***

Pool rules will be distributed to all residents at the beginning of the summer. The pond has been designated as an Ecological Area and NO FISHING is permitted.

12. ***Pets (One Per Unit)***

Any pet creating a nuisance or unreasonable disturbance may be permanently removed from the property upon ten (10) days written notice by the Board of Directors and/or Managing Agent. IMPORTANT: Pets are not allowed to roam unattended. Pets must be leashed at all times. Residents are required to clean up after their pets. Anyone observed violating any of these rules is subject to a $50.00 fine.

(continued)

Exhibit 9.1 *(Continued)*

13. **Heat**

Unit owners are responsible for their heating Flair valve. This valve can be installed by Jake the Plumber, Telephone Number 800-987-6543. You can also use the plumber of your choice. Note that boiler room access is restricted to Jake the Plumber and Home Oil. Other vendors must request that the system be shut off and turned on by one of these companies. Also, if you do not have heat, your system could be air-bound and need bleeding. This is a unit owner's responsibility.

14. **Hot Water**

We have been told that it is imperative to use the shut-off valve on your washer when it is not in use. If this is not done, the water temperature can fluctuate dramatically.

15. **Flip Charge**

A "FLIP CHARGE" of $250.00 is due immediately and payable each time a resident vacates the premises. If the unit is shared and two separate moves occur, you are subject to $250.00 for each move-out. This should be automatically mailed to the CMS office by the unit owner. Make the check payable to "Pine Valley Condominium Association." Be sure to mark on the check "Flip Charge" and indicate your unit number. NOTE: When a move-out occurs and the $250.00 Flip Charge is not automatically mailed to the management office (within no more than three days from vacancy), and the building representative calls in the move, an additional charge of $50.00 will be charged to the unit account on the eighth day and another $50.00 on the ninth day over and above the regular $250.00 Flip Charge. The Flip Charge will then total $350.00. This fee helps to cover the cost of repainting, repairing, and cleaning carpets, especially where there is a heavy turnover.

16. **Carpeting**

Carpeting is required on the floors throughout all units located above ground level (exception for baths and kitchens).

17. **Stereo Speakers**

Speakers may not be mounted on walls as this causes undue reverberation.

18. **Window Treatment**

Proper window treatment MUST BE installed within thirty (30) days of occupying a unit.

(continued)

Exhibit 9.1 *(Continued)*

19. **Emergency Service**

The Managing Agent provides a 24-hour, 7-day-a-week answering service. AFTER 5:00 P.M. WEEKDAYS AND ALL DAY SATURDAY AND SUNDAY only *emergency calls are accepted.*

20. **Work Orders**

Repair items are best handled by using work order forms provided by the Managing Agent, which are available in the lower mailbox in front of units 451–456. Place completed form in the top box. Call the management office for emergency repairs ONLY; otherwise, use the work order forms provided. This will guarantee your request will be addressed promptly.

21. **Snow**

When a snowstorm is over, the snowplow will clear roads first, then parking areas. IMPORTANT: IT IS EACH RESIDENT'S RESPONSIBILITY TO MOVE HIS/HER CAR TO A CLEARED SPACE SO THAT ALL PARKING SPACES CAN BE CLEARED.

22. **Air Conditioners**

Must fit built-in sleeve properly so birds, etc., cannot nest. If no A/C is in sleeve, sleeve must be covered with a cover that is painted the exact dark brown color as trim.

23. **Signs**

No signs are permitted to be displayed either on units or parked vehicles.

24. **Air Valve**

Do not turn off your heat completely, even if you are going away for a day. The heating system at Pine Valley is a loop system, and, if you turn your heat completely off, the hot water cannot circulate through the system and your heating pipes will freeze. If you need to have work completed on your inside heating system, please remember that the heat control valve is the unit owner's responsibility. If the boilers need to be turned off, the plumber will have to contact Home Oil and the unit owner will be responsible for a service call charge payable to Home Oil.

25. **Water Leaks**

Please remember that unit owners above ground level are responsible for the repair of damage resulting from water leaks emanating from their units. It is the unit owner's responsibility to contact the owners below and/or adjacent to his/her unit to determine the extent of damage outside of his apartment. For any necessary repairs, it is his or her responsibility to

(continued)

Exhibit 9.1 *(Continued)*

reach an agreement with the owners of those units affected. Pine Valley Condominium Association, Inc., is only involved in the notification of responsibility and does not become involved in the negotiation of the painting, plastering, or repair process.

Should you have a leak in your unit or have water damage as a result of a leak emanating from another unit, please contact the management company immediately.

26. *Guests*

Should you have guests staying with you for a few days, you are required to notify the management company prior to their arrival. You will be asked for the make, model, and license number of a guest's vehicle. Management Services will then notify the security firm and your guest(s) will not be ticketed.

27. *Signs*

No signs can be installed on Pine Valley property or rights-of-way without permission from the Pine Valley Condominium Association, Inc., Board of Directors. This includes holiday signs and large greeting signs installed by party companies.

28. *Washing Machines*

The installation of full-size washing machines is not permitted. Unit owners who presently have full-size washing machines may continue to use them under the following terms and conditions:

(a)   Full-size washing machines may only be filled to one-half capacity.

(b)   Unit owners with full-size washing machines will be held responsible for any damage or destruction to the common elements of other units or unit owners' property.

(c)   Unit owners who continue to use full-size washing machines at full capacity will be required to remove the machines.

(d)   Full-size washing machines must be replaced with smaller machines when they reach the end of their useful lives.

[Author Note: Pine Valley HOA issued this washing machine rule because of a plumbing deficiency within the building. On occasion, the washer discharge connection breaks and spills out water. A half-load or smaller capacity washer minimizes the damage that is created due to a big spill.]

29. *Bird Feeders*

Since bird feeders attract rodents, squirrels, etc., and we have had problems with rodents and squirrels getting into attics and walls, the Board of Directors MUST ENFORCE the rule that Bird Feeders are not allowed. They will be removed and the unit owner will be charged $50.00.

(continued)

Exhibit 9.1   *(Continued)*

30. ***Frost-Free Outside Faucets/Hoses***

[These] MUST NOT be left connected. Hoses must be disconnected from the outside faucets at all times during freezing weather. If this is not done, the water backs up into the pipes and causes them to freeze/crack.

31. ***Disputes between Neighbors***

The Board of Directors CANNOT become involved in civil matters. Also, if another unit owner causes damage to your unit, it is this unit owner's responsibility to pay for all damages. The unit owner who has incurred damage should immediately contact the unit owner who has caused the damage.

32. ***Porch Lights/Security***

A security suggestion is to keep your porch lights on in the evening. If you have an emergency, day or night, please call 911 for help. Security is hired to control speeding and parking and to deter intruders. The security company does not have back-up or emergency equipment similar to that of the police department.

33. ***Lease***

A unit may not be leased or rented for a term of less than one year. All leases and rental agreements shall be in writing and subject to the requirements of the documents of the Association. Unit owners shall provide the Association with a copy of all leases and amendments thereto. Landlords who fail to mail Management Services an updated lease (within and no more than seven days from the move-in date) will be charged $10.00 per day each and every day until such time as the management company is in receipt of the new lease. No warning letter will be sent. Landlords will be fined and their accounts automatically billed.

The lessee(s) of the unit must reside in the unit. No unit may be leased to or for the benefit of a business entity for the purpose of providing housing to its agents, servants, employees, or guests.

Owners are responsible for their tenants' actions. This includes violations of rules, fines levied, and damages created by tenants and/or tenants' guests.

34. ***Toddler Playground***

The playground must be kept free of litter, trash, etc. No children over the age of six (6) years old are permitted on the playground equipment. Please close the gate when leaving the playground. No pets are allowed within the playground area.

(continued)

Exhibit 9.1   *(Continued)*

35. **Halls**

Articles such as rubbers, shoes, boots, bicycles, strollers, chairs, garbage, recycling bins, bottles, etc., CANNOT BE STORED/KEPT IN THE HALLWAY. (No personal property of any kind can be stored in the common hallways.) Front entrance doors should remain closed at all times for your safety and security.

36. **Additions, Alterations, or Improvements by the Association**

Whenever, in the judgment of the Association, common elements shall require additions, alterations, or improvements costing in excess of $10,000, said alterations or improvements shall not be made unless they have been approved by a majority of the Unit Owners present and voting at a meeting at which a quorum is present. When said approval has been obtained, all Unit Owners shall be assessed for the cost thereof as a common expense.

37. **Additions, Alterations, or Improvements by the Unit Owners**

(a)   All condominium units shall be and remain of like exterior design, shape, color, and appearance as other condominium units of the same class and type. No owner shall alter or modify the size, shape, color, or structure of any exterior surface of his unit, including entrance doors, windows, shutters, screens, stairs, porches, or balconies, nor improve, plant, replant, or replace any trees, bushes, or sod, or remove fill dirt, without obtaining prior written consent of the Developer (so long as it is managing the Condominium) and the Association.

(b)   Occupants of condominium units shall not suffer, permit, or maintain in their premises loud noises or obnoxious odors, nor interfere with the rights of other unit owners or annoy them by unreasonable noises.

38. **Right of Access**

Each Unit Owner shall grant a right of access to his unit to the manager and/or the managing agent and/or any other person authorized by the Association for the purpose of making inspections and for the purpose of correcting any condition originating in this unit and threatening another unit or common element or for the purpose of performing necessary installations, alterations, or repairs to the mechanical or electrical services or other common elements in his unit or elsewhere in the building within which the unit is located, provided that requests for entry are made in advance and that any such entry is at a time reasonably convenient to the Unit Owner. In the case of an emergency, such right of entry shall be immediate, whether the Unit Owner is present at the time or not.

39. **Utility Services**

Electrical services shall be supplied by Hartford Electric Co., Inc., directly to each unit through a separate meter for each unit, and each unit shall be required to pay the bills for such electric services consumed or used by his/her unit and in the limited common elements serving the unit. Water shall

(continued)

Exhibit 9.1   *(Continued)*

be supplied by, and the charges therefore paid to, the First Taxing District Water Department. Sewers will be connected to the public sewer system. Charges for sewer and water shall be a common expense.

40. ***Right of First Refusal***

No Unit Owner may effectively dispose of a unit or any interest therein by sale or lease in the Association without first offering the same for sale to the Association upon the terms and conditions hereinafter provided for. The provisions of this section shall not apply with respect to any sale, conveyance, or lease by any Unit Owner of his interest to his spouse, to any of his children, or to his parent or parents, or to his brothers or sisters, or any one or more of them, nor shall it apply to any unit owned by the Association.

(a) The Unit Owner intending to make a sale or lease of his unit or any interest therein or the purchaser or lessee thereof shall give to the Association notice of such intention together with the name and address of the intended purchaser or lessee and the terms and conditions of the sale or lease including the price. The Association shall thereafter have a period of 15 days within which they may buy or lease said unit on the same terms and conditions as contained in the outside offer. If the Association is going to buy said unit, then within said 15-day period the Association shall deliver or mail by registered mail to the Unit Owner an agreement to purchase said unit upon said terms and conditions. The price shall be paid in cash and the sale shall be closed on the date specified in the original proposed sale. If the Association is going to lease said unit, then within said 15-day period the Association shall deliver or mail by registered mail to the Unit Owner an agreement to lease said unit upon the said terms and conditions. The lease shall start on the date specified in the original proposed lease. If the Association shall take the lease on the unit, it shall have the right to sublease the unit. Upon the failure of the Association to exercise said right of first refusal, the Unit Owner shall be free to sell or lease the unit without regard to the right of first refusal. If the proposed transaction is a lease, however, the lease must state that the lessee agrees to abide by all of the terms and conditions and covenants of the Declaration of Condominium and these Bylaws and any rules and regulations as may hereafter be established from time to time by the Association.

(b) If the Association elects to exercise its right of first refusal in the manner set forth in subparagraph (a) of this section or if it does not elect to exercise its right of first refusal within 15 days after receipt of the notice described in subparagraph (a) of this section, the Association shall, in addition to the foregoing, and within 10 days after the Association acts on

(continued)

Exhibit 9.1 *(Continued)*

such request and no later than 40 days, furnish to any Unit Owner, or purchaser or lessee requesting the same, a recordable statement certified to any exercise, waiver of, failure, or refusal to exercise this right of first refusal in all cases where such exercise, waiver, failure, or refusal does in fact occur. Failure or refusal to furnish such a statement within 40 days after delivery of a written request by a Unit Owner, or purchaser or lessee in accordance with the provisions hereof shall make all such rights and restraints inapplicable to any disposition of a condominium unit in contemplation of which such statement was requested. Any such statement shall be binding on the Association and the Unit Owner. No action may be commenced to enforce such right unless commenced and a notice recorded on the land records within six months of the recording of such conveyance.

(c)   The Association shall not exercise any right of first refusal set forth herein without the prior approval of at least seventy-five (75) percent of the Unit Owners in the Pine Valley Community.

41. *Selling and Soliciting*

Selling, soliciting, or commercial enterprises are prohibited within the Community without first obtaining the consent of the Corporation. If a solicitor comes to your door, notify the office immediately. Residents are encouraged to notify the Board immediately if any solicitors cause a personal disturbance. This rule refers to Commercial Soliciting only, and in no way is intended to limit the rights of the residents to freely canvass or to otherwise infringe upon their rights.

42. *Enforcement of Rules*

Complaints of violations of the rules of this community should first be reported to a member of the Rules Committee, who will then call a meeting of said committee. The Committee will review the matter and refer their recommendations to the Board. The Board will then issue an order to desist, impose a fine, or take whatever other action is necessary to protect the interest of the community residents.

43. *Attorney's Fees*

If Pine Valley takes court action for a violation of these Rules and Regulations, the prevailing party shall be entitled to reasonable attorney's fees.

44. *General*

If any provision of these Rules and Regulations be contrary to any law of any jurisdiction in which Pine Valley is located, it shall not apply or be enforced. However, the other provisions of these rules and regulations shall not be affected and shall continue in full force and effect.

(continued)

Exhibit 9.1   *(Continued)*

---

45. *Door Mats*
Reasonably sized door mats may be installed in front of the residents' unit doors.

Addendum: Effective 10/1/97, no moving trucks over 45 feet long are allowed on the property.
Addendum: Effective 10/1/97, to clarify existing rules and regulations, storage of items on decks and balconies deemed to be unsightly and/or not in keeping with the character of the complex, by the Pine Valley Condominium Association, Inc., Board of Directors, is not permitted.
Note: The Board of Directors can impose a fine of up to $50.00 per occurrence/per day for violations of the rules and requirements of Pine Valley Condominium Association, Inc.
Important: The above information is not intended to replace the Declaration and Bylaws. It is a brief summary for quick reference. In the event of discrepancy, the Declaration and Bylaws and recent Board of Directors' decisions represent current official position and take precedence.

Exhibit 9.1   *(Continued)*

Board rules typically promote community values.

the Pine Valley HOA, you will find no rule that seriously violates any reasonable standard of common sense or responsible freedom.

What Rules and Why?

Similar to the style of Chapter 7 (bylaws) and Chapter 8 (the declaration), this chapter will go through the what and why of board-issued rules. Because many of these rules essentially explain themselves, I discuss only those that might need some clarification, elaboration, or emphasis. However, because all HOAs draft their rules to fit their own needs and inclinations, Pine Valley serves as a suggestive example, not a comprehensive listing of every conceivable rule that you might run into.

Many HOA rules need no explanation.

Also, recall that although various HOAs may apply similar rules, the source of those rules may differ. In one HOA, the board may prohibit white shutters or enclosed balconies. In another HOA, you might find those types of restrictions in the declaration (which means a rule change will prove more difficult). Let's see how the Pine Valley HOA tries to carry out its rule-making responsibilities and the implications that such rules might have for you as an investor (and for your tenants).

Maintenance of Unit (1)

As in all HOAs, investors and homebuyers must carefully clarify the line between HOA expenses and unit owner expenses. Some HOAs do take responsibility for windows, screens, and certain plumbing and electrical connections, but Pine Valley pushes more of these maintenance expenses into the owner's realm of responsibility. (In terms of plumbing, rarely would any HOA assume responsibility for owner- or tenant-created problems. The HOA won't answer a call to fix a stopped-up toilet or a broken garbage disposal.)

Board rules clarify maintenance responsibilities.

Unit Occupancy and Use (2)

Occupancy restrictions need not violate fair housing laws.

HOAs and investors must comply with local, state, and federal fair housing laws. But within that context, HOAs and investors may still restrict occupancy to prevent overcrowding. Toward that end, Pine Valley does not permit owners or tenants to use a den as a bedroom (see Exhibit 9.2). Some HOAs also attempt to prevent multiple roommate types of occupancies. Senior citizen HOAs may limit occupancy by age (typically 55 years, but in some instances, 62).

Management Services, Inc.

Condominium Management & Consulting

28 Westin Avenue
Columbus, OH
(800) 987-6543

June 1, 2003

The Ohio Board of Realtors
45 King Street
Columbus, OH

To Whom It May Concern:

We sent you a letter on July 31, 2002, attaching a copy of the Two Changes to the Declaration at Pine Valley Condominiums.

We still see ads stating that the Den can be used as a second bedroom. This is against the Declaration.

Please be sure that when listing these units that the "Den" can only be used as a Den. If a unit is sold and the Den is used as a bedroom, the Board will take action in accordance with the Declaration and Bylaws.

Attached you will find a copy of the Two Changes to the Declaration.
Thank you for your cooperation.

Very truly yours,

Ariel Lyndon, Manager
PINE VALLEY CONDOMINIUMS

Exhibit 9.2   Letter to Realtors.

Residential Uses Only? With so many people working from home (or running home businesses) these days, some HOAs have acquiesced to this trend. Others, though, (such as Pine Valley) have not. So, you will want to read the rules closely to determine how tightly the HOA defines residential use. The rules of one relatively permissive HOA state, "Unit may be used as a professional office, subject to applicable government regulations and the prior written approval of the Board." Another HOA goes even further to permit home businesses: "No business may be conducted . . . except such businesses as is solely and exclusively incident to each unit, provided that no such business shall put up signs, displays, or advertising visible from the outside of the unit."

> **When allowed, business or professional uses must not annoy other residents.**

No Nuisances Permitted Even when HOAs permit some type of business of professional use, such a use will rarely give the unit owner (or tenants) the right to create a nuisance. If the nonresidential activity means that delivery trucks will come and go every day, if customers or clients traipse in and out, or if noise or commotion accompanies the use, the board will undoubtedly clamp down.

Balcony/Terrace (3)

> **Unregulated balconies can create the look of a tenement.**

Have you noticed some apartment and condo buildings where residents use their balconies, terraces, or patios for hanging out wet towels or clothing, storing bicycles, or piling up cardboard boxes full of who knows what? It looks messy and unattractive, right? That's why well-run HOAs police the use and appearance of those areas. Boards do not want their buildings to become tenements. Nor should you.

Charcoal Grills (6)

Hot charcoal presents a fire hazard and a disposal problem. In addition, if a grill is accidentally knocked over, it could rain hot charcoal on people below. In this mid-rise building, "no *charcoal* grills" seems like a sensible precaution. Such a rule also might give the HOA a break on the premiums it pays for fire insurance.

Parking (9)

Without tight rules on parking, the aesthetics of the parking areas could deteriorate. In addition, by prohibiting boats, trailers, and

> **Parking rules often exclude trucks, vans, and motorcycles.**

trucks, the HOA frees up parking spaces for the primary vehicles of the residents and their guests. Increasingly, HOAs prohibit trucks, vans, and cars with commercial messages or company names printed on their exteriors. In the eyes of many residents, such vehicles cheapen the appearance of the complex. (See Exhibit 9.3).

---

1. TRUCKS ARE PROHIBITED FROM PARKING AT PINE VALLEY.
2. MOTORCYCLES ARE PROHIBITED FROM PARKING AT PINE VALLEY.
3. VANS ARE NOT PERMITTED WITH ANY TYPE OF ADVERTISING OR LETTERING. [THE] ONLY VANS ALLOWED MUST BE USED FOR *TRANSPORTATION ONLY AND MUST HAVE WINDOWS ON THE SIDE*. Vans must park on the outer perimeter of property *only* as it is difficult for other vehicles to see when backing out due to the size and height of Vans.

All residents must have a parking permit sticker in order to park at Pine Valley. If you have a visitor that will be parking overnight for any length of time, inform the security officer on duty.

IMPORTANT: When preparing a lease, it is the responsibility of the Unit Owners to inform their tenants of all the rules and regulations and to inquire what type of vehicles the tenants will be parking at Pine Valley.

Exhibit 9.3　　Parking at Pine Valley.

Pool/Pond Rules (11)

Swimming pools create a liability insurance expense, and frequently pool noise can annoy residents who live within audible range. (See Exhibit 9.4.)

---

1. Pool hours are from 6:00 A.M. to 11:00 P.M. Residents must be able to present passes at all times. Pool attendant hours are from 10:00 A.M. to 6:00 P.M. Residents are to register daily in the attendant's presence by name, unit number, and the number of adult and child guests entering the pool area.

    Special times are reserved for adult swim/quiet hour (age 14 and over) as follows:

    Saturday and Sunday 8:00 A.M. to 10:00 A.M.

2. *No* lifeguard is on duty at any time—swim at your own risk. In compliance with State regulations, the gate *must* be kept closed at all times.

3. Any user in the Pine Valley pool swims at his/her own risk. The Pine Valley Association will not be liable nor assume any responsibility for loss of personal property or injury of any kind.

4. Each Pine Valley resident will assume *complete responsibility* for any of his/her family, guests, etc. Each resident is responsible to ensure that no diving, running, shouting, throwing of objects, or general horseplay occurs.

5. Use of the pool is restricted to residents *only.* On weekends and holidays, the Board and/or pool attendant may exclude guests, as conditions warrant.

6. Pool guests (*other than family members who are Pine Valley residents*) are limited to four (4) daily (including children) and must be accompanied by a resident at all times. Nonresident owners may visit the pool area with a valid pool tag.

7. No pool toys, rafts, or floats are allowed in the pool. Children under the age of 14 must at all times be accompanied by and be under the supervision of a parent or adult resident. The attendant cannot be used as a babysitter. Parents are responsible for children's behavior, especially in such matters as unruly or loud behavior, diving into any area of the pool, etc. Buoyant devices worn by children are permitted. Diapered children must wear rubber or plastic outer covers.

(continued)

Exhibit 9.4   Pine Valley Condominium Association Pool Rules 2003.

8. Light snacks may be consumed in the lounge chairs but the picnic tables should be used for fuller meals. As a safety concern, only plastic containers or cans should be used for beverages. Glass containers are not allowed. Residents must clean their area and discard all wrappers, cans, etc., in the wastebaskets.
9. Residents' cooperation is requested in removing litter.
10. The proximity of living units to the pool and courtesy to other pool users requires that use of radios or tape players around the pool be permitted only with earphones.
11. *No pool parties* without prior written permission from the Board of Directors. Requests for permission must be in writing to CMS office at least *two weeks* before the party date. Residents may contact the office if no response is received within seven days.
12. Proper bathing attire is required in the pool area (proper swim wear only). You must shower before entering the pool.
13. *No* pets are allowed in the pool area.
14. The above rules are in effect at all times, whether or not a pool attendant or Board member is present.

FAILURE TO ABIDE BY THE ABOVE RULES MAY RESULT IN A $50.00 FINE.

IT IS ALSO THE RESPONSIBILITY OF THE UNIT OWNER TO ENSURE THAT HIS/HER TENANT ABIDES BY THE POOL RULES AND TO BE CERTAIN THAT THE TENANT RECEIVES AND UNDERSTANDS THESE AND ALL RELEVANT REGULATIONS.

Exhibit 9.4 *(Continued)*

Pets (12)

Pet rules differ enormously among HOAs. Read such restrictions carefully. Oddly, the Pine Valley HOA has written its pet rule rather ambiguously. Presumably, a literal interpretation would prohibit a resident from owning a hamster cage with several hamsters or a well-stocked aquarium. But the resident could own a falcon, a pot-bellied pig, or a pet boa constrictor. It also appears that the rule does not limit the size of a pet. Could a resident keep a mild-mannered miniature horse?

> **Crafting pet rules demands great wisdom.**

Most pet rules not only specify a number (typically one or two), but also a size (less than 15 pounds) and sometimes type of animal (dog or cat). Maybe the HOA feels this rule is strict enough because it allows the board to eject a nuisance. If no nuisance is caused, who would care whether someone houses a poodle or a panda?

Flip Charge (15)

As an investor, you may resent having to pay a special $250 charge every time a tenant moves in or out. However, this rule is necessary at Pine Valley because move-ins and move-outs tie up elevator time, soil carpets, and damage walls. If you pass this charge along to your tenants, it may reduce your tenant turnover.

Signs (23)

At first glance, you may think that the HOA should not restrict your ability to display a FOR RENT or FOR SALE sign on your unit. However, in the past, I have visited complexes where 20 to 30 percent of the units were up for sale at one time. Potential buyers (renters) would take one look and think, "Wow, there must be something wrong with this place. Why else would so many units be on the market?"

> **Limits on FOR SALE and FOR LEASE signs enhance the marketability of units.**

No FOR SALE or FOR RENT signs prevent a desperation complex and add an aura of dignity to the building or development. (As a potential buyer, though, always learn the complete condo inventory in a project. Not only will this knowledge expand your choice, it will also give you ammunition for negotiating.)

Guests (26)

Guest rules promote security and safety.

Pine Valley (as do many HOAs) require multiday visitors to register. This procedure serves to enhance security. It, too, though, will help you as an investor. It prohibits your tenants from moving additional persons into the unit without your knowledge or permission.

Lease (33)

Pine Valley requires all investors to file current copies of their leases with the Pine Valley management. Again, this rule may seem like a bother. But it adds to the security of the building (development) because management will always know who's living where. Also, the one-year minimum stay reduces transiency within the project (as does the flip charge).

Note also that the lease rule imposes liability on investors for the rule-breaking behavior of their tenants or their guests. Investors must know and understand all HOA rules (declarations and board-issued), so that they can fully explain them to their tenants. Again, this rule may seem negative at first glance. But in fact the

Investors need to educate their tenants about HOA rules.

lease requirement works in your favor. It should give you peace of mind to know that the HOA board and other unit owners will be keeping an eye on your tenants. If, for some unknown reason, your tenant screening fails to exclude a less than perfect tenant, the HOA will definitely notify you. See Exhibit 9.5 for lease rules defined by the HOA.

Capital Improvements (36)

In some HOAs, boards can ultimately budget for capital improvements and assess the unit owners as necessary to pay for these re-

Pine Valley Condominium Association, Inc.

This is to clarify the procedure for absentee owners regarding the leasing of their unit effective January 1, 2003. There will be no exceptions.

In compliance with the Pine Valley documents, one of the following must be in the Pine Valley files at the management office at all times.

1.   If your *lease* is expired you must hand-deliver or send by certified mail a copy of your *new lease within thirty days after expiration date.*

2.   If you are *not preparing a new lease,* a *letter of extension* must be hand delivered or mailed certified mail to the management office within thirty days after expiration date of present lease. The letter must indicate new term of lease and must be signed by the tenant and the owner.

3.   If the *unit is vacant,* a letter indicating this must be in the Association file. As soon as the unit is rented (before the tenant moves in), a copy of the lease must be mailed certified or hand delivered to the CMS office.

4.   If on a *month-to-month agreement,* a letter must be hand delivered or mailed certified mail to the management office to verify this. A month-to-month agreement must be renewed in letter form each January. The tenant as well as the unit owner must sign this agreement letter.

A $50.00 lease fine will automatically be added to your unit account for failure to comply with one of the above.

Below is the information we now have in our records on your unit. Please update as per above instructions.

When a tenant moves out, the unit owner is responsible for automatically sending a $250.00 flip charge, payable to Pine Valley and mailed to the Management Service address. Write your Unit Number on check face. This means each time any individual(s) occupying any unit alone or together moves from that unit with his/her belongings or the unit is completely vacated, a $250.00 flip charge for each type of move-out is due to the Association.

Exhibit 9.5   Lease Rules for Pine Valley.

> **Some HOAs require a member vote before approving large capital expenses.**

> **This rule can contribute to creating a rundown building.**

pairs or replacements. Pine Valley does not grant its board this sort of unrestrained power. Instead, the majority of owners present at a member meeting get to approve or reject those types of expenses when they exceed $10,000.

Is such a limit on board powers good or bad? It all depends. It prevents a runaway board from single-mindedly pursuing its own agenda. But if many unit owners are pressed for cash (as is possible in some HOAs overly represented by senior citizens or first-time homebuyers), they may reject improvements that could actually save money over the longer run.

As a general observation, I advise investors to avoid condo projects (or buildings) where penny-pinching owners refuse to make timely improvements to preserve the values of their units.

Owner Additions and Alterations (37)

The rule refers to the distinction made earlier between uniform monotony versus universally beautiful. All HOAs should strive to draw the line in a way that promotes uniform beauty and individual freedom. Unfortunately, some HOAs are populated by one or more self-appointed condo commandos who spend their time issuing orders and searching for unit owners who depart from some real or imagined architectural decree (or other type of rule).

> **Uniform beauty versus uniform blandness.**

Although condo boards should not take an "anything goes" approach, they should encourage unit owners to accent their units with flair that falls within a reasonable definition of good taste. When you carry out your prepurchase conversations with board members and unit owners, try to feel out the tenor of the HOA's ar-

> **Boards should encourage artistic flair within the bounds of good taste.**

chitectural approval and enforcement standards. When deciding between too loose or too rigid, I favor too rigid. It's easier to ease up on standards than it is to pull them back into good taste once they escape and create havoc throughout the community.

Utility Services (39)

In some condo projects, the unit owners directly pay all utility bills. In others, the HOA may assume responsibility for such items as hot water, heat, cable service, and waste disposal. When comparing the monthly fees among various condo developments, projects, and buildings, make sure to compare like to like. Oak Park may bill HOA fees at $250 per month. Sunset Ridge may bill $210 a month. But if Oak Park fees include cable TV, heat, and waste disposal, whereas unit owners individually pay all of their utility bills at Sunset Ridge, Oak Park offers the better deal.

> **Discover whether HOA fees pay for any utilities of the unit owners.**

You might also check to see how the HOA handles property taxes. I've seen projects where the HOA pays all, and I've observed situations in which unit owners are billed directly for all property taxes assessed against the units and the common elements. State law will generally determine the property tax billing and payment procedures.

> **Determine whether HOA fees pay the property taxes of unit owners.**

Right of First Refusal (40)

The right of first refusal gives the HOA an opportunity to approve your buyer or tenant. If it disapproves, it must then buy (or lease)

> **The right of first refusal helps preserve the character of the development.**

your unit on the same terms written out in your sales contract or lease agreement. However, before the Pine Valley HOA could choose to execute this right, 75 percent of all unit owners must vote for the acquisition. Given that arduous hurdle, HOAs exercise this right only in unique situations.

The right of first refusal can help the HOA prevent undesirables from moving into the project—without denying unit owners the economic advantage that they might achieve through the transfer. It may also deter undesirables from even trying to buy or lease a unit in a development (or building) in which the HOA exercises the refusal power.

> **The right of first refusal could cause you to lose an impatient tenant or buyer.**

On the other hand, some desirable buyers or tenants may not want to cool their heels for 15 to 30 days while the HOA weighs its choices.

On the whole, for mid-priced to upscale buildings and developments, the right of first refusal probably does more good than harm. That's especially true if the HOA tends to give a quick thumbs up to the great majority of acceptable buyers and tenants.

Enforcement of Rules (42)

> **Many HOA sct up rules committees to police violations.**

At Pine Valley any resident who notices a material violation of the rules can report the offense to the rules committee. The rules committee will render its judgment and recommend its decision to the board. The board then chooses the remedy. Generally, neither the rules committee nor any other committee can bind the association or act independently of the board.

Remember, too, that in most states, an individual unit owner may proceed independently against a violator through court action. This right of the unit owner can circumvent a board that fails to act for some reason. If a unit owner suffers a legally compensable loss because of the violation, he or she can recover monetary damages from the violator.

For example, a noisy neighbor could cause your tenants so much grief that they claim constructive eviction and move out to

> **If a neighbor's violations cause you a loss, you can recover damages.**

find the quiet that they rightfully expected when they leased your unit. Or, imagine you're trying to sell your unit. But your neighbor (in violation of the rules) leaves a junked car sitting up on blocks right in front of your unit. In that case, the judge might award damages to you and issue an order that requires the renegade owner (or tenant) to remove the vehicle from the property.

$50 Fine per Occurrence per Day

> **Courts uphold legally authorized fines by HOA boards.**

Depending on the condo documents (and state law), many HOAs such as Pine Valley can fine unit owners for violating the rules (or permitting their tenants to violate rules). When legally authorized, courts will uphold these fines, and if the unit owner fails to pay them, the HOA can foreclose the unit.

Fines Aren't Cheap   Note also that Pine Valley rules give the board the right to fine violators $50 per day per occurrence. Presumably, if an owner left a junk car wrongfully parked for 30 days, the board could levy a fine of $1,500. Even though the total amount of the fine seems outrageous, most courts would not substitute their notion of fairness for that of the HOA legal documents.

Condo buyers must realize that HOAs can only preserve community values when individuals agree to live under the principle of majority rule.

Rebellious Owners Create Great Trouble for Themselves I have seen cases where courts have forced rebellious owners to pay HOA fines of $40,000 or $50,000 for painting the exterior of their units an unapproved color. Though this outcome seems even more absurd than the $1,500 parking fine, the absurdity is not the rule or the amount of the fine. The true absurdity lies with the unit owner who voluntarily joins an HOA and then refuses to adhere to the principle of majority rule.

CHAPTER 10

Choose a Profitable Location

Think of location as you would think about investing in a company. You want to find the best-priced stock, not necessarily the best firm. Likewise, when you choose a location in which to invest, you're not looking for the *best* location (or even the *best* project or the *best* unit). Instead, you're trying to figure out which location will give you the highest return. As a refresher on this point, consider the following analogy.

> **The best company doesn't *necessarily* make the best investment. Nor does the best location.**

In Which Company Should You Invest: General Motors or Microsoft?

To again emphasize this point, I ask you to think about this question: Which company will provide investors the highest return: General Motors (GM) or Microsoft? Most inexperienced investors answer Microsoft. If you're market-savvy, you answered, "It all depends on the relative price of their stock."

Too Optimistic on Microsoft

> **Market prices tend to reflect well-known facts.**

Undoubtedly, Microsoft earns much higher profits and is growing its revenues far faster than General Motors. But everyone already knows those facts. So the stock price of Microsoft already accounts for these positive expectations. Indeed, in January 2000, near the peak of the tech stock boom, investors showed so much hope for Microsoft that they pushed its stock price up to record highs.

Negative Outlook on GM

In contrast, in January 2000, GM continued to lose market share. Its heavy liabilities for pensions chewed up a large chunk of its earnings, and the company still hadn't convinced Wall Street analysts that its newly announced corporate strategy could really turn the company around. With less than stellar operating performance and pessimistic investors, GM's stock price kept itself locked in the basement.

GM's Stock Outperforms Microsoft

> **Current market prices tend to reflect what's hot, what's not.**

Nevertheless, investors who at that time dumped their Microsoft stock and poured their money into GM would have earned huge profits, whereas investors who continued to hold Microsoft watched that investment fall by 40 percent. Contrary to popular perception, you cannot make money with stocks if you follow naively rules such as:

◆ Always buy growth companies.
◆ Always avoid companies that operate in the old economy.

- ◆ Buy only companies with strong management.
- ◆ Stick with companies that boast a durable consumer franchise (e.g., Coca-Cola, McDonald's).

Likewise, to make the most money in real estate, you should not follow naively clichéd advice, among which the following two seem to be most ingrained:

- ◆ Never buy into a complex that's tipped toward renters.
- ◆ Always buy in the best location you can afford.

During the Texas real estate crash, for instance, a friend of mine bought a condo for $12,000 with a cash advance on his credit card. The project was located in a somewhat less than desirable part of Houston. Fewer than 20 percent of the units in the complex were occupied by owners. Three years later (after modest fix-up work), my friend sold the unit for $26,000 to another investor. During the three years he owned the property, he kept the unit rented at $375 a month. The new investor successfully raised the rent to $425.

> **At the right price, almost any condo can reflect good value.**

Personal or Financial?

Naturally, I'm not specifically urging you to buy run-down, renter-dominant condo projects in the seedy parts of town, even though, you might find some great bargains there. Instead, I'm pushing you to open your mind to a range of possibilities. Explore the market and look for the best profit potential; compare features, compare prices, compare locations, and compare relative values.

In the end, you may choose to avoid some types of properties in some types of neighborhoods for purely personal reasons. That's fine. But in this book, I want to educate you about how to

> **Analyze properties from both a personal and financial view. But don't confuse the personal with the financial.**

make the most money you can with condos. That goal requires me to point you toward well-reasoned decisions, not merely tell you to follow overly simplified rules or off-the-rack advice.

Location Incorporates a Milieu of Features

Moreover, when assessing location, you can't really think of it as just one feature of a property. Because, in fact, *location* refers to a milieu of features, attributes, negatives, and positives. Plus, features that some buyers or renters might prize, others might judge less acceptable. Many people wouldn't live in a condo canyon even if you gave them a unit for free. True urban dwellers could not imagine living in one of those garden-type townhouses located in suburbia.

As you think through the various ways that locations differ from each other, think what types of tenants might be drawn to that area. To what types of tenants would you like to rent? College students? Young professionals? Retired folks over the age of 55? Working-class families? Section 8 recipients? Empty nesters? Single

> **The "best" location differs by target market.**

women? Single men? Gay and lesbian couples? When you evaluate market appeal, keep coming back to the question, What type(s) of people would find this area (unit) desirable (or at least, affordable)?

With that said, let's review the basics of location in three major categories:

1. Accessibility/convenience
2. Environment
3. Investment potential

Convenience: Easy Come, Easy Go?

To judge the relative convenience of a neighborhood, pull out a map. Identify and zone all of the places that residents of the neighborhood can reach within say, 5, 10, 15, and 30 minutes. The precise relevant zones will vary according to local attitudes about the meaning of the term *convenient*.

In my close-in neighborhood, most residents would reject as convenient any place more than 5 or 10 minutes away. To many

> **Convenient differs among geographic areas and target markets.**

people in the Los Angeles area, 30 minutes may seem like just down the street. In other words, take note of the neighborhood's convenience, but only in the context that your target market will appreciate. What places should you map? Virtually everywhere that your target market of tenants might show an interest. I would suggest at least the following:

- Major employers
- Minor employers
- Parks, tennis courts
- Lakes (fish, ski, swim)
- Beaches
- Police and fire stations
- Childcare facilities
- Colleges or universities
- Churches
- Libraries
- Bus stop, commuter terminals
- Places of worship
- YMCA/YWCA
- Golf courses
- Dentists and doctors
- Hospitals/clinics
- Office supply
- Public elementary school

- Public middle school
- Public high school
- Private schools
- Shopping centers (districts)
- Bus stops/El or subway stops
- Newsstands, bookstores
- Restaurants
- Groceries
- Convenience stores
- Bike baths, jogging trails
- Fitness (health) clubs
- Home improvement centers
- Coffee houses/cafés
- Movies, playhouses
- Nightlife
- Racquet clubs
- Banking
- Playgrounds

Once you've tallied up the places of potential appeal, try to discover those unique shops, cafés, and restaurants that add character to the neighborhood. No doubt, your survey of an area will come up with places that I've not mentioned. Catalog those places, too. When you compare the convenience of various condo/townhouse projects, explicitly notice as many details as you can. With detailed knowledge of the area, you will be able to develop a slam-dunk marketing program for the units you do buy.

Let Me Count the Ways

When measuring convenience of a location, don't just think about automobiles and driving times. Increasingly, people want to live in areas where you can walk to shops and cafés, bike to campus, or even jog to the office. Although not as important in most cities today as in years past, easy access to a bus stop may rank highly as a desirable feature for some target markets. For big-city commuters, convenience to the subway or commuter train stations will score points.

> **Some target markets prefer locations with multiple modes of accessibility.**

Overall, a location that offers multiple convenient means of easy access stands out from those locations where you can't go anywhere without getting into a car.

Times of the Day or Week

You may look for properties on Sunday afternoon, but be sure to think about rush hour. Many locations that seem convenient in off-peak hours turn into stalls and tangles at 8 A.M. Monday morning.

I recall when some of the new apartment and condo developments were built along the Interstate 4 corridor in Orlando. "Just 10 minutes to downtown," their ads boasted. Although these projects do stand 10 or 15 minutes from downtown at 3 A.M., at any reasonable hour of the day, travel to and fro can require an hour or more (even without accidents). As to alternative routes or modes of transportation, forget it. The freeway's your only real choice.

Bad Weather, Bridge Out, Road Work?

For locations where you can't walk to everything, consider what happens to convenience when a snow storm hits, a bridge is out,

> **Does the location lack highly predictable travel times?**

or for the third time this year the roads are torn up for repair work. Do the ferries, buses, and commuter trains always run on schedule? Do those schedules change by season (or time of day)? If so, how? Do any of these potential blocks to easy travel negatively impact the desirability of the area(s) you're evaluating?

Environment

Today, when someone mentions the word *environment,* you might immediately think of saving redwoods, snail darters, and spotted owls. In terms of evaluating location, though, *environment* refers to all of the influences surrounding a property that may bear on its desirability and market value. Experts in the field of real estate identify these environmental categories of influence as:

- ◆ Economic base
- ◆ Demographics and psychographics
- ◆ Aesthetics
- ◆ Legal
- ◆ Fiscal
- ◆ Political
- ◆ Safety and security
- ◆ Weather patterns/microclimates

Economic Base

> **Jobs, incomes, and wealth support all housing prices.**

> **Don't get caught unprepared in an economic downturn.**

Many naive real estate investors forget that their local economy supports the prices of all types of properties. When the local economy strengthens, home values typically jump ahead. When the local economy sags, home prices tend to stabilize or even slide backward. Indeed, because condos compete with both houses and apartment complexes, economic downturns can prove especially troublesome for condo investors who can't weather the storm.

To gain juicy long-term profits, try to avoid (or at least prepare for) those economic cycles that can create short-term setbacks. Recall the experiences of New England and southern California in the early 1990s.

Economic Cycles   In 1989, as reports of New England's slide into recession caught national attention, homebuyers in southern California lined up to buy homes as fast as they came onto the market. Multiple offers became common. Eager prospects for new homes even camped at development sites while waiting for the sales campaign kick-off. "We were afraid that if we didn't buy now, we'd lose our chance forever," said Theresa Nham at the time of her purchase in May 1989. "Forget New England—Southern California's economy is too diversified to suffer a downturn. Home prices here always go up."

In one sense, of course, the mid- to late 1990s proved Theresa right. Home prices did go up. But she should have added "over the long run." In the short run, home prices can weaken. Layoffs and unemployment can bring home prices down. Such a crash is all the more likely when speculation runs amok, as it has at times in the Farm Belt, the Oil Belt, and, more recently, the Defense Belt. As is now well known, even large companies like United Airlines, Mi-

> **Persistently weak local economies can pull down condo prices in the short term.**

crosoft, AT&T, and IBM can hit a profit crunch and lay off thousands of people.

Evaluate Your Local Economy (Don't Fall for Dot-Com Mania)   Looking back it's easy to see that at times too many homebuyers and real estate investors have focused only on the economic present—or, even worse, carried overly optimistic projections into the future. To prevent this mistake, check the strength of your local economy. Is it stable and growing steadily? Does it show signs of weakness? Is it exploding with speculation (as was the NASDAQ in the late 1990s)? What do the economic signals indicate?

- Are unemployment claims increasing or decreasing?
- Is help-wanted advertising in the local newspapers expanding or contracting?
- Is credit becoming more or less available for local businesses?
- Are office building occupancy rates and rents increasing or decreasing?
- Are used car prices (especially for the luxury or more expensive models) increasing or decreasing?
- Are bankruptcies of local businesses decreasing or increasing?
- Are home prices increasing moderately, or have they been going up by 12 percent a year or more for the past three years? Are home prices falling? Are rents falling?

During the past 20 years, some areas of the country—Rust Belt, Farm Belt, Oil Belt, Sun Belt, Defense Belt—have experienced economic downturns. As we advance into the twenty-first century, each of these areas has made a strong comeback. In looking to the future, you can again expect increasing home prices.

But exceptions can and will occur (Silicon Valley?). So don't assume the strength of your area's economic future. Investigate

> **If your local economy looks weak, develop an offsetting strategy.**

the facts. Many areas go through ups and downs. If the short-term economic outlook for jobs in your area seems shaky, you might want to delay investing. Or better, focus on finding a soon-to-be-hot neighborhood, a bargain-priced condo (unit, building, or development), where you can create value through improvements in the property and the HOA.

Demographics and Psychographics: Incomes, Lifestyles, and Attitudes

Check out the Census Bureau's Web site at www.census.gov. Talk with real estate agents. Visit neighborhood stores, restaurants, and coffee shops. Find out the types of people who live in the area. Get to know the area's demographics and psychographics.

Demographics   *Demographics* refers to "people" characteristics, such as age, education, family size, type of household, occupation, ethnicity, religion, income, wealth, geographic origin, and many other personal attributes. By paying attention to demographics, you can answer the questions: Who's living in the area? Who's moving in? Who's moving out? Once you learn the "who" of an area, you can decide whether this fits the profile of your target market. You can better judge the direction in which the neighborhood is heading.

> **Who's moving in? Who's moving out?**

Compatibility, not bigotry.   In an age of hypersensitivity, I should emphasize that I am not advocating racial or religious bigotry. It is a fact of life, however, that most people choose to live in areas (or housing developments) where selected demographic characteristics predominate. For example, in Prince George's County (Washington, D.C., area) many affluent black families choose to live in predominately black developments where home prices start at $350,000 to $400,000. Throughout the Sun Belt, age-restricted 55-plus communities are common. In Miami Beach many Jewish retirees and second-home owners prefer condos occupied by a heavy percentage of Jewish people.

South Beach in Miami, Oak Lawn in Dallas, and Azalea Park in San Diego attract a high percentage of gays. Many South Americans buy condos in Miami because of its large Hispanic population and the ease with which they can shop and dine without the need to speak English. If you have kids ages seven and nine, chances are that you chose an area to live that caters more to families with children than to the plus-65 set (such as Naples, Florida). It is not bigotry to notice that demographics matter.

Censorship of real estate agents. Although the First Amendment guarantees free speech, courts and government regulators have written real estate agents out of the constitution. As a result, agents face constant threats of lawsuits, fines, and license revocation if they answer questions that pertain to area demographics. (In fact, government regulations even try to prohibit realty agents from using language such as "walk-in closet," "exclusive neighborhood," "walking distance to schools," "master bedroom," and dozens of other everyday words and terms.)

> **Real estate agents fear to talk about demographics.**

If you would like to know the demographic profile of an area (or neighborhood), your realty agent may not be willing to provide this information. Don't worry, though. In typical government irrationality, various federal, state, and local government agencies (especially the Census Bureau) publish volumes of demographic data. You can find it at public and academic libraries. Good real estate agents and reference librarians are able to direct you to relevant reports and publications.

Other sources of demographic data. In addition to government reports, demographic data make up the stock in trade of marketing research firms. In fact, many firms now post such information on their Web sites, or they can issue specifically re-

> **Rely on close, firsthand observation.**

quested reports that you can download for a nominal charge. Of course, nearly all of us use word of mouth and observation to draw conclusions. However, try not to rely on merely superficial and casual inquiry.

Instead, walk and talk the areas, neighborhoods, and developments that you are considering. Decide on the demographic characteristics that are important to you (if any). Then ask questions. Keep a sharp eye. Take notice of whether you find the area demographically promising.

Psychographics In addition to demographics, you can identify a population by its psychographics. The compatibility of people depends on something more than age, income, education, wealth, ethnicity, and other demographic characteristics. It also relates to their attitudes, values, and lifestyles. Within an area, are you more likely to find a bridge group or poker party? Do residents most often think of sports as Monday night football with a six-pack and chips? Or do they prefer a 10-mile Sunday morning run followed by brunch at an outdoor café and *The New York Times?*

> **What neighborhood attitudes and lifestyles prevail?**

Do you see too many people hot-dogging their eardrum-bursting Trans Ams, Firebirds, and Harleys? Can you hear rap music playing six blocks away from its source? Do people leave the beach and parks littered with soda cups and fast-food wrappers? Does the area attract people who demand a good selection of tattoo parlors and body-piercing shops?

It's not just downscale areas that can be affected. During a period of time that I lived in Virginia, I maintained a second residence in the high-priced area of Washington, D.C., known as Georgetown. On Friday and Saturday nights, Wisconsin Avenue, the major neighborhood commercial street, became notorious for "wilding." Hundreds of rude, offensive, and sometimes felonious teenagers would swoop in and disrupt life for all residents, diners, shoppers, and merchants.

> **Even upscale neighborhoods may suffer from disruptive behavior.**

In upscale Santa Fe, New Mexico, for a while on Saturday nights, punkers dressed in black would overtake the town square, the prime area of town that is surrounded by upscale art galleries and restaurants. Although I believe the Santa Fe and Georgetown problems have been remedied, they illustrate an important point: Don't assume that tranquility reigns. Don't assume that upscale areas and housing prices cannot or do not attract some people who choose to behave contrary to acceptable community standards.

Aesthetics: Sights, Sounds, Smell

As with all other ingredients of location, your first defense against mistake lies with a close personal inspection. Walk competing projects. Walk neighborhoods. Focus your attention on a neighborhood's overall attractiveness and appeal. Talk with residents. What do they like or dislike? Search for answers to questions such as the following.

1. *Noise.* Does the neighborhood suffer from any undue traffic noise, airport flight paths, industrial sounds, or other disturbances (loud barking dogs, nearby construction, etc.)?
2. *Upkeep.* Do residents maintain their properties? Do the lawns of houses and apartment buildings sparkle with pride of ownership? Or do properties lack upkeep and maintenance?
3. *Parking.* Are the streets relatively free of cars? Or does the neighborhood lack sufficient off-street driveways and garages? Or worse, do you see cars parked in yards? (Neighborhoods heavy with student rentals sometimes display this type of eyesore.)

4. *Bad Mix.* Does the neighborhood abut or merge into any commercial, industrial, or otherwise incompatible land uses? Do you notice unsightly vacant lots or boarded-up properties?

5. *Views.* Do neighborhood residents enjoy pleasant views of lakes, parks, woods, bay, or mountains?

6. *Overall Feel.* What's your overall feel of the neighborhood? Most critically, what changes will occur over the next five years? Will the appeal of that location advance or decline?

Zoning and Other Related Ordinances

As a condo investor, you want to consider zoning and other related ordinances for three major reasons:

1. Weigh the potential for new development.
2. View the quality of neighborhood life.
3. Learn the restrictions by which you and your tenants must abide.

Weigh the Potential for New Development Property owners love to rail against zoning and other similar land-use regulations. But to a large degree, those regulations hold down competition. What if cities gave carte blanche to builders and developers (as did Dallas and Houston during the 1980s)? Within no time at all, these overeager entrepreneurs would swamp the market with new product.

> **Zoning is your friend. It reduces competition.**

Overall regulatory environment. Why have California housing prices appreciated faster than most other areas of the country? Population growth? Yes. Job growth? Certainly. But the flip side of demand is supply. And California pits builders against tightly restrictive zoning and environmental controls. If not for this hostile regulatory environment, home builders would double the number of houses, condos, and apartments that they put up each year.

Although such a quickened pace of development wouldn't halt price increases, it would surely impose some moderation. What does this point mean to you? Try to locate desirable areas where tight zoning and regulatory controls force builders to fight through years of hearings, delays, protests, and lawsuits. With growing demand pressing against a tightly regulated supply, you will earn above-average rates of appreciation.

> **Condo (apartment building) conversions can glut the market.**

Be wary of condo conversions. When tight building controls force home prices higher and higher, condo conversions begin to look profitable. Unfortunately for individual condo investors, a converter can bring hundreds of apartments to market far faster than any builder can. That's what happened in Chicago in the early 1980s.

> **Does your city strictly limit condo conversions?**

Rental apartment buildings were selling "wholesale" at $50,000 a unit. Individual apartments sold as condos would command a price of $100,000. With such large discrepancies in price, a sterling opportunity for arbitrage presented itself. Buy a 200-unit rental apartment building and convert it to condos. Even after the costs of legal, marketing, and fix-up work, one could earn a quick net profit of $25,000 per unit.

Today, wide-scale arbitrage as existed in the 1970s (especially in Manhattan) and the early 1980s do not seem too likely in most cities. The real estate investment trusts (REITs) have bid up the prices of quality apartment buildings to levels too high to support profitable conversions. But just as important, many cities now regulate the number of rental apartments that converters can bring to market each year. Or they may tangle the converter in myriad delays and a cost-increasing permit process.

If the areas that you're investigating have enacted such laws—or otherwise make condo conversions legally difficult, consider that fact a major positive for that location.

Check the zoning of surrounding sites.   When I accepted a temporary job in Chicago several years back, I leased an apartment on the 39th floor of Columbus Plaza. When I moved in, the unit gave me panoramic views of Grant Park, the Loop, and Lake Michigan. By the time I moved out of that unit eight months later, a newly constructed 60-story office building blocked 85 percent of the view from that unit.

Never forget: What exists today may not exist tomorrow. Vacant fields morph into shopping centers. A 4-story building might get knocked down in favor of a 40-story building. The bulldozer may take out a beautiful stand of trees and leave nothing but razed earth that awaits the next gas station and convenience store.

> **What changes will zoning allow for the neighborhood?**

To avoid unpleasant surprises, check the zoning and other restrictions that govern surrounding sites. Is it likely that new developments or a change of land use could negatively (or positively) impact the locational desirability of a condo that you're considering, not just in terms of new competition but also in terms of traffic, noise, views, and the overall character of the neighborhood.

Quality of Neighborhood Life   You find what appears to be a good buy on a unit. Yet as you drive around the area, you begin to worry a bit. You see an old refrigerator sitting on the front porch of a house and also spot several disabled vehicles up on blocks. You hear a loud stereo blaring from a nearby apartment building. "Oh, oh," you think, "this place is heading downhill."

But wait. Maybe someone just needs to complain to the city. Chances are that every negative you viewed violates some type of local ordinance.

> **Use local ordinances to stamp out undesirable conduct.**

Ideally, cities enact zoning and other related ordinances (noise control, maximum occupancy, parking, signage, trash disposal, etc.) to preserve the character and quality of neighborhoods. If the neighborhood looks good, verify that local laws will uphold its desirability. If an area appears to be slipping into deterioration, call out the code enforcers to arrest the decline before it picks up too much momentum to easily reverse.

> **Local ordinances will regulate you and your tenants.**

"It's My Property" Zoning and related ordinances won't regulate just the surrounding properties. They will also regulate you and your tenants. More than likely, though, your HOA rules will control the use of your condo unit far more than any local law. Nevertheless, as you explore the rules that govern an area, take note of any that may impact you directly. Even though it's your property, neither you (nor anyone else) can do with it as you please.

In fact, as Chapter 8 points out, the declarations of most HOAs specifically require their HOA members (unit owners) to scrupulously adhere to all federal, state, and local laws. Even if the city chooses not to act, the HOA could. Consider these possible types of violations:

- ◆ Running a home business in an area zoned exclusively for residential use.
- ◆ Renting to three or four unrelated roommates in violation of single-family occupancy laws.
- ◆ Use of "recreational" drugs by your tenants.
- ◆ Hosting (illegal) Friday night poker games.
- ◆ Illegal discrimination or failure to follow local landlord-tenant laws.

In our regulated society, real estate investors must understand the legal environment in which they plan to operate. Generally, such laws don't present any real difficulties—as long as you dot your i's and cross your t's. The investors who run into trouble are those who don't bother to learn the legal requirements that they should follow.

Safe and Secure

Naturally, people wish to feel safe in their homes and on their neighborhood streets. Low crime makes for higher property values. But it's not just the quantity of crime that counts. More important is the type of crime. Drug dealing, gang shootouts, and house break-ins weigh much differently than occasional car thefts or domestic quarrels.

> **Before you say "high-crime" area, define what type of crime you're talking about.**

Often, too, perceptions don't match reality. Check facts with the police. Recognize that statistical reporting areas may not accurately apply to various submarket neighborhoods. Beware of broad generalizations. Pinpoint as closely as possible the actual street boundaries that delineate high-crime areas. Note the relative differences among reputed high-crime and low-crime areas. These differences may not range as far apart as many people think.

Although people seem most threatened by neighborhoods with dangerous people, natural disaster can also claim life and property. If pertinent, think about the neighborhood's susceptibility to mudslides, sinkholes, earthquakes, floods, hurricanes, or fire. Higher risk areas may also push up your property insurance premiums and require more extensive coverage.

Fiscal Soundness

Nearly everyone would like more government services, better schools, *and* lower taxes. But many Americans are getting just the

Do revenue shortfalls foreshadow high property taxes?

opposite. Some cities, counties, and states throughout the United States are incurring revenue shortfall. But aside from political semantics, the results are usually the same: higher taxes and cutbacks in schools, libraries, street repairs, fire and police, and social services. "The month after we moved in," says Shannon Brown, "they jacked up tax rates, canceled the bus service, and raised the tolls for the bridge."

If you're buying a property in a city that's running a fiscal deficit, beware. Because state and local governments can't borrow with the same reckless abandon as the federal government, at some point—sooner rather than later—someone's got to pay. Likely as not, that someone will be you. Property tax rates will head up. You pay more for less.

Look to the Future   As you look to the future, find out the financial condition of the community. Does it balance its books? Or is it headed toward a financial crunch? As an added precaution, ask your realtor or the city treasurer's office about the level of the community's bonded indebtedness. Sometimes communities that expect rapid growth float bonds (borrow money) to pay for new streets, roads, sewage facilities, parks, libraries, schools, and fire stations to support development and an increasing population. (In California, these are called Mello Roos bonds.) Over time the bonds will

Examine the fiscal soundness of the taxing districts that govern your condo investments.

be paid off by taxing all the residents in the new developments. As long as growth continues as expected, financing improvements with bonds doesn't create a problem.

However, if growth stalls, or the local economy falters, early residents may end up with a serious problem. After the 1980s Colorado oil bust stalled growth in that state, new developments and communities went bankrupt. Some owners of $100,000 houses were getting property tax bills for as much as $12,000 a year.

Most owners didn't pay. They just walked away from their houses. Lawyers for the tax authorities, mortgage lenders, and bond holders were left to litigate over the remains.

The Colorado experience was extreme. But it illustrates a basic rule: Understand the risks of investing in a community that extravagantly spends more than it takes in—and then requires property owners and property taxes to pick up the tab.

Political Responsiveness

"A great advantage of our neighborhood," says Juanita Morena,

> is you can call the council member from this district and get her on the phone immediately. If a pothole needs fixed or a fallen tree needs to be hauled away, it's usually done within a couple of days. When older people have some heavy trash or junk furniture to get rid of, someone calls and asks them, "When will you be home? We'll get the men to come to the house and carry it out for you."

It is true that many people avoid high-property-tax districts. But when you're looking at a neighborhood's tax rates, also check out the services it provides. How quickly do the police and fire departments respond to emergency calls? How long does it take to get the streets cleared after a winter snow storm? How good are the public schools, parks, libraries, and recreational programs? If the neighborhood asks the city to attend to a special need (street repairs, speed bumps, stop lights, crime control, graffiti, gang activity), can the property owners get action?

> **What services do property owners receive for the taxes they pay?**

Does neighborhood politics come close to that democratic ideal: a government of the people, by the people, and for the people? Do the neighborhood property owners really get what they pay for?

Discover Your Area's Microclimates

Does your metropolitan area have "microclimates?" In and around some cities, within commuting distance of a central business district, a July day might bring fog and 60-degree temperatures in one neighborhood, 70 degrees and rain in another, and 90 degrees and sunshine elsewhere. Oceans, lakes, rivers, hills, mountains, bays, and even tall buildings can affect weather patterns.

> **Weather patterns may differ throughout a metro area.**

Within a 15-mile radius of downtown Vancouver, British Columbia, rainfall varies from 15 inches to more than 100 inches a year. In San Francisco, the Cow Hollow and Marina District neighborhoods enjoy noticeably less fog and more sunshine than other neighborhoods located near the zoo and the Pacific Ocean. If you live in Walnut Creek (20 minutes from the San Francisco Bay Bridge), you'll find many summer days hotter than 80 degrees. To city residents, though, 80 degrees feels like a heat wave. In the Los Angeles metropolitan area, Ventura residents breathe (relatively) clean air, whereas in Palmdale residents have suffered up to 150 smog warnings a year. Skyscraper buildings not only block sunlight but can create strong gusts of wind. (Don't try walking near the Sears Tower in Chicago on windy days.)

If you live in a metropolitan area with microclimates, you may know how weather differs among local neighborhoods and communities. If you are investing elsewhere, talk to Realtors or perhaps call a local weather station. To avoid unwelcome surprises, it pays to know the microclimate weather patterns before you invest in a neighborhood.

Location: Summing Up

Many experts in real estate advise homebuyers and investors to "buy in the best location you can afford. The best locations always

> **The "best" neighborhoods don't always appreciate the fastest. Appreciation potential depends on relative prices and relative benefits.**

appreciate the fastest." Apart from mathematical impossibility, this advice falls flat because *best* means different things to different people. Some people value convenience to work; some value a pleasant environment. Others put their emphasis on quality schools, abundant nightlife, or even affordability. Different strokes for different folks.

As a real estate investor, you will profit most when you take notice of these differences. Then balance the full range of neighborhood (area) strengths and weaknesses against the prices that homebuyers and renters seem willing and able to pay. When you compare and contrast along these lines, you won't necessarily invest in the best locations. But you will invest in the locations that will prove most profitable.

Note: Recently, many neighborhoods have been going online with chat groups and e-mail lists. By tapping into this bird's eye information, you can really get some insights into the strengths, weaknesses, and social milieu of a location. Ask Realtors or neighborhood residents whether the areas you're interested in are providing this "cross between a town meeting and a kaffeeklatch." See, for example, "The Right Neighborhood: Finding the Sense of a Community Online," (*Chicago Tribune,* May 18, 2003).

Predict the Future

Almost universally, books on real estate investing tell you to search out properties that you can buy at a bargain price. Sounds good.

> **Look beyond market value and the past prices of supposed comp sales.**

Except here's the rub: Nearly all of these books define "bargain price" only in terms of buying at less than market value. Unless you can immediately flip this property and take a quick profit, it may or may not prove to be a bargain. Just like the prices of stocks, property prices can go up or down. You must look beyond the "less-than-market-value" approach to finding a bargain.

How to Define "Bargain"

Famous investor Warren Buffet has said he would rather buy a great company at a fair price than get a lousy company at a bargain price. Of course, ideally, the goal of every investor is to get both: (1) a great company, and (2) below-market value price (as Buffet did with the *Washington Post*).

Essentially, Buffet made his statement in response to the simplistic and frequent reporting that smart investors are bargain hunters. Buffet wanted to emphasize that to true-value investors, the term *bargain* does not mean absolutely low-priced, but only low-priced relative to an investment's expected future cash flows (income, appreciation). No one should interpret "bargain-priced" to narrowly mean "low-priced" relative to the present or the past.

What good does it do you to buy Amazon.com at $50 off its market price of $200 a share if, in fact, its intrinsic value could easily sit at less than $10 per share? The same principle applies in real estate. By all means, look for a property that you can buy for less than its market value. But before you buy, make sure that market fundamentals point to increases in market values, not declines (as Silicon Valley homebuyers are now experiencing).

> **If the price falls, you haven't snagged a bargain.**

Appraisals Shortchange Fundamentals

As a starting point for condo investing, do closely calculate the market value of every unit in which you're interested. Normally, that value should set the top limit for your purchase price. If you pay more than market value for a property, even with market appreciation, you could wait years before the market catches up to the price you overpaid. On the other hand, if you buy an appreciating property for less than its market value, you create an instant boost to your equity in excess of the amount of your down payment.

> **Appraisals never tell you whether you're buying at a bargain price.**

Notwithstanding the above advice, even though an appraisal may help you decide how much to offer for a property, in and of itself, a market value appraisal can never tell you whether you *should* buy a property—regardless of how much of a below-market price you expect to get. Why? Because market value appraisals:

1. *Focus on the Past.* By drawing data only from the past (albeit the recent past), appraisals say nothing about the future.
2. *Ignore Other Neighborhoods or Condo Developments.* By drawing sales prices from comparable condos in the same location or from the same development, appraisals say nothing about the relative price advantages/disadvantages of condos/townhouses located elsewhere near or far.
3. *Shortchange Area Economics.* Most market value appraisals ignore (or at best shortchange) the economics of an area. Because market value appraisals look chiefly to the sales price of comparable properties, they do not dwell at length on matters of jobs, incomes, population trends, new developments, land-use controls, and the other fundamental factors that support (or diminish) property values.

Focus on the Recent Past

Savvy investors in real estate must realize that market value represents a snapshot of the recent past. Essentially, an appraisal says, "Because these similar units *have sold* for these prices, then this subject condo *should sell* for this price." As a practical matter, though, the sales of those comparable units may actually have occurred three to six months ago—sometimes longer. In fast-changing markets, such out-of-date comparable sales not only fail to speak to the future, they do not even speak to the present.

If a market has recently slowed, an appraiser's (or your) estimate of market value may overshoot the mark. You can easily err in this way when property prices have been marching up at 1 or 2 percent *a month* for a year or more. You look at recent comparable unit sales, extrapolate from recent trends, and set a market value figure. You bid 10 percent less. After negotiations, you buy at a perceived 5 percent discount.

> **Appraisals view the market through a rearview mirror.**

In this case, you think you paid less than market value. In fact, due to the economic slowdown that you had not yet picked up on, you really paid above market value. Naturally, given these difficulties, always keep in mind that comparable sales data will leave you with much less market knowledge (present and future) than you actually need.

Appraisals Ignore Other Areas

In any given urban area, some neighborhoods, subdivisions, and HOA communities (buildings) may offer far better value for the price than others. Yet appraisals only draw on properties from the same location (or same complex if sufficient sales are available).

> **Appraisals never compare or point out bargain-priced neighborhoods.**

As a result, many investors never think to compare the strengths and weaknesses of various locations and rank them according to their relative prices and benefits (as I have stressed in Chapter 10).

By remaining fixated on buying at a price below market value, these investors miss another type of bargain hunting: buying in an undervalued neighborhood or HOA community.

Appraisals Shortchange Economic Fundamentals

Imagine the year is 1975. Assume you must buy one of two investment choices:

- ◆ *Oakland Hills, California:* This three-bedroom, two-bath townhouse in Hiller Highlands is firmly (non-negotiably) priced at $50,000. Its market value sits at $45,000.
- ◆ *Terre Haute, Indiana:* You can buy this three-bedroom, two-bath home for $40,000. An accurate appraisal shows a market value for this home at $50,000.

> **Appraisals never forecast longer-term trends in supply, demand, or appreciation.**

Which of these properties would you choose? If you define "bargain" or "good buy" as a price less than market value, you would choose the house in Terre Haute. If you believe houses appreciate faster than condos, you would choose the house in Terre Haute.

If you were astute enough to understand the importance of economic fundamentals, you would have chosen the Oakland Hills town-house—even though you must pay an above-market price. Since the mid-1970s, homes in the Oakland Hills have multiplied in value at least sixfold; house prices in Terre Haute have little more than doubled.

Economic fundamentals account for this huge difference. Yet, when you only compare market value appraisals on similar properties (then or now), you miss serious mention of any of these fundamentals. To invest wisely, broaden your perspective.

Summing Up: The Market Value Mistake

Many real estate investors mistakenly believe that market value represents the ultimate touchstone for finding a bargain. When they buy for less than market value, they brag to the world about the good buy they snagged. When they can't negotiate a sharp deal, they walk away.

Smart investors take a more complex approach. Sure, they would like to acquire each of the properties they do buy at a price less than market value. But they also know that the real test

> **Don't fall for the market value mistake.**

of a bargain price comes on the date of sale—not the date of purchase. To achieve success toward that end, they bolster their market value appraisals and comparable price data with more extensive and more expansive market information.

Current Market Data

In addition to recent comparable condo sales price data, your investigation of the current market should include several other market facts. These facts can help you develop a better picture of the here and now, as well as help you forecast short-term changes. Available primarily from local Realtors and mortgage lenders, these data include:

1. Time on market
2. Asking price/selling price
3. Inventory of unsold homes/condos
4. Properties under contract
5. Mortgage applications, delinquencies, and foreclosures
6. Vacancy rates/FOR RENT ads

Time on Market

In most areas of the country, Realtors keep tabs on how long it takes for listed properties to sell. When the real estate cycle starts to cool, homes sit unsold for greater periods of time. If last year, homes sat with FOR SALE signs in their front yards for an average of 77 days, and now the time on the market stands at 98 days, be careful.

In Manhattan, for example, between 2000 and 2001, time on market for condos and co-ops increased from 118 days to 132 days. As the time on the market lengthens, the sales slowdown signals that sellers are asking too much for their properties. What is true of the market in general is also true of particular properties. Before you put in an offer for a property, find out how long it has been up for sale—not just with the brokerage firm that has the current listing but also whether the property was previously listed unsuccessfully with some other firm. As a general rule, the slower

> **How quickly are houses and condos selling?**

the market, the longer a specific property has languished unsold, and the more carefully you should weigh your investing decision.

Asking Price/Selling Price

In very strong markets, homes sell quickly at (or sometimes over) their asking prices. Bidding wars and multiple offers create buyer panic. On the down cycle, the reverse occurs. Not only do homes take longer to sell, on average, the eventual selling price of a property might fall to, say, only 80 to 85 percent of its listing price. Either of these markets should cause you to step back and evaluate where the market is likely to head in the near future.

> **Are sellers cutting their price—or forcing buyers into bidding wars?**

Caution in a slowing market is obvious. But why caution in a super-hot market? Because buyer panic, bidding wars, and multiple offers often push prices up too quickly (e.g., Silicon Valley 1997–2000). Once the buying fever passes, prices get a dose of market reality. In 1984, I put a property up for sale in Dallas, and I got three offers at the full asking price. Buyers were in a frenzy. Eight years later, the people I had sold to put the house back on the market at the same price they had paid. In contrast, I had picked up a 30 percent gain in two and a half years of ownership. (Note: Had I continued to own that rental property for those eight years of zero appreciation, I would still have earned a high rate of return on my initial investment. That's because during that eight-year period rents increased by more than 50 percent and interest rates fell from 13.5 percent to 7.0 percent. My annual cash flow would have jumped by 150 percent.)

Inventory of Unsold Properties

In slowing markets the inventory of homes (houses and condos) for sale steadily piles up. Buyers tend to disappear. Everybody wants to sell. During San Diego's early 1990s down market, the local Realtor's multiple listing service accumulated more than 18,000 listings. By the time the area's recovery was in full swing, the number of listings had shrunk to fewer than 14,000 homes. Today, inventory has fallen to 11,000 units.

Indeed, at least for now, real estate agents in many areas still try desperately for more listings. Scarcity, rather than surplus, prevails. Illustrating this point, a Vermont sales agent reports, "We're not in a sellers market, but inventory is depleted and prices are tending to go up." In contrast, this agent reports that "in 1991, I had a ski resort condo complex with fifty-two units on the market. Now only seven are for sale. I'm begging owners to list." Keep an eye on the number of homes for sale. When realty agents begin to

> **Are Realtors begging for listings or buyers?**

beg for listings, the market typically is signaling to buy now, and price increases are nearly certain. A piling-up inventory of unsold properties indicates that prices may be above the levels buyers are able and willing to pay. That's the time that investors hang back and wait for sellers to become desperate and thus far easier to work with.

Properties under Contract

You can also detect market tempo by keeping count of properties going under contract. Realtors typically track homes by the number listed, the number going to contract, and the number of closed sales. Essentially, going to

> **How many homes went to contract during the past 30 or 60 days?**

contract represents a pipeline for property sales just as new orders represent pipeline activity for manufacturers.

When the number of properties going to contract rises relative to the number of new listings, the market can be expected to tighten and prices will increase. When contracts begin to fall off relative to the number of new listings and closed sales, you can expect the market to cool and prices to soften.

Mortgage Purchase Applications, Delinquencies, and Foreclosures

Because mortgage financing plays such a key role in real estate markets, as a smart investor you should keep a record of mortgage trends, especially as they relate to new buyer mortgage applications, payment delinquencies, and foreclosures.

Mortgage Applications (Purchase Originations) Relatively few homebuyers or investors pay cash for their properties. So, tracking purchase mortgage applications (as opposed to refinancing) over the past 6 to 12 months can further signal whether the market is picking up (or losing) steam. In addition, learn whether lenders are easing up on credit standards or if they are pulling back.

Starting in the mid-1990s, mortgage lenders created an enormous array of easy-qualifying, little or nothing down mortgage loan programs for first-time homebuyers, minorities, inner-city neighborhoods, credit-impaired buyers, and many other segments of borrowers. Some lenders were even making investor loans with 90 percent loan-to-value ratios. "Have money, will lend" became the banker's motto.

This aggressive lending helped to fuel the real estate boom that began in the late 1990s. Low interest rates and the National Homeownership Strategy also played a big role. Now, though, with subprime lenders, FHA, and VA taking some hits, you might find that mortgage lenders will return to a more prudent approach to qualifying borrowers (especially investors) and setting loan terms.

Is there a slowdown coming? When lenders tighten their lending after a run of easy money, they choke off property financing and sales. In turn, fewer sales turn into larger inventories of unsold homes and place downward pressure on property prices. Savvy investors monitor credit standards.

Delinquencies and Foreclosures   Under adverse circumstances, out-of-work or otherwise financially strapped homeowners (mostly overextended recent buyers) can't sell at a price high enough to cover their outstanding mortgage balance and selling expenses. Mortgage delinquencies and foreclosures tend to increase. More downward pressure comes to bear on property prices. More opportunities for true-value investors become available.

> **Are homebuyers and investors falling behind on their mortgage payments?**

Regulatory law requires most mortgage lenders to report their 30-day, 60-day, and 90-day delinquencies. By following these trends, real estate investors can forecast a likely fall in (or stabilizing) market values. In addition, mortgage delinquency gives advance notice on foreclosure rates. Because foreclosures compete with owners who are trying to sell their properties, a larger inventory of foreclosures makes selling more difficult.

From the mid-1990s through early 2003, most areas of the United States experienced small inventories of foreclosed properties—especially as compared with the tumultuous late 1980s and early 1990s. During more recent years, most investors have found slim pickings in the foreclosure files. However, as lender excesses come back to haunt them, you can expect to see a jump in the number of foreclosures in those areas of the country where job losses spike up.

In any event, stay abreast of delinquencies and foreclosures. It will serve as your early warning system. Falling mortgage delinquency rates signal market recovery and rising prices. Upward trends in late payments, foreclosure filings, and foreclosure sales signal a market slowdown or housing recession.

Vacancy Rates

Because you will want to get your condos rented quickly, you also should survey vacancy rates and rental amounts for rental apart-

> **Are vacancy rates for rentals going up or tightening?**

ments and single-family houses. Vacancy rates (and rent levels) don't necessarily move in the same direction as do property sales prices. For example, falling interest rates improve home-buyer affordability and can draw people out of rentals and into homeownership. On the other hand, fear of falling home prices scares off many would-be home-buyers. They cling to their rentals and vacancy rates tighten. Rents may even go up.

Summing Up: The Current Market

Even when comparable sales price data seem to show that you're buying at a bargain price, you still need to look for other confirm-

> **Focus on the future, not the past.**

ing (or conflicting) evidence. Comparable sales data *lag* the market. Other indicators, such as time on market, asking price/selling price ratios, inventories of unsold homes, mortgage applications, mortgage delinquencies, and mort-gage foreclosures, signal where the market is heading.

So in addition to market value, look to these leading market indicators to help you predict markets that are about to turn up or down. Sharp investors avoid bubbles about to burst; they arrive early for the next housing party. When you stay tuned to leading indicators, you materially decrease your chance of loss and disap-pointment. More profitably, you position yourself for beat-the-market gains in appreciation.

Boom and Bust Cycles

Most so-called efficient (or quasi-efficient) stock market theorists believe that market timing never works. Random walks prevail.

You might as well throw away your charts of past stock price and volume movements. Whether or not you accept this efficient market theory for stocks, you certainly should reject it for real estate. Lags in new construction, time on market, employment trends, and other slower-paced factors of home building, buying, and selling mean that you can accurately forecast (more or less) short- to mid-term market movements in the housing market.

Unlike stocks, housing prices do not wander around like a drunk in a parking lot looking for his car. Nor does housing typically experience massive selloffs that immediately send property prices plunging or massive bursts of buying that can immediately push prices skyward.

Boom and Bust Myth

Although some residential property markets throughout the United States and Canada do swing in so-called boom and bust cycles, most do not. During the late 1980s and early 1990s, the national media published a continuing stream of negative articles that would have led any foreign observer to conclude that housing nationwide was suffering a cataclysmic and never-ending downturn. In part, this negativity was fueled by a famous article by two Harvard researchers titled "The Baby Boom, the Baby Bust, and the Coming Collapse of Housing Prices."[1]

> **Relatively few housing markets really go through booms and busts.**

However, if the journalists (and professors) who were writing these stories had traveled outside of the Boston–Washington corri-

---

1. Gregory Mankin and David Weil, "The Baby Boom, the Baby Bust, and the Coming Collapse of Housing Prices," *Journal of Regional Science and Urban Economics* 19 (fall 1989): 117–123.

dor and California, they would have cured their myopia. They would have found some housing markets going strong, others in modest slowdown, and a few markets in severe distress (Texas, for example).

Media Distortion versus Local Market Experience

Like all of us, national journalists tend to extrapolate from the experiences they are close to. With severe housing recessions (following extravagant booms) in Manhattan, Boston, Washington, D.C., and Los Angeles, the national press imagined that everywhere else must be facing similar difficulties. They weren't. And they won't.

> **Journalists love to exaggerate and sensationalize.**

Before you accept the real estate boom and bust myth, check the experience of your local market. You will likely find relatively modest ups and downs. More important, market segments matter. The media tend to focus on homes in the higher ($400,000+) price ranges. Naturally, because rent levels typically won't come close to supporting such high prices, this market segment of housing will show far more price volatility than lower-priced housing. Whenever your cash flows support the price you pay (as they should), you need not fear a bust. Even if property prices fall in the short run, your annual returns will persist. Even better, maintain a strong position of cash and credit. Use downturns to pick up true bargains.

The "Market" versus Market Segments   In the early 1990s when $1 million homes in La Jolla, California, were falling in value by $200,000 to $300,000, home prices in nearby Clairemont were holding firm. When $5 million homes in Beverly Hills were falling in market value by $1.5 million, home prices in Watts (south central Los Angeles) were continuing to climb.

> **Low- to moderate-priced housing shows more stability than the volatile upper end.**

Whenever you hear about the real estate "market" doing this or doing that, probe further. Ask, what market? Condos, co-ops, single-family houses, apartment buildings, retail, or offices? What communities or neighborhoods? What price ranges? What rental rates? What sizes (square footage, room counts)? What types of buyers? What types of tenants?

Even within the same local area and within the same period of time, various real estate submarkets may be going against the prevailing market conditions and trends.

Don't jump to conclusions about the market until you know what precise market segment you're referring to. Just as with stocks, gross perceptions about the real estate market frequently mislead. You may believe that the market is overpriced, suffers too high vacancies, or is bereft of good tenants. But none of these or any other generalizations are likely to apply wholesale. Market segments matter.

When discouraged by overall market trends, don't give up. Look for "undiscovered" submarkets. I have never seen the time

> **You can nearly always find profitable market segments.**

when a local market did not offer at least a few opportunistic paths to follow. Similarly, don't naively fall for talk of a market boom either. Just as busts don't affect all properties equally, neither do booms. For true-value investors, a strong market never displaces the need for thorough analysis.

In fact, because booms tend to dull reasoned thought, too many investors adopt a "can't-wait, got-to-buy-now, prices-can-only-go-up" mentality. Avoid this amateurish mistake. Before you quickly buy into an condo boom, play the devil's advocate with yourself. Honestly evaluate whether you've really discovered the best market segment in which to invest. A quick trip through the condo experience can illustrate this point.

Condos: Boom, Bust, and Recovery

Some years back, Paul Maglio bought a two-bedroom condo located near Boston Harbor. He paid $120,500 for the unit. At the time he bought, 200 other potential buyers had put their names on the complex's waiting list. Everyone wanted this sure-fire investment opportunity. With appreciation rates running at 20 percent a year, condos were geese laying golden eggs.

Then the geese died. Throughout Massachusetts, as well as other areas in New England, New York, much of the Southwest, and southern California, many condo (and co-op) prices fell 30 to 70 percent off their peaks. Bruce Hopper, another Bostonian who lost a bundle on his condo, sadly regrets his decision to buy. "It's too bad," Hopper says, "because condos were the ideal situation for a lot of people—first-time homebuyers who wanted the American dream. But it didn't pan out and now we're stuck." Upon hearing about experiences like these, many investors hesitate to buy a condo. They fear getting stuck with a condo that can't be sold for anywhere near its purchase price.

> **Condo mania displaced good sense.**

Don't Prejudge: Weigh Risks against Potential Rewards

As historical price increases have shown, long-term concerns about condos cannot be justified. Those Boston condos now sell at twice their late 1980s peak prices. Nevertheless, as with all investments, weigh potential risks against potential rewards. Overall, as I wrote in Chapter 2, the outlook for condos in most areas will remain quite positive over the coming decade. When compared to the prices of single-family homes in many cities, condos once again appear to offer good value and good opportunity for appreciation. Even better, search the market and the odds are at least 50–50 that you can find a condo bargain.

How to Spot a Condo Bargain

In nearly every case, the majority of condo buyers and investors who have lost money have been those who were carried away by condo mania. They paid no attention to cash flows. They played the game of speculative appreciation. In contrast, longer-term owners nearly always have come out ahead. Second, condo investors who could see the market softening and sold out near the top often made thousands of dollars. Third, buyers today who can learn to spot opportunity (and smell potential danger) stand to make good profits.

By learning the lessons of history, you can reasonably judge whether condo prices in your area stand a good chance of going up (or down). Here are the signals to look for:

1. Many people hold pessimistic views about the future.
2. The monthly after-tax payments for principal, interest, property taxes, insurance, and HOA fees total less than monthly rentals on comparable apartments. In other words, you can generate positive cash flows—right now.
3. The market values of existing units sit substantially below the cost of constructing similar new units.
4. Vacancy rates for rental apartments are less than 5 percent.
5. Local economic indicators (number of people working, retail sales, new car sales, bank deposits, new business starts, etc.) are showing strong positive gains.
6. The condo units that you are considering enjoy some *unique* and *highly desirable* advantages (design, views, location).
7. Relatively few new apartment or condo complexes are being built or planned. No major conversions of apartments to condos are under way or planned. Government restrictions limit apartment conversions.
8. Compared to single-family houses, condo prices sit relatively low.

9. The condo complex you are looking at is stable: strong financial reserves for repairs and replacements; no adverse litigation; few units occupied by renters (less than 20 percent is good, less than 10 percent is excellent); relatively little turnover of owners and residents; well-maintained common areas; and cooperative relations among owners. When, on balance, these and the previous eight signals look positive, you can buy with confidence.

On the downside, history shows that, in most cases, a fall in condo prices usually is foreshadowed by one or more of these danger signals:

1. A sharp downturn in local employment.
2. Large numbers of apartments being converted to condos, especially when accompanied by very easy qualifier financing.
3. Large amounts of new condo or apartment construction.
4. The current monthly costs of owning greatly exceed the monthly costs of renting.
5. More than 30 to 40 percent of a complex's units are investor-owned and are occupied by renters (or even worse, vacant).
6. Everybody "knows" values are going up at least 10 to 15 percent a year. The market runs rampant with speculation.

Condos in many cities offer great long-term investment potential. Even ignoring appreciation, when you can earn a good positive cash flow, your condo will yield an attractive financial return. As you pay down the mortgage balance, you build up your equity. For investors who want an inflation-protected income stream, owning one or more investment condos will prove quite profitable. Because the HOA will take care of all (or most) external upkeep and maintenance, condos make for low-effort investments.

Use market downturns to pick up bargains. Use location analysis to predict the next hot area. Use your knowledge to

> **Apply your knowledge. You will choose great investments.**

closely compare the features of various HOAs and condo developments (buildings). When you put this market-savvy knowledge to work, you will achieve the ultimate low-risk, high-return, low-maintenance investment.

CHAPTER 12

Buy and Finance Your Condominium(s)

Okay, you've studied the market. You've weighed the pros and cons of different locations. You've compared various condo and town-house communities. You know their prices, advantages, and disadvantages. Now it's time to choose the unit(s) and HOA(s) that offer the best opportunity for profit, negotiate a good buy, and arrange financing.

Negotiate a Win-Win Purchase Agreement

Negotiators typically adopt one of three negotiating styles: (1) adversarial, (2) accommodating, and (3) win-win. Most lawyers rely on the adversarial style. They make outrageous demands. Then they push, pull, or threaten to move you as close as possible to their position. Adversarial negotiators care not whether their "opponents" end up satisfied. All they care about is winning for themselves.

> **Never adopt the lawyerly adversarial approach.**

In contrast to the adversarial approach, an accommodating negotiator easily gives in to every request. Accommodators feel powerless

| Avoid becoming an accommodator. |

to create the outcome they really want. They often feel helpless due to lack of money, time, information, knowledge, or experience. Accommodators detest conflict. They would rather lose than stand their ground. When negotiating through a real estate agent (or other third party), accommodators typically delegate too much responsibility. "Oh, just do what you think is best" or "Let's just agree and get the whole thing over" are two common responses of accommodators.

In pursuing a win-win method, negotiators adopt a little of the adversarial style and a little of the accommodating style. Most important, though, they adopt a more complex perspective. Win-win negotiators recognize that every negotiation brings forth multiple issues, priorities, and possibilities. They also recognize and respect the other party's (not *opponent's*) concerns, feelings, and needs. Win-win negotiators don't think along a single line of contention—especially that of price.

Win-win negotiators primarily work to secure a strong, mutually beneficial agreement that everyone is committed to seeing through to completion. By reading through this chapter, you can see how to shape a win-win agreement. In addition, you can learn to avoid falling prey to the win-lose transactions of the adversarial hard-ballers, or becoming one of those passive accommodators whose eagerness to do a deal traps them into unwise concessions.

Win-Win Principles

To set the stage for effective negotiations, here are 12 principles that should guide you to a win-win agreement.

Cooperate with Empathy   Find common interests that can precede the negotiation. Don't just jump into talk about price and terms. Use some chitchat to warm up the relationship before you get down to business. Don't provoke a competitive spirit or a win-the-game attitude about the negotiation. You win the game when you buy a property at a low price, not when you drive off a potential seller because you failed to yield on a relatively minor point.

Recognize that negotiation is a cooperative enterprise. It provokes an emotional experience with both parties having needs, wants, and feelings that have to be considered. Learn as much as you can about the sellers. Engage in empathetic conversation.

Don't Push for Total Victory   Recognize the proper time to stop negotiating. Successful negotiators can feel tension building. Pushing the negotiations for that last dollar in purchase price or that last concession has killed many sales. Beware, too, of pushing so hard that you destroy the trust of the relationship. If parties lose trust in each other, negotiations become much more difficult to maintain on a win-win basis.

Understand Seller Objections   Listen carefully to the objections and arguments of the seller. Try to determine what the seller really wants. Often people seek results indirectly. If what a person actually wants is brought forth, the negotiations will yield a better outcome. Many times, disagreements arise simply because two parties are not communicating what they think they are communicating. Listen far more than you talk.

Use Gentle, Probing Questions   Use questions in negotiations as a way to identify needs. Carefully notice that the phrasing of questions can be just as important as knowing what questions to ask. An old story goes that a clergyman asked his superiors "May I smoke while praying?" Permission was denied. Another clergyman, though, used a different approach. He asked, "May I pray while I am smoking?" Of course, you know the answer. A skilled negotiator should be adept at phrasing questions to identify a seller's needs without causing offense.

Dialogue, Not Monologue   Give logical and practical reasons to support your viewpoints. Likewise, seek explanations for what the seller is wanting. Never quickly say no to a proposition suggested by a seller even when you think the offer is ridiculous. Take time to reflect so that the seller's input seems important. Always try to return the negotiations to the goals you hold in common with the seller.

Speak of Negatives through Objective Comments   Remind the seller of the property's negative features. But do so in a way that doesn't arouse retaliation—especially if you are negotiating with a homeowner. Speak in terms of the market, the features, or the decorating schemes that tenants prefer. Don't insult the seller's tastes or handiwork. Say, "Tenants usually prefer neutral carpet colors such as beige or earth tones." Don't say, "How could I possibly get this place rented with that awful orange shag carpet and that pink foil wallpaper?"

"Take It or Leave It" Seldom Succeeds   Because many sellers expect to negotiate (as opposed to agreeing flat-out with your requests), leave room for bargaining in your offer. Even though price and terms may rank most critical to the negotiations, possession date, closing date, personal property, repair escrow, and other issues can present other trade-off points.

Don't Ask for the Moon and the Stars on a Stormy Night   Stay realistic. You may face a seller's market or a buyer's market. You may face a timid seller or an assertive one. You may meet sellers where the wife is eager to sell the house, but the husband doesn't care. Each negotiating situation differs from all others. Don't lose sight of the realities of the transaction in which you are participating. This recommendation brings up another important point: Only the seller benefits when two or more buyers compete for the same property. Avoid getting involved in a bidding war. The heated competition makes it difficult to obtain a good buy. Besides, why compete head to head when other potential bargains are available down the street?

Concede with Care   Don't make concessions easily. A sophisticated seller will press for more easy victories. Always hesitate before acting. Suggest quid pro quo. Give only when you ask for something in return.

Beware of oral concessions. Oral concessions tip your hand to a higher price or other unfavorable terms that you are willing to accept. Or they may be used as a ploy by sellers to get you to orally commit to a price. Once the seller feels you are committed that far, he or she may write up the offer for an even higher amount. Each time you offer or counteroffer, make sure the terms are written. Use a contract of sale form and change the relevant terms that are subject to the negotiation with each party initialing those changes.

Counters Kill Offers   Recognize the risks of negotiating. When you reject a counteroffer from a seller, that counteroffer is dead unless the seller chooses to revive it. Likewise, when you counter a seller's offer, your counter kills the seller's proposal. Also, the seller is free to withdraw an offer (counteroffer) at any time before you accept it. A seller or buyer may withdraw an offer without any obligation even if the party has promised to keep the offer open for a certain period.

Stockpile Information Early   Stockpile information from the very beginning. The more you learn about a seller's financial capabilities, family situation, likes and dislikes, priorities, time constraints, available options, previous offers (accepted or rejected), past real estate experiences, perceptions about the property's condition and value, and any other factors that might bear on the transaction, the better you can adapt your offer and negotiating strategy to the seller's situation and personality. You not only need to secure this information, you need to secure it as early as possible, while you are in the relationship-building stage of your negotiations.

If you jump into a hot-and-heavy debate over price and terms before you've built an information stockpile, you generally will find that the sellers clam up. They guard their disclosures much more closely. As another point, most sellers aren't stupid or naive. They put forth their own information agenda in terms of what they would like you to believe. Don't accept the information you obtain as unvarnished fact. Look for nuggets of truth, but keep your bunkum detector finely tuned.

Learn and Control the Seller's Reference Points   Control the reference points of the negotiation. All sellers base their asking price and terms on certain reference points. The seller may believe that comparable rental condos have sold with a monthly gross rent multiplier of 125 and will therefore apply that norm to figure a fair price for his or her unit.

To negotiate effectively with this seller, you must learn the reference points the seller is using and why. Once you gain this information, attempt to explain why those norms aren't applicable and why the reference points you've selected are fairer or more appropriate. You might point out that the comparable units are newer (better location, better views, lower HOA fees, more stable residents, better condition, etc.) than the seller's unit or HOA. For instance, true comparables to the seller's property have typically sold at only $150 per square foot, not the $180 that the seller is asking.

The seller may know the unit down the hall just sold for $180,000 but doesn't realize those owners carried back financing at 5.0 percent and gave the buyers $15,000 worth of furniture. Although you can try a no-frills approach—"I'll give you $155,000. That's my top offer. Take it or leave it"—it's more effective for you to first set the price reference points on which you and the seller can agree. Persuade the seller to accept a reference point that's favorable to your offer and you'll edge closer to the agreement you want.

The Purchase Contract

Except for several unique features of purchase contracts for condos (see Box 12.1), your condo purchase agreement will include the same types of terms and provisions as any other real estate sales contract. You'll see terms such as:

Legal Description:	Must include unit, associated limited common areas if any, and percent of undivided interest in common areas.
Common Assessment:	State current assessment as levied by the HOA for payment of common expenses, how and when payable and when next reassessment expected (list expenses included).
Special Assessment:	List any outstanding assessment as levied by HOA for payment of special expenses, remaining currency, and the purpose of assessment (also list anticipated special assessments).
Reserves:	Recite any reserves of the HOA credited to the owner not included in the sale price. (In new projects there is often a payment required to establish initial operating reserves.)
Presale Requirements:	Recite terms of presale requirements, if any. (New projects often require percent of project that must be sold and ready to funding of the construction loan.)
Management Agent:	Identify management agent.
Insurance:	Recite extent of insurance provided, and not provided, by HOA. Identify agent.
Condo Documents:	A statement acknowledging approval (and possibly receipt) of all pertinent documents listed (i.e., declaration of conditions, covenants, and restrictions; bylaws; articles of incorporation; house rules; budget; etc.).
Liabilities:	Recite all known violations to condo documents or health and building codes and all pending or anticipated litigation involving the unit and/or the HOA and all outstanding judgments.
Right to Cancel:	Recite terms of any applicable laws or provisions of the documents which grant rights to cancel.

Box 12.1 Unique Terms of Condo Purchase Agreement.

- ◆ Earnest money
- ◆ Possession date
- ◆ Owner financing (terms, cost)
- ◆ Personal property
- ◆ Settlement costs (who pays what and how much)
- ◆ Purchase price
- ◆ Pro-rations of taxes, fees, assessments
- ◆ Repairs
- ◆ Warranties
- ◆ Default remedies (liquidated damages, specific performance)

> **Don't negotiate price. Negotiate a total win-win agreement.**

To negotiate a successful purchase agreement, don't just tug and pull on price. See if you can give and take on other issues, too. Remember, never negotiate price per se. Negotiate a win-win agreement.

Maximize Your Leverage with Owner-Occupancy Financing

By far, the easiest, safest, surest, and lowest-cost way to borrow all (or nearly all) of the money you need to buy a condo involves owner-occupied mortgage financing. Numerous high loan-to-value (LTV) owner-occupied loan programs are readily available on single-family homes, condos, townhouses, and two- to four-unit apartment buildings that offer 95, 97, or even 100 percent financing. With sterling credit, some lenders will even lend you 125 percent of an owner-occupied property's purchase price. In contrast, if you do not qualify for owner-occupied financing (i.e., the desired loan fits into the investor category), most lenders (banks, mortgage bankers, savings institutions) typically limit their mortgage loans to a 70 to 80 percent LTV ratio.[1]

---

1. From the late 1990s to the present, some lenders were willing to make investor loans with LTVs as high as 90 percent. If (when?) property markets soften, these liberal lenders will undoubtedly raise the amount of their required down payments.

> **When possible, use owner-occupied financing for your first condo investment.**

In addition to lower down payments, lenders also qualify owner-occupants with less exacting standards. Plus interest rates for owner-occupants can sit 1 (possibly 2) percentage points below the rate charged for investor loans. If lenders are charging, say, 5.0 to 6.5 percent for owner-occupied loans, the rate for investor condos may sit in the 7.0 to 8.5 percent range. If you are a beginning real estate investor, you definitely should explore owner-occupied mortgage loans.

Owner-Occupied Buying Strategies

If you don't currently own a home, you can begin building your wealth in income properties very easily. Simply select a high LTV loan program that appeals to you. Buy a one- to four-family property, live in it for one year, then rent it out and repeat the process again. Once you obtain owner-occupied financing, that loan can remain on the property even after you move out. Because the second, third, or even fourth homes you buy and move into will still qualify for high LTV (low or nothing down) financing, you can quickly accumulate several rental houses as well as your own residence—all without large cash investments.

Although you will be able to go through this process two, three, or maybe four times, you can't pursue it indefinitely. At some point, lenders will shut you off from owner-occupied financing because they will catch on to your game. Nevertheless, serial owner-occupancy acquisitions makes a great way to accumulate several income properties.

Homeowners, Too, Can Use This Method

Even if you already own a home, you should definitely consider the advantages of using owner-occupied financing to acquire your

Try this homeowner investment strategy.

next several properties. Here's how: Locate a condo or townhouse that you can buy and move into. Find a good tenant for your current home. Complete the financing on your new property and move into it. If you really like your current home, at the end of one year, rent out your most recently acquired property and move back into your former residence. Otherwise, find another "home" to buy and again finance this property with a new owner-occupied, high-leverage, low-rate mortgage.

Why One Year?

To qualify for owner-occupied financing you must tell the lender that you *intend* to live in the home for at least a year. Intent, though, does not mean *guarantee.* You can (for good reason or no reason) change your mind. The lender will find it difficult to prove that you falsely stated your intent at the time you applied for the loan.

Nevertheless, to succeed in real estate over the short and long term, you must establish, maintain, and nurture your credibility with lenders—and everyone else with whom you want to make deals or build a relationship of trust. Slipping through loopholes, making false promises, side-stepping agreements, or any similar slights will tarnish your reputation for integrity. Unless you really do encounter an unexpected turn of events, honor a lender's occupancy requirement.

Where Can You Find High LTV Owner-Occupied Mortgages?

Everywhere! Look through the Yellow Pages under "Mortgages." Then start calling banks, savings institutions, mortgage bankers, mortgage brokers, and credit unions. Also, many mortgage lenders

> **Nearly all mortgage lenders now offer low-down-payment loans.**

advertise in local daily newspapers.[2] Also check with your state, county, or city departments of housing finance. Home builders and Realtors also will know various types of low or nothing down home finance programs. Sixty minutes on the phone will help you.

Previously, I wrote, "not enough money no longer serves to justify procrastination. Lack of self-discipline, yes. Lack of motivation, yes. Lack of knowledge, yes. But not lack of money. If you think 'cash short' blocks you from buying property, think again."[3]

High Leverage for Investor-Owned Financing

Let's say you've maxed out your high LTV (low down payment) owner-occupancy financing possibilities. Or maybe you're happy in your present home. There's no way you (or your spouse) will move (even temporarily) to another property. In this situation, what are some of the ways that you as an investor can avoid putting up 20 to 40 percent of the purchase price in cash from your own savings? In other words, what high leverage (low down payment) techniques can you use to buy income properties?

> **Investors can buy using little of their own cash.**

High Leverage versus Low (or No) Down Payment Before we go through various high-leverage techniques, note a subtle (but critical) distinction: High leverage does not necessarily require a low down payment. In investor lingo, high leverage means

---

2. For a more detailed discussion of mortgage lending, see my book *106 Mortgage Secrets All Homebuyers Must Learn—But Lenders Don't Tell* (John Wiley & Sons, 2003).

3. *The 106 Common Mistakes Homebuyers Make (& How to Avoid Them), Second Edition.* (John Wiley & Sons, 1998), 261–273.

that you've been able to buy a property using little cash (10 percent of the purchase price, or less) from your own funds.

Imagine you've found a condo priced at $100,000 and your lender agrees to provide a first mortgage in the amount of $70,000. If you can't (or don't want to) draw a full $30,000 from your savings to make the required down payment, you have to think of some other way to raise all (or part) of these funds. If successful, you will have achieved a highly leveraged transaction. You will control a $100,000 property with relatively little cash *coming from your own pocket.*

In a nutshell, you can gain the benefits (and risks) of high leverage in either of two ways: (1) originate or assume a high LTV first mortgage, or (2) originate or assume a lower LTV mortgage. Then, to reduce (or eliminate) your own cash input, use other sources of funds (loans, equity partners) to cover much of the difference between the amount of the first mortgage and the purchase price of the property.

Creative Financing Revisited   *Creative financing* means running through multiple financing alternatives. The term gained wide popularity when housing prices shot up and millions of Americans felt shut out of the real estate market because they lacked sufficient cash, credit, or both. "The central theme of my course," wrote Ed Beckley, "is to teach you how to acquire as much property as you can without using any of your own money. . . . Starting from scratch requires that you become extremely resourceful. You need to *substitute ideas for cash.*"[4]

> **Creative finance means coming up with ideas to raise money.**

Okay, then, how might investors use creative thinking and resourcefulness to substitute for cash? Here are some of the most popular ideas and techniques.

---

4. *No Down Payment Formula* (Bantam, 1987), 69.

Look for a liberal lender.   Most banks and savings institutions will only loan 70 to 80 percent of a (non owner-occupied) income property's value. However, some financial institutions will make 90 percent LTV loans. In addition, some wealthy private investors provide high LTV mortgages. You often can find these private investors through newspaper classified ads: Either you can advertise in the "Capital Wanted" section, or you can phone those who list themselves in the "Capital Available" section.

You also can call mortgage brokers who may have contacts with as many as 20 to 100 sources of property financing. Through their extensive roster of lenders, mortgage brokers may be able to find you the high LTV you want.

Second mortgages.   Some income property lenders will permit what are called 70–20–10 loans, or some other variation such as 75–15–10, or maybe even 80–15–5. The first figure refers to the LTV of the first mortgage; the second figure refers to the percentage of the purchase price represented by the second mortgage; and the third figure refers to out-of-pocket cash contributed by the buyer. A 70–20–10 deal for the purchase of a $100,000 house would require:

First mortgage	$70,000
Second mortgage	$20,000
Buyer cash	$10,000

Typically, the property seller is the favored source of second mortgage loans. Often called "seller seconds" or "seller carry-backs," such loans require little red tape, paperwork, or closing costs. Plus, you can often persuade a seller to accept an interest rate that's less than a commercial lender would charge. At a time when first mortgage rates were at 11 percent and commercial second mortgage rates were at 16 percent, I was able to get a seller to carry back a $25,000 interest-only seller second at a rate of 8 percent.[5] The deal looked like this:

---

5. In this case, the seller second primarily served to reduce my overall cost of borrowing due to its low interest rate.

Purchase price	$106,500
First mortgage at 11%	$ 60,000
Seller second at 8%	$ 25,000
Cash from buyer	$ 21,500

If sellers won't cooperate, *and the deal still makes sense,* look to private investors, mortgage brokers, banks, and savings institutions. However, before you turn to loan-sharking commercial second mortgage lenders, think of friends or family members who might like to earn a relatively safe return of 7 to 10 percent (more or less) on their money. Compared to certificates of deposit and passbook savings that typically pay 2.0 to 5.0 percent, a 7 to 10 percent rate of interest might look pretty good.

Borrow against other assets.   If you're a homeowner with good credit, you can raise seed money for investment real estate by taking out a home equity loan (i.e., second mortgage) on your home. With many lenders pushing 125 percent LTV loans for homeowners, you may be able to raise a fair amount of cash—even if you haven't yet accumulated substantial equity. Alternatively, consider a high LTV refinance of your first mortgage.

What other assets could you borrow against? Retirement accounts, cars, jewelry, artworks, coin collection, life insurance, or vacation home? List everything you own. You may surprise yourself at what you discover.

Convert assets to cash (downsizing).   Rather than borrow against your assets, downsize. Friends of mine recently sold their 6,000-square-foot Chicago North Shore residence for just over $1 million. With those proceeds they then bought a vacation home, a smaller primary residence, and an in-town condo. Could you, too, live comfortably in a smaller or less expensive home? Are you wasting money on unproductive luxury cars, jewelry, watches, or clothing? Are you one of the many Americans who lives the high life—for

> **Sell unproductive assets.**

now—but is failing to build enough wealth to really support the twin goals of financial security and financial independence?

In their study of the affluent, Thomas Stanley and William Danko (*The Millionaire Next Door,* Longstreet, 1996) interviewed many high-income professionals whom they called underaccumulators of wealth. In contrast were prodigious accumulators of wealth—who worked in less prestigious jobs and earned less income. Yet because of wise budgeting and investing, their net worths far surpassed the net worths of the high-income prodigious spenders. Downsizing now will pay big dividends later.

Use credit cards. Although it's one of the more risky techniques of creative financing, some investors take advantage of every credit card offer they receive in the mail. Then when they require cash to close a deal, they quickly raise $5,000, $10,000, or even $50,000 from cash advances. Investors have been known to pay all cash for a property with the entire sum raised from credit cards.

| Use cash from credit cards cautiously. |

Naturally, no one should use cash advances for long-term financing. On occasion, though, you might find plastic a good source to cover short-term needs. You may, for example, find a terrific bargain that you can renovate and immediately flip (resell) at a great profit.

Personal loans. In the days before credit card cash advances (which are the most popular type of personal loan), personal loans were called signature loans. As you build your wealth through growing real estate equity, you'll find that many lenders will gladly grant you signature loans for $10,000, $25,000, or even $100,000 if your credit record and net worth can support repayment. You can use the money from these signature loans to buy even more real estate. (Signature loans typically charge lower fees and interest rates than credit card cash advances.)

Although many mortgage lending institutions set rules against using personal loans for down payments, beginning and experienced investors alike routinely find ways over or around those rules. Property owners who offer seller financing (OWC) will seldom inquire about where you're getting your down payment money. So if you're short on cash, don't let that stop you from buying rental properties. Don't arbitrarily rule out using some type of cash advance or signature loan to raise money for your down payment.

If you do rely on this type of financing, weigh the risk factors. Ill-conceived borrowing can easily push you into those ugly toss-and-turn, sleepless nights, if not financial ruin. Make sure your plan of repayment does not depend on any type of speculative (uncertain or unpredictable) contingency.

What Underwriting Standards Do Lenders Apply?

Before you originate any type of new financing from an institutional mortgage lender (bank, credit union, mortgage banker, etc.), you'll complete a mortgage loan application.[6] To evaluate your loan request, lenders apply a variety of mortgage underwriting guidelines. The more you can learn about these guidelines, the greater the chance that you'll be able to locate a lender who will approve the loan you want. In addition to owner-occupancy and LTV ratios, here are six other standards:

1. Collateral (property features)
2. Amount and source of down payment and cash reserves
3. Capacity (monthly income)
4. Credit record and credit score
5. Personal characteristics
6. Compensating factors

---

6. For a much more extensive discussion of financing properties, I remind you to see my book *106 Mortgage Secrets All Homebuyers Must Learn—But Lenders Don't Tell* (John Wiley & Sons, 2003).

Before you apply for a loan—or even before you shop for your investment—talk with several savvy mortgage brokers. Learn the standards that will apply to you in your market.

Automated Underwriting

In recent years, mortgage lenders have increasingly turned to automated underwriting. Under this system, a loan rep gathers all pertinent data, enters it into a computer program, and within minutes, out pops a loan decision. Although each of the underwriting items discussed still counts toward the approval (or rejection), many loan reps (especially new ones) don't understand the actual underwriting criteria. As a result, they simply accept the verdict of the computer output.

> **Learn your credit score on the Web at www.myfico. com. Credit scores really count.**

If your credit profile matches the acceptable profile in the computer program, that's great. It means a faster, less costly path to closing with a shorter stack of paperwork. On the other hand, if your personal situation needs "outside the box" personal consideration, many of today's loan reps (computer clerks) won't be willing or able to help you reverse a "no" decision to a "yes."

So, if you find yourself facing this dilemma, make sure you locate a savvy rep from the "old school" who can apply the skill and knowledge necessary to get your loan approved—or at least tell you the areas where your application falls short and how you can work to remedy any deficiencies.

As a starting point, to see how you might fare with automated underwriting, go to the Web site at www.myfico.com. From this site, you can learn your automated credit score and general pointers on how to improve it. Nevertheless, especially when applying for investor financing, you want a smart loan rep who not only knows how to improve the look of your application but also knows the right lender and loan product for your needs.

CHAPTER 13

Tailor Your Lease Agreements

Many investors who own rental properties rely on rigid, fine-print leases that require the tenant to pay rent, care for the property, and follow all house rules and policies. As a result, these owners never realize that the lease itself can become a powerful part of their overall market strategy.

Use Your Lease in Your Market Strategy

In fact, leases can do far more to advance your market strategy than they can to force a bad tenant to go straight. You primarily deal with bad tenants through careful screening, not by going to court to enforce a lease.

Don't get me wrong. In these litigious times of tenant rights, you must bind your tenants with a well-crafted and legally enforceable written agreement. I'm not encouraging you to do otherwise. However, I want you to go beyond legal necessity and consider how you can use the language of your lease to attract great tenants.

Competitive Advantage

Before you decide on the specific terms of your lease, closely review the leases of other owners of rental units. Look for ways to differentiate your rental agreement that would encourage tenants (your target market) to choose your property over competing properties. For example, to gain a competitive advantage, you might, lower up-front cash requirements, offer a repair guarantee, shorten your lease term, guarantee a lease renewal without an increase in rent, or place tenant security deposits and last month's rent in the investment of the tenant's choice to accrue interest for the tenant's benefit.

> **Your lease can help you differentiate your rental units from those of your competitors.**

You could even develop tightly restrictive lease clauses. Then, position your property as rentals that cater to more discriminating and responsible tenants. Include severe restrictions on noise and other nuisances common to rentals. In exchange, you might offer a rent level slightly less than market.

You create competitive advantage not only by choosing units and HOAs that will appeal to the wants of your tenant market but also by custom-tailoring the clauses, language, and length of your lease to match tenant needs.

Explain Your Advantages   By adapting leases to better fit the needs of your target market, you can increase net rental revenues, achieve a higher rate of occupancy, and lower operating expenses. To fully realize these benefits, though, you must make sure that prospective tenants recognize and understand the advantages you're offering. Adopt an effective sales strategy. Rather than show the property perfunctorily, point out and explain (from the tenants' standpoint) the desirable features of both the unit, the HOA, and your lease.

> **Show and tell.**

Understandable, Easily Readable English Language   As a starting point, consider doing away with those multipage, fine-print lease forms that are filled margin to margin with legal jargon. Instead, work with an attorney to construct a more reader-friendly agreement. Besides, those excessive legalisms can sometimes work to your disadvantage.

Legalisms bite back.   When you take an overly legalistic approach with your tenants, don't be surprised when they respond in kind. The more pages your lease entails and the more arcane its language, the more likely your tenants (or *their* lawyers) will find some word or clause to argue about. (Lawyers pull in far more money from litigating a lease than they do from drafting a lease.)

> **What good is a lease that no one can or will read?**

Originally, fine-print leases were used primarily to intimidate tenants. Today, that purpose is as outdated as feudalism. Today, if pushed, your tenants and their lawyers can become equally creative in their interpretation of lease clauses. Even worse, your tax dollars may actually pay your tenant's attorney.

The myth of a "strong" lease.   Supposedly, a "strong" fine-print lease is one in which every clause binds the tenants into doing exactly what you want them to do. (Oh, if it were only that easy.) All too often, though, tenants do what they want to do—lease or no lease. Don't believe in the myth of a strong or airtight lease. In most cases, it's not the strength of the lease that determines whether your tenants conduct themselves in a manner consistent with your wishes. Rather, it's the quality of the tenants themselves.

A strong lease can never substitute for careful tenant selec-

> **Bad tenants break strong leases every day.**

tion. When push comes to shove, a strong lease *may* help you mitigate the aggravation and losses caused by troublesome tenants. But regardless of the language in your lease, good tenants alone will make your days as a property owner both profitable and enjoyable.

Joint responsibilities?   Because most leases are ostensibly drafted for the primary benefit of property owners, they slight tenant rights and owner responsibilities. In contrast, as part of your market strategy to attract quality tenants, your lease might display a more balanced treatment.

Without a doubt, many tenants view owners of rental properties with suspicion and distrust. When you adopt a more just approach, you will display your good faith. It also will reveal you to be a cut above other property owners. Plus, because you do intend to fulfill your responsibilities, a listing of them will help educate your tenants. More than a few tenants believe that owners of rental properties do little more than collect rent and get rich. You gain when you disabuse them of this notion by listing your responsibilities and expenses within the lease.

Joint drafting?   People feel more committed to agreements when they help shape them. To put this fact to your advantage, try discussing and drafting the terms of your lease agreement with tenant participation. Naturally, you'll have a good idea of which clauses, conditions, and responsibilities you want to address. But some give and take will make the tenants feel like contributing partners rather than just vassals or serfs.

> **Ask your tenants for their input.**

Win-win negotiating.   Joint drafting also can provide another benefit. Your proposed tenant may suggest trade-offs whereby you both win. Some years back when I first moved to Florida, for example, I tried to rent a place to live for a period of three to six months. Before buying a home, I wanted time to learn the market and explore options. I desired a short-term tenancy and I owned a pet (a Yorkshire terrier), so I faced slim and undesirable pickings. As a result, I stayed at a Holiday Inn for 14 weeks.

If I had been able to secure a satisfactory rental house or apartment, I would have been a perfect tenant. I also would have been willing to pay a premium rent and large security deposit. Yet all of the property owners and managers I talked with simply stated their

> You can boost profits with a flexible, open mind.

"no pets" rental requirement. None even hinted at the possibility of negotiating win-win.

Think carefully before you adopt such a rigid policy. Even if you don't jointly draft a lease agreement, at least keep the negotiating door open. Let the prospective tenants know that you are open to win-win flexibility and mutually advantageous changes. When you ask for tenant input, you discover the issues of most concern and value to the tenant. It's in those instances that you can price for maximum profit, yet still offer tenants the value proposition they will prefer.

What Terms Might You Negotiate?

Theoretically, you could open up the entire lease to negotiation. That's certainly the practice for leases that apply to large office buildings and shopping centers. But I fear that excessive flexibility would prove unworkable for owners of condos. In my experience, here are the issues where you might voice flexibility:

- Screening criteria
- Amount of rent
- Amount of deposit
- Improvements for tenants
- Pets
- Wear and tear
- Terms of the lease
- Strict rules

In suggesting these possibilities for negotiation, I want to again mention that all of your negotiations must take place within the context of applicable fair housing laws and the rules and regulations of the HOA. Generally, you can't steer the terms of your lease toward a person's race, religion, ethnicity, gender, age, disability, or any other category that's protected by federal, state, or city housing laws.

However, fair housing doesn't deny you the right to mutually tailor a lease with your prospective tenants. As analogy, mortgage lenders discriminate and negotiate every day of the week. They do not, however, discriminate on nonpermissible grounds. Neither should you.

Tenant Screening   Many property owners set one minimum standard for credit and income. Applicants either pass or fail. This screening policy will generally prove simple and legally defensible. In contrast, to again draw on the analogy from mortgage lending, mortgage applicants don't suffer this same fate. Years ago borrowers were either accepted or rejected, but today lenders quote different interest rates, down payments, and closing costs to hopeful borrowers who differ in terms of credit quality, affordability ratios, and job history. In addition, contrary to popular belief, most lenders will negotiate your loan costs.

> **Don't arbitrarily screen out good people.**

In other words, if you have earned a FICO (overall credit profile) score of 780, nearly all lenders will charge you less and give you a lower down payment than someone who displays a 620 FICO score. Would this same tactic work for you?

Good people, bad credit.   For example, say you're asking $750 a month and you require a $1,000 security deposit. You receive an application from a couple whose credit score of 575 sits below your cutoff number of 625. They explain that their bad credit resulted from a spell of unemployment. They always paid their past rent on time. They really like your unit. They're willing to pay $800 a month and give you a $2,000 security deposit.

What do you do?   Do you accept or reject this couple? Of course, many owners would never get this far. Their rigid minimum would rule this couple out. But for this very reason you might want to set a policy of flexibility—as long as you're compensated accordingly.

Amount of Rent   Some owners prefer not to quote a rental rate over the phone. Instead, they quote a price range. When

Let tenants tell you how much they will pay.

prospective tenants show up to look at the apartment, the owner says, "Okay, what will you give me for it?" Well, he might not use those exact words, but something similar sets the stage for discussions about the amount of rent the prospects would be willing to pay. This approach can prove profitable for at least two reasons.

Find the high bidder.   First, you might get a high bid from someone who particularly likes your unit because it offers one or more critically important features that the prospect has not found elsewhere. Of course, that's precisely why you gather market research. You are trying to discover and incorporate such features into your market strategy such that you can extract higher rents yet provide more tenant satisfaction. If you use the bid procedure, you could end up with a higher rental amount than you would have dared to ask.

Also, I do not know why more owners don't use a bid process when tight markets or their superior properties yield a battalion of applicants.

Twenty phone calls? Fifteen applications? Raise the rents.

In these situations, owners typically accept the best qualified. But rather than pick and choose from among a number of candidates, let each prospect bid. That way the unit will go to the persons who value it most highly. As noted previously, in hot markets home sellers use the bid process to sell for amounts in substantial excess of their asking price.

Secure market information.   When you price your units according to bid, you also gain valuable market information. Think back to the discussion about those owners who brag, "We never suffer a vacancy. Our units always rent the first day they hit the market." In fact, any owner who makes this claim is really admitting, "We don't know how much tenants would pay for our units. But we do know that we're under the market."

Bids beat test marketing.

Other owners take a little more market-savvy approach. A unit comes on the market, they advertise it at $650, and it rents the first day. Three weeks later, a similar unit becomes available. The owners advertise it at $675. It rents the first day. One month later, another unit comes on the market. They ask $750. No takers for a full week. They back off to $715 and the unit rents in three days.

Obviously, the trial-and-error approach works better than continual error without trial balloons. Nevertheless, had these owners run an auction or other type of bid procedure, they would have learned early on that the market had jumped substantially ahead of where they thought it was.

Gain market downside, too.   Bids also yield market information on the downside. If you show a unit to 12 prospects over a period of three weeks and get no takers, the rent's too high (or

Bids help weather soft markets with minimum loss.

you're marketing the wrong product to the wrong people). When markets do soften, the faster you learn that fact, the quicker you can adjust your strategy. Don't merely complain that your vacancies are caused by a glut of new apartment complexes offering two months of free rent. Revise your rents (or features) to reestablish your favorable competitive position.

Security Deposit   As noted, you might vary the amount of your security deposit based on the credit score of the applicant. Or instead of a cash deposit, you could accept a lien against the tenant's car or another type of asset. You might also waive (or reduce) the deposit if the prospects will get someone with a strong financial profile to co-sign the lease. (Mortgage lenders use both of these techniques to make loans to borrowers who otherwise would not qualify on their own.)

Especially in soft markets, you must try harder to qualify prospects without jeopardizing your own profitability. Think of all

Structure your
screening
standards to
accept as well as
turn down.

of those credit card companies that have figured out ways to qualify the "unqualified." Or just imagine what type of slump the auto industry would face if these companies only sold new cars to people who could truly afford them.

Want to bring in more income? Avoid rigid standards. Think of alternative ways to satisfy your financial (risk) parameters. Look for ways to accept, not reject.

Improvements for Tenants You're talking with a prospect who is sitting on the fence of indecision. You need to persuade her to sign up for your unit. You ask, "What is it that you don't like about the apartment? What can I do to encourage you to make our building your home? Are you thinking of some changes that would better suit your preferences or needs?"

Again, this conversation will reaffirm that you're an open and flexible type of property owner who wants to keep the building's residents pleased. But also, when you candidly talk with prospective tenants, they will provide you with many good ideas that you can put to strategic advantage throughout your operations.

"Yes, I believe that if you moved the refrigerator over here, that would make the kitchen easier to work in. Then you could put in a pass-through for the dining room. And why don't you have a microwave hung under the cabinet over here?"

"Great ideas. I'll get these things done tomorrow. We're very pleased that you've chosen one of our units, and we know you're going to love it here."

Pets Many tenants will pay a substantial rent premium for the privilege of being able to keep a small pet in their apartment. However, the problem for property owners is not so much pet damage to their property (which can be covered by a large security deposit). Rather, misbehaved pets (and pet owners) can annoy other residents of the community.

> **Pet policies will bring in more revenue and create more problems.**

No one wants to hear a dog yelping all day as it is left alone in the apartment. No one wants to hear a cat fight at 2 A.M.

Your mission, should you choose to accept it, is to figure out a way to capture the extra revenue that pet owners are willing to pay. But you should do so with an absolute tenant guarantee that their pets will not disrupt the peace, quiet, and enjoyment of the premises for others. If you can negotiate an agreement that satisfies both of these objectives, you will earn the King Solomon award for shrewd wisdom. (I have at times succeeded in this, but I have also failed. Thus, I regret that on this point I cannot relay any firm principles to guide you.)

Wear and Tear   So-called standard leases often state that tenants are responsible for all damages *except* normal wear and tear. I would never use such a clause. It invites tenant neglect and abuse. Many tenants believe that soiled carpets, cracked plaster, broken screens, and numerous other damages reflect nothing more than normal wear and tear.

I disagree. If a tenant properly cares for a property, that property will not suffer any noticeable wear and tear during a tenancy of one year or less. For such short-term periods of residence, tenants should leave the property in essentially the same condition in which they accepted it. Eliminating the wear and tear clause will save you money and argument.

If prospects don't accept this condition, I ask them what wear and tear damage they expect to do to the property throughout the year. Because they won't admit to causing damage, that usually settles the discussion. If they do come back with a response that will create wear and tear, then I try to negotiate for more rent, a higher deposit, or some other trade-off. In the end, I don't take a hard line. But I do want prospects to under-

> **Tenants on one-year leases should not create wear and tear.**

stand that my rental rates do not include an allowance for damages—wear and tear or otherwise.

Terms of the Lease Do not reflexively set the term of your leases at one year. As I related earlier, many good tenants need a place to live for a shorter period of time and will pay a healthy rent premium for that opportunity. You might even be able to coordinate a "weak and peak" type of timing. You get a vacancy in June (slow season). If you leased for a year, you would face a vacancy again during next June at the slow time of the year.

Instead, offer a six-month lease until December (peak season) or perhaps a lease for 18 months. I know an owner of apartments in Flagstaff, Arizona, who rents his units on nine-month leases for college students (September to May). Then, during the summer tourist season, he accepts 30- to 90-day rentals at steeply inflated prices (still cheaper than what the better motels and hotels charge—and also less than the time shares).

Strict Rules Property owners frequently misunderstand the prime purpose of rules that govern tenant behavior. These owners think that rules exist primarily to protect their property. This is not true. Look at the long, detailed house rules that govern the homeowners of a $1 million Manhattan co-op or a $2.5 million Longboat Key condo. These rules exist to preserve the nature of the community. The residents clearly want strict rules because they are the people who create and enforce them.

Make strict rules part of your market strategy. The best tenants are those who appreciate tight rules (e.g., rules that pertain to pets, noise, parking, smoking, cleanliness, partying, etc.). In other words, you don't so much use your rules to control behavior. Rather, by adopting strict rules, you appeal to people who conscientiously behave as good citizens and want others to behave likewise.

Overall, structure your rules for the good of the residents, not as some punitive dictate of a feudal landlord. Also, seek input from tenants

> **Let tenants suggest changes.**

as to what rules they would like to see implemented, modified, or discontinued. It's your unit, but it's their home. Give them a voice in how you can enhance their satisfaction and everyday living.

Lease Options

Many tenants would like to own their own homes. Yet for reasons of blemished credit, self-employment (especially those with off-the-books income or tax-minimized income), unstable income (commissions, tips), or lack of cash, they believe that they can't currently qualify for a mortgage from a lending institution. For

> **A lease option truly offers the lazy investor's way to wealth.**

these renters, the lease option (a lease with an option to purchase) solves their dilemma. Properly structured, the lease option permits renters to begin to acquire ownership rights in a property. Simultaneously, it also gives them time to improve their financial profile (at least from the perspective of a mortgage lender).

Here's How It Works

As the name implies, the lease option essentially rolls two different types of contracts into a combination contract. Under the lease agreement, the tenants sign a rental contract that covers the usual terms and conditions that we've just mentioned, such as the following:

- ◆ Monthly rental rate
- ◆ Term of lease
- ◆ Responsibilities for repair, maintenance, and upkeep
- ◆ Pets, smoking, cleanliness
- ◆ Permissible property uses
- ◆ HOA rules (noise, parking, number of occupants)

The option part of the contract gives tenants the right to buy the home at some future date. As a minimum, it will include (1) the amount of the option payment, (2) the option purchase price for the house, (3) the date on which the purchase option expires, (4) right of assignment, and (5) the amount of the rent credits that will count toward the purchase price of the house.

Benefits to Investors

Although you can structure lease options in many different ways, they nearly always provide these benefits to *investors:* (1) lower risk, (2) higher rents, and (3) guaranteed profits.

Lower Risk   As a rule, tenants who shop for a lease option will take better care of your unit than would average renters. Because they intend one day to own the unit, they will treat it more like homeowners would than tenants. Also, they know that to qualify for a mortgage they will need a perfect record of rent payments. (If your tenant-buyers don't know that fact, make sure you impress it into their consciousness.) As a minimum, lease option tenants expect to pay up front first and last month's rent, a security deposit, and, more than likely, an option fee of $1,000 to $5,000 (possibly more). Considered together, all of these factors spell lower risk for you the property owner.

Higher Rents   Lease option tenants will agree to pay higher than market rents because they know you will apply a part of that monthly rent to the home's purchase price. The tenants view these "rent credits"—actually they should be called purchase price credits—as forced savings that will contribute toward a lender's required down payment.

From your immediate standpoint, the higher rent payments increase your monthly cash flow and boost your cash-on-cash return. In high-priced areas where newly bought rental properties awaken a hungry alligator, the increased rent of a lease option may turn a negative cash flow into a positive.

Guaranteed Profits   Experienced investors know that (on average) fewer than 50 percent of lease option tenants take advantage of their right to buy their leased home. Sometimes they change their mind. Sometimes their finances fail to improve as much as they hoped. Sometimes their personal circumstances shift (separation, divorce, job relocation, additional children).

Whatever the reason, the tenants (at least in part) forfeit their rent credits, option fee, and any fix-up work they have performed around the house. As a person you may feel badly for the tenants. But as an investor, their loss means your gain. By not following through with their purchase, you end up with more profit than you would have earned under a traditional rental agreement.

> **Lease options give you the best of both worlds.**

Even if the tenants do buy, you still win, because in setting your option price, you built in a good profit margin over the price you originally paid for the unit. This technique works especially well in those transactions where you have bought at a bargain price. In addition, you gain more than you would have from a straight sale of the property because you didn't have to pay high marketing costs or Realtor commissions.

For investors, the lease option makes for truly a win-win agreement. You win when your tenants buy, and you win when the tenants don't buy and relinquish their right.

CHAPTER 14

Your Easier Path to Wealth and Income

No one knows the future for Social Security, stock prices, bond returns, or inflation. Consequently, as long as the population and economy continue to increase, rental housing will provide the safest and surest path to both long-term real wealth and high spendable cash returns. A $10,000 to $20,000 down payment today will steadily grow into an equity of $50,000 to $100,000 over a period of 10 to 20 years. During this same period your rent collections will increase by at least 50 percent, and they could even double if you choose a soon-to-be hot area.

Less Risk

You will also enjoy great safety of capital with rental housing. Even in recessions, condo values and rent collections for owners of small properties generally remain stable. In such down periods, home building and apartment construction falls, thus reducing new supply. Bad times also tend to draw more households toward renting and away from homebuying. In good economic times, rents are pushed up by rising employment, incomes, and general prosperity. Plus, households "unbundle." People who were living with others to save money now start renting a place of their own.

Personal Opportunity

When you rely on stocks, bonds, and even Social Security, your fate is out of your control. Other than buying, selling, or perhaps voting, you can do nothing to influence the returns you would like to receive. This is not the case with condos.

When you depend on rental properties to build wealth and a lifetime of income, you gain the personal opportunity to achieve good returns, even in a recession. (Or, as some might say, especially in a recession, because that's when you can easily pick up bargain-priced units.) Overall, investing in rental properties provides you with a large variety of personal opportunities unavailable to stock market investors (or speculators):

- ◆ Buy properties at prices substantially less than their current market value.
- ◆ Through creative financing, acquire properties with little of your own cash.
- ◆ Improve properties to enhance their current market value.
- ◆ Improve your market strategy to boost rents and lower vacancies.
- ◆ Cut operating costs to increase net operating income.
- ◆ Sell your existing properties and trade up without paying a tax on your capital gains.
- ◆ Refinance your properties and pull out tax-free cash. (Of course, you can borrow against a stock portfolio. But margin requirements, price volatility, and low or no cash dividends make that choice costly and risky.)

To profit from some or all of the real estate opportunities just listed requires knowledge, effort, and market savvy. Unlike those who buy stocks, condo investors don't whimsically follow hot tips from their barbers, auto mechanics, or CNBC. You can't buy, own, sell, and profit from real estate simply with the click of a mouse.

But that "disadvantage" explains why, over time, real estate provides a safer, surer path to wealth and income. For today, a majority of investors still foolishly believe that they and tens of millions of other Americans can achieve wealth without work. Just buy stocks, and voilà—your portfolio will grow. Easy Street awaits *everyone* who faithfully continues to contribute money into their 401(k)s, Keoghs, 529s, and IRAs. But it won't happen. It can't happen.

At some time in the future, Americans will realize that returns from corporate stocks can never exceed the total amount of corporate profits (or in reality, corporate dividends). These amounts will never grow large enough to support the more than 50 million individuals and households who continue to send monthly checks to Wall Street.

At present, only rental real estate provides true *investment* opportunities. Of course, you can *speculate* in stocks. You can even speculate in real estate. You can buy lottery tickets. You can shoot craps in Las Vegas. Maybe any or all of these will pay off for you. But the odds are stacked against you. In contrast, selectively acquire just two to five rental condos, and you will begin to build an income for life—a monthly cash flow that will generously finance the life you would like to live.

With condos you will enjoy the cash flow and wealth-building benefits of owning rental properties. Yet you eliminate and delegate most of the chores of landlording that deter many investors from real estate. Well-chosen condos truly do offer an easier, surer path to income and real asset values.

I wish you the best. Should you have any questions or comments about investing in real estate, please telephone me (800-942-9304, ext. 20691) or send me an e-mail (garye@stop renting now.com). I enjoy hearing from my readers.

INDEX